DECENTRALISED GOVERNANCE, REGIONAL DEVELOPMENT AND WOMEN EMPOWERMENT

DECENTRALISED GOVERNANCE, REGIONAL DEVELOPMENT AND WOMEN EMPOWERMENT

Edited by
Annpurna Nautiyal
Himanshu Bourai

GYAN

Decentralised Governance, Regional Development and Women Empowerment

ISBN: 978-81-212-1152-9

Published in 2013 in India by
Gyan Publishing House
23, Main Ansari Road
New Delhi-110002
Phones : 23282060, 23261060
Fax : 011-23285914
E-mail: books@gyanbooks.com
Website: www.gyanbooks.com

Laser Typesetting : Quick Media, Delhi
Printed at : Chawla Offset Printers, Delhi

Contents

SECTION-III

CASE STUDIES

Preface

The basic philosophy of decentralisation, which is an alternative system of governance, is adopting the 'people-centric' approach for resolving the local problems and ensuring economic and social justice at the grass roots level. The entire process aims to put people at the centre of power so that in place of just being the beneficiaries of any schemes, they can become the real agents and the engines of growth and development. Due to its people-centric approach, the decentralised governance has not only emerged as a powerful tool but it is being universally accepted as the main instrument of empowering people at the grass-root level. The merits of decentralised governance have established that for fulfilling the goals of holistic development, large scale decentralisation of powers and functions are not only desirible but it is also equally important to harness the local resources in accordance to local needs and local knowledge. Actually, a democracy working for equity and justice must base itself on the willing assent of the people, not on coercion; therefore, there is an urgent need to devise ways and means to willingly involve people both at the level of formulation and implementation of plans made for development.

The Indian model of decentralised governance is based on three tier model and functions at the district, block and village levels. The most important responsibility of all the three bodies is to prepare need-based plans for their respective regions and people. However, it has been observed that these institutions usually remain ineffective, in performing their basic role because of the unwillingness of the governmental agencies to share information, power and resources. Sometimes the dominance of the rural elites in these bodies, their vested interest and the lack of political will to carry out the plans also hampers the effectiveness of these bodies. The failure to regularly hold elections and the propensity of the political elite to blindly follow the dictates of the bureaucracy which do not seem to have taken the notion of decentralisation of decision-making power very kindly also makes these bodies defunct.

Actually, the objectives of fulfilling the developmental needs of the local people in a better way, identification of local problems, better use of local manpower, natural resources and environment, management of financial resources for regional development, better mobilisation of resources, implementation and monitoring of development programmes, and the real participation of the people cannot be achieved without the decentralised political institutions, administrative structure and data collecting machinery. As the decentralised political institution with a representative character provides every section or group of the people, an opportunity to register their participation in the decision-making process, therefore, to encourage people's participation, decentralisation at every level needs to be promoted. The autonomy of the decision-making is also necessary for the decentralised governance as the decisons made independently without pressures, either from the state or the central government, can only accomplish the objectives of need-based development. The participation of the people can also be acertained by affirmative action of making a certain percentage of reservation of seats mandatory for the weaker sections of the society and also for the backward regions. In view of this, the 33 percent reservation provided to the women in the institutions of the local self government is one step in this direction, as this has encouraged even the non political women to venture out from the confines of their homes and enter a different and unknown world. Since the goal of regional development, decentralised governance and women's empowerment could not be achieved without the qualitative and full involvement and participation of the women in all the plans and programmes, therefore, there is a need to work seriously towards the eradication of disparities and ensuring gender equality through the decentralised governance.

The present book on "Decentralised Governance, Regional Development and Women Empowerment" attempts to assess and analyse the role of the local self government institutions in achieving the aim of regional development and women empowerment. Though, the conceptual and diverse issues, covered in this book, focus on the intricacies and problems but the specific case studies highlight the constraints and challenges of these institutions in the Garhwal Himalayas. Since, Uttarakhand was created as the 27th state of the Indian union in November 2000 to fulfill the concerns of just, equitable and holistic development of this mostly remote, rural and mountanous region, therefore, the Panchayat Raj Institutions can play a tremendous role in realising the aim of the village and regional development. Moreover, as women in Uttarakhand are the real players and backbone of economy and society, therefore, their participation and involvement in these institutions can make a difference in the scenario of regional and village level development.

This book mainly consists of the papers presented during the National Seminar jointly organised by the department of Political Science under its UGC-SAP-DRS programme and the Women Studies Centre with the financial assistance received by the University Grants Commission, New Delhi to discuss the role of decentralised governance in regional development and women empowerment. The editors are thankful to the University Grants Commission, New Delhi for providing financial support under both the programmes. The financial assistance received from the HNB Garhwal University is also duly acknowledged. We are also thankful to the authors who have contributed their papers for this book. The kind assistance extended by the faculty, staff and research scholars of the department of Political Science, HNB Garhwal University, is also thankfully acknowledged.

Annpurna Nautiyal
Himanshu Bourai

Introduction

Annpurna Nautiyal and
Himanshu Bourai

Development, which is always multi pronged, aims for providing the basic facilities to all the people, particulary the poor people, so that their productivity and income could be increased and their contribution in the developmental process can also be ascertained. In view of this, development is not a matter of charity which can be bestowed on the people or an administrative discretion but it is obligatory for any political system to fulfill the aspirations of the people related to their holistic development. Actually any political system that believes in people's empowerment should be more concerned about people's welfare and proper use of resources, for providing basic education, health care, and social services to satisfy their needs. People's satisfaction brings an increase in their productivity levels, growth, and overall development of the community and society. The societies where people are not bothered about the availability of the basic facilities, have registered immense growth and progress, but on the other hand, the societies, where people are even deprived of the basic facilities, agitations and movements, tend to become the most sought after means for registering their anger and frustration towards the policy-makers or the governmental policies.

However, the objectives of fulfilling the need and aspiration of local people in a better way, identification of local problems, healthier use of local manpower, natural resources and environment, mobilisation of resources, improved management of financial resources required for regional development, implementation and monitoring of development programmes, encouraging the local self government and the real participation of the people cannot be achieved without the decentralised political institutions, administrative structure and data collecting machinery. As the decentralised political institution with a representative character allows every section or group of the community an opportunity to register their participation in the decision-making process, therefore, to encourage people's participation, decentralisation of authority at every level needs to be promoted. The autonomy of the decision-making authority is also necessary for the decentralised governance so that decisions can be made independently, without pressures either from the state or the central government. Advocates of political decentralisation believe that decisions made with greater participation of the people will be based on right information and actual needs of the community and the local representatives, because of their familarity with the problems, and the people would also be able to deliver good results. Decentralisation can also help the locals by cutting short the complex bureaucratic procedures and making the officials sensitive to local conditions and needs. It can allow the central and state governments to provide services efficiently to the remotest of the areas and also motivate people to take interest in the formation of poicies and plans for local area development by providing more opportunities for greater political representation, for diverse political, ethnic, religious, and cultural groups in the political and decision-making process. Decentralisation can be a good tool for promoting local experiments for development, as per the vision of the local people and by allowing the involvement, participation and a system of testing the programmes and plans by the local people—such interest and attachment for the programmes can be generated among the people. The involvement of the local people in the political process besides creating an atmosphere for a more imaginative, ground-breaking and responsive programmes for the development of the local area can also increase political stability and national unity by allowing citizens' control on the programmes being undertaken for the development of the area.

The Indian model of decentralised governance is based on three-tier model and functions at the district, block and village levels. The most important responsibility of all the three bodies is to prepare need-based developmental plans for their respective regions and people and also encourage people's participation and involvement in preparing these plans. The involvement and participation of the people is important to not only earn a sense of their belongingness towards the plans, but also in their implementation as people's plans. However, it has also been observed that, these institutions meant to increase people's direct participation, usually remain ineffective in performing their basic role, because of the unwillingness of the governmental agencies to share information, power and resources. Sometimes the dominance of the rural elites in these bodies, their vested interest and the lack of political will to carry out the plans also hampers the effectiveness of these bodies or earn people's goodwill or motivate them to take active part in their activities. Morover, the weak administrative machinery and technical support system leads to the poor and inefficient delivery of the services resulting into people's distance and apathy from such programmes and plans. The transferring of administrative responsibilities to local levels, without adequate financial resources also makes the equitable distribution of services and goods more difficult. Due to these factors, decentralisation can sometimes make coordination with the national policies and their implementation difficult and thus undermine the goals of good governance and people's participation. The distrust of the people, lack of their prticipation and dominance of the local elites in the decentralised structures also affects the productivity of these institutions and leads to malpractices among the local people. Due to this people, particularly the women population, most of the times do not find any interest in participating in the institutions meant for their empowerment, which is not a good sign for any democracy. This needs to be changed to ensure people's involvement, participation and empowerment.

Besides the routine and normal procedures of promoting people's involvement in the institutions of local self-government, their participation in these bodies can also be acertained by affirmative action like reserving a certain percentage of seats for the weaker sections of the society or for the backward regions. In view of this, the 33 per cent reservation provided to the women in the institutions of the local self government, can be cited as an example of such affirmative action which has encouraged even the non political women to venture out from the confines of their homes and enter in a different and unknown world of politics. The decentralisation of fiscal responsibility and authority to the local level has opened new prospects for women and other weaker and marginalised groups to become part of the policy planning, budget allocations and monitoring. But this is only one step, because, though women constitute nearly 50 percent of the total population in India and contribute substantially to the economic resources of the family, yet they are still considered unequal in every sense of the term: economically, socially, educationally and politically. Women shoulder almost all the responsibilities for meeting basic needs of the family, but unfortunately they are denied the resources, information and freedom of action which is not only required to fulfill their responsibilities but also deciding the course of action for the family welfare. Since the goal of regional development, decentralised governance and women's empowerment could not be achieved without the full participation and involvement of the women in all the plans and programmes meant for the development of the community, society or area therefore, there is a need to work seriously towards the eradication of disparities and ensuring gender equality through the decentralised governance. There is also a need to expose the men and women towards the regional and political realities for entering into politics at every level of governance and also adopting appropriate planning and focused approach towards development.

With the above frame in mind, if we talk in the context of the women of the hill areas, we find that though the total economy of hill areas revolves around the women, yet, they not only lack economic independence/power but they also survive amidst many hardships. The gender disparity in Garhwal Himalayas has become more acute due to the intensity of out-migration of the male population, the lack of literacy, tough topography and growing problems of the environmental degradation. In the absence of the men in the family, the dual responsibility of the women in domestic and agricultural field only adds to their miseries in the form of excessive work load without any monetary benefit. It is ironical that despite several technological advancements and better facilities available to the women in the urban areas, the condition of the women in the remote and rural areas and their drudgery has almost remained the same for the last many decades. Although, there are governmental schemes but since, they are generally not made on the basis of the ground realities, therefore, they have failed to make much difference in the life and drudgery of women. Often mountain women's workloads and limited mobility makes it impossible for them to take advantage of health, education and training facilities due to which one does not find any drastic change in their life styles. Due to over work, majority of the women neither get time to participate in any training or educative programmes meant for their development and awareness, nor do they get any incentive for doing so. Therefore, in the absence of knowledge, interest and awareness about their rights and duties, the clauses of empowerment also fail to make a major difference in the lives of a large number of women in the hill areas. The dependence on the male members of the family for knowledge, awareness and execution of the responsibilities in some cases also creates problems and hampers the empowerment of the women. In view of the developmental problems of the hill areas and to create a vision to promote women's participation, there is also a greater need to promote decentralised governance more religiously.

Since decentralised governance can provide an answer to the problems of regional development and people's aspiration, resentment and frustration. Therefore, the need for devising ways and means for strengthening such infrastructures, which supports decentralisation, development as well as women's participation and empowerment, assumes greater significance. The issue of decentralised governance also becomes important in view of the fact that Uttarakhand has also witnessed several people's movements like Chipko and the Uttarakhand movement, staged against the insensitive policies of the governments, neglect of the region in terms of development and infrastructure facilities, displacements, environmental degradation etc. As the focus of the movements or the people's worries has largely centred on the problems of development, therefore, it can be said that there is a close connection between deprivation and movement because the capacity of the deprived people to assess the conditions of the privileged class as well as the realisation among the people that they are capable of doing something to undo the deprivation encourages them to stage protest and movements. (Kothari, 2002, p. 443) In Uttarakhand, such realisation among the people is very deep-rooted due to which it has seen many people's movements and presently also people's frustration with the inaction and non fulfillment of the developmental aspirations vents out through movements. Since 80 percent population of Uttarakhand is rural, therefore, it is said that Uttarakhand's soul lives in the villages and the target of the real development cannot be achieved fully, unless all remotely situated villages are equipped with facilities and brought into the mainstream. A large section of the society believes that there is a need to endorse the Gandhian idea of the self-sufficient village republics in Uttarakhand, because majority of the population still lives in villages, and agriculture is their mainstay. The development of all the remotely situated villages, which are so far cut off from the mainstream and deprived of the basic facilities, would be the only barometer of development in Uttarakhand.

Actually, the biggest task of today is to implement regional development plans through decentralised governance in such a way that not only greater gender equality and growth could be ascertained but a balance between people's aspirations, natural resources and the environment is also maintained. The Gandhian Model of development, that proposes and emphasizes on the capacity building which would automatically lead to women's empowerment, also needs to be followed as women have immense tolerance management and capacity to handle all kinds of situations. But at the same time, it is also true that being part of an age-old culture and system of male domination, they need to be constantly reminded of their capacities of multitasking and producing good results. The present book which consists some of the papers presented in a three-day national seminar organised by the Department of Political Science, and Women Studies Centre, HNB Garhwal

University, Srinagar, Garhwal, in February 2010 to deliberate on the issues of "Decentralised Governance, Regional Development and Women Empowerment" seeks to identify the problems which slow down the process of regional development, get in the way of women's empowerment in the decentralised governance and suggest the steps for women's improved and greater representation and participation in the system of decentralised governance.

The first paper of this book, delivered as the key note address of the seminar, by Kumud Sharma, of the Centre for Women's Development Studies, New Delhi on "Framing the Discourse on Decentralised Governance and Women Empowerment" actually forms the base of this book. Her paper not only takes up the issue of decentralised governance and women empowerment but also emphasises that these cannot be separated from regional development. She has argued that in a liberal, multi-party democracy, arguments for democratic decentralisation have shaped the liberal democratic discourse in India because of the thought that it will allow greater efficiency, transparency accountability, and responsiveness in the local governments and also provide more opportunities for people's participation. Actually, in a plural and diverse society, based on class, caste, ethnicity, religion, the economic complexities and diversities need decentralised governance to respond to diverse developmental needs of the region and social groups. Demand for decentralisation and political representation, is seen as a legitimate means for protecting the interests of the marginalised or excluded group. Within democracy the demand for greater representation is also seen as an instrument for redistribution of power and resources; and expected political engagement through representation and participation can introduce new interests and concerns. While advocating the need for greater decentralisation, she has also stressed that decentralisation can not guarantee expected outcomes but can only provide opportunities to participating in planning and local governance. Moreover, outcomes of decentralisation are shaped by many other factors, such as, local capacity, political and social histories, local social organisations and social stratification, land and tenurial relations, strength of local power elites and bureaucracy and its commitment to decentralisation; the role of development agencies, civil society organisations and NGOs. In fact decentralised governance is a political process, therefore, there are winners and losers and it also carries the risks of interest groups capturing local government and reinforcing existing inequalities; consolidating existing alliances with local elites (patronage); corruption; politician and bureaucratic nexus etc.

She has also clarified that the notion of women's 'political empowerment' is caught in the conflicting agendas, because, the political institutions and electoral processes which influence women's access to power, largely remain male dominated. She feels that in view of the societal relationship even the greater representation of women may not actually challenge existing hierarchies of power, because of the temptation to either run down women's achievements or romanticise the heroism of a few women or bringing in 'proxy women'. To her, representation does make an impact on local self-governance, but not necessarily on policy decisions. Therefore, women's empowerment approach is not a grand narrative and it is difficult to approach the issue within conventional category of political analysis. It is a concept which focuses on everyday resistance and struggle of women who contest the power configuration in day-to-day life, claim spaces dominated by developmentalist state and patriarchal structures; create spaces to negotiate and emphasise collective agency of women. She has also stressed that gender accountability of institutions of local governance does not flow from increased representation of women. There is a link between strong political representation and a high incidence of female poverty. While women's empowerment issues need to be discussed in the context of power and capabilities of Panchayat Raj Institutions, there is a need to strengthen the institutional framework with adequate resources and sensitivity to women's issues backed by capacity building, sensitisation, poverty reduction, resource monitoring and gender audits. She feels that unless budgetary allocations for health, education and support systems for women are earmarked, an increasing number of women will drift into poverty. She has emphasised that gender accountability in decentralised governance systems, does not flow from increased representation of women. But institutional norms and practices play an important role in determining women's entitlements and participation. There is also a need to expand spaces of civil society organisations, local women's groups and networks as support mechanisms, user groups and ideologically grounded programmes like Mahila Samakhya for decentralisation of power, to mobilise women around their concerns and building their capacities to effectively participate in local planning, implementation and monitoring of programmes. While suggesting these steps for strengthening the local government, she also questions whether the community based organisations (CBOs) could influence allocation of resources and local development priorities and enhance women's voice and capacities to participate in local government. For the success of decentralised governance, she feels that the political mobilisation has to go with economic mobilisation and advocacy and also to strengthen the negotiating spaces for women in the present paradigm of state, market and civil society.

The second paper of this section, by I.D. Mishra, on "Democracy Accentuates Decentralisation" focuses on how decentralisation dissolves the power to flow to its constituents to make it meaningful, useful and significant. He has stressed that decentralised power is the core principle of democracy and development. Power centralised is neither citizen centric nor democratic, because it uses coercive means to achieve its target of retaining the power centralised in the interests of its holders. In his view, power holders are the power enjoyers at the cost of those who are being powered or controlled. Power holders keep their interests desired conscious, and keep them protected and fulfilled by the power they hold. Power, even if institutionalised in such situations, remains much more personalised. Power in this form becomes coercive, and sometimes even beyond limit, and legitimacy of the claim remains dependent upon the holders and not upon those who are being powered or controlled. Conclusively, he has observed that decentralisation is actually the living centre of democracy. It integrates individual and their groups to the democratic system and its institutions with their full autonomy and participation for growth and development. Plurality remains intact with minimal chances of intervention and eruption of disharmony provided that the culture of plural co-existence is promoted and nourished. Therefore, he says that if decentralisation ensures many things, it also demands many things to get their full expression as well. It ensures individuality and its expression, recognition of groups and society, plurality and plural culture, regionalism and rationality in democratic tune, governance and government with democratic culture; and above all, strengthens state with people's democracy at all levels. But he feels that it is not possible to avail opportunity where people at large are illiterate and uneducated, poor and sick with a weak citizenry. Such people remain unable to support and strengthen the state which guarantees them of their rights and provides opportunity to enjoy their rights. Since decentralisation is a multi-fold concept, it needs to be unfolded at policy-making level and due attention to be paid at every fold at the level of implementation. He says that in the past we have failed to uphold the balance of relations between the various folds, such as, regional and central, rural and urban, social, economic and political at both the above levels. Our urban and economic centric policies have marginalised the social and political objectives of decentralisation. Although he has opined that the urban centric approach as a model of development cannot be justified as a code of development for rural India, because decentralisation to be successful should aim to rehabilitate rural India in its resources and self reliance, but its anti-urban flavour would also not serve the purpose of holistic development.

Himanshu Bourai in the third paper of this section on "Decentralised Governance and Women: Special Reference to Panchayats in India" has focused on the three aspects of political system—Decentralised governance, Women empowerment and Panchayts—in India. The first part of the paper discusses the theoretical aspects of decentralisation. She emphasises that decentralisation aims to promote democracy (at the grass-root level), protection of freedom and human rights (vertical check and balance), increasing efficiency through delegation of responsibility, rendering higher quality of services, and promoting social and economic development and without these goals decentralisation is meaningless. In the second part of her paper, with the help of the historical background of decentralisation, she has explained the major aspects of 73rd and 74th constitutional amendment acts which make provisions of reservation for the women in Panchayats. The third part of the paper discusses the role and contribution of women in Panchayats. She has stressed that for long, community activism and political aspirations have remained a closely held preserve of the male-dominated society, with involvement of the 'weaker sex' in public domain, largely remaining both negligible and insignificant. Through the 73rd Constitutional Amendment ushered in 1993, though one-third of the seats were reserved for women in local self-governance, however, the impact of women panchayat members and head of the Gram Sabha (pradhans) in these bodies remained peripheral for a long time. This is not imaginary, but based on facts highlighted in various studies on the functioning of local bodies that have women as chiefs. As the male panchayat members call the shots by carrying out most of the proposals for developmental schemes, the women are left with little or no work and thus remain unable to leave their mark in these bodies. However, if there is a will, there is a way and in this context the case of the women of Uttarakhand can be taken as not long back women pradhans in this northern state of India also used to be manipulated by the male members of their families to further their own political and personal agenda. Women's lack of knowledge about the functioning and procedures of panchayats, the prevailing conservative traditional system which restricts women from speaking freely in front of elder male relatives and little experience in attending the male-dominated meetings, placed the women at the receiving end and also affected their full participation in discussions and decision-making process at policy level. But slowly, the subdued women, who got elected to the panchayats through the reservation, have started asserting their rights with the result; local self-governance in the state has received a new direction and thrust. The author concludes that, by and large, PRIs have not delivered the desired services to rural people, even though they are empowered to prepare plans for economic development and social justice. They have not yet become the real institutions of self governance, largely, because of the lack of people's participation, especially, the women, the poor, and other marginalised groups on account of their ignorance, poverty, lack of distributive justice; reluctance of the higher tiers of the Government to devolve financial and administrative powers to them as the Line Departments and District Rural Development Agency continues to control the planning and implementation of developmental projects; apathetic attitude of bureaucrats and politicians; insufficient capacity and resources of the PRIs (and Gram Sabha) in running their activities effectively; and, lack of organic linkages among the three tiers.

In the second, section, Abdulrahim P. Vijapur in his paper on "Gender equality in Islam and Muslim Women in India: An Agenda for Reforms", has discussed the greatness of Islam as a religion and practices from the gender perspective. Briefly discussing the history of Islam and naming it as one of the great religions of the world with followers throughout the world, he has opined that as an egalitarian belief system, it introduced the concepts of universal brotherhood and non-discrimination among Muslims on the ground of sex or race. Islam gave the women fundamental rights and championed all movements to improve the status of women, at a time when societies were overtly traditional and socially underdeveloped. He has focused on finding answer to the questions whether Islam provides for gender equality? And to what extent the equality of sexes is found in practice in Islamic societies? Are there any deviations from the scriptural precepts of gender equality? What reformative measures have been undertaken in Muslim countries as well as in India to improve the status of women by enacting laws? While discussing these issues he has opined that no serious attempts have been initiated in India to reform family laws with a view to improving the status of Muslim women. He suggests that such initiatives should come from the leaders, theologians and cross-section of the Muslim community, because the government initiative will be misconceived by the community as a step towards Uniform Civil Code.

He feels that the gap between precepts and practices is quite glaring, with respect to women's inheritance rights. In his opinion except for the Arab populations which was responsible to develop Shariah under the guidance of the Prophet, Shariah posed serious problems for other people who became Muslims later on, because its basic concepts were often wholly alien to the traditional structures of their societies. Therefore, despite being Muslims, they could not strictly adhere to Shariah. He has also argued that after India's independence, legal reforms were initiated in the sub-continent, but in India these acts did not make any difference in the life of the Islamic women. He has highlighted that the Pakistani Parliament, on the other hand, initially passed the West Punjab Muslim Personal Law (Shariat) Application Act in 1948, which included agricultural land in its purview. In 1962, it passed the West Pakistan Muslim Personal Law (Shariat) Application Act, which was applicable to whole of West Pakistan, except the "Tribal Areas" in North West Frontier Province. It made women legally entitled to inherit agricultural property as full owners. The Bangladeshi (formerly East Pakistani) Muslims were also not affected by the legal reforms enacted in West Pakistan as the 1937 Act of India was in force but despite the absence of subsequent amendments, Shariah applied to the agricultural land also. In India too, even after the independence, the 1937 Act has continued to be applicable. In his opinion, however, it was gratifying to note that in Tamil Nadu and Andhra Pradesh the Act was amended in 1949 to include agricultural land, in 1963 Kerala did the same. In Assam, Maharashra, Gujarat, and West Bengal, there was no strong preference for customs even before the Act was passed; hence in these states, the Shariah rules could be applied to agricultural land as well. But in several states of north-west India such as Uttar Pradesh (which included till recently Uttrakhand region too), Punjab, Himachal Pradesh and Haryana, the Act has not been amended to include agricultural land. Despite the land reform laws, customary law still governs the succession of such land. Thus, in these states, severe gender inequalities still persist as far as the succession of land property among the Muslims is concerned. He has advocated the need by the Muslim intelligentia and leaders (both political and theological) to mobilise public support to amend/reform the 1937 Shariah Act to remove gender inequality. As empowerment means to give somebody the power or authority to act, therefore, to bring the women at the centre stage, he feels that women should be given the power or capacity to regulate their day-to-day lives in the social, economic and political fields. Since, the main motive of women's empowerment is to protect their rights, to enrich their quality of life and involve them in decision-making process at all levels, particularly related to their lives and families, therefore, the empowerment of Muslim women should involve: higher literacy level and education, better health care for the women and their children, awareness about their reproductive rights, implementation of Shariah law to give inheritance rights, abolition of triple talaq, a practice followed in India in contradiction of Quranic dictum, punishing those demanding dowry (as it is against Shariah), ensuring the payment of Mehar (dower) to women at the time of marriage, encouraging their participation in local and urban governments as elected representatives. These measures would require reforms in Muslim Personal Law and such initiatives need to come from the Muslim community itself, because if these are initiated by the Government, a political party or Supreme Court, the community leaders, both religious and political, would consider it as interference in their personal laws and threat to their identities. Moderate Muslim intellectuals and women's groups from the Muslim community should initiate debate and discussion in this direction. He feels that for providing gender justice, the women's NGOs and Hindu women's organisations in place of insisting on the need of drafting Uniform Civil Code, should advocate reforms in all personal laws of different communities because the changes made in the family laws with the initiatives of the respective communities would be more acceptable to them than the uniform laws, which may threaten their distinct cultural identities.

In the second paper of this section on "Gender Concerns and Development Debates" Bijayalaxmi Nanda has focused on the fact that without women's participation, development has no meaning. She feels that gender bias in developmental programmes indicates that women are particularly disadvantaged with respect to access to health care, education, political rights and labour force and other forms of participation. Voices, for the inclusion of women in the development, emerged in the 1970s and over the past two decades, it has passed through three stages: women in development, women and development and gender and development. Nanda has clearly stated that development can only be achieved, if women could get equal share and opportunity to participate in all spheres of development. The strategies, under the national policies in India, need to be critically examined in this context. She has highlighted that, an analysis, of all the five year plans and efforts in these plans for development of women, reveals the gaps between rhetoric and reality. The literacy levels, morbidity and mortality levels, participation levels, all show that the status of women in India remains abysmally low. She has opined that due to the lax attitude the economic reforms and the process of liberalisation and economic globalisation, that have followed since 1990s, have affected the women and vulnerable groups adversely. This indicates, that faster economic growth does not necessarily lead to more secure employment and reduction of poverty. Therefore, there is a need to address the interconnections between poverty, education, cultural inhibitions and gender factors. The vision of the Beijing Conference's 'Growth with Equality' can only be realised by a consideration of these factors and a set of multiple strategies where the state is involved. Women have to be integrated at all levels, in the mainstream of development and economic activities and their status can be enhanced by removing social and cultural barriers that impede progress and increase women's vulnerability. She has emphasised the need to visualise development as empowerment through participation and removal of hurdles in the path of participation. Only by adopting such approach, the gap between the rhetoric of women's development and the reality of development can be bridged.

In her rather unusual paper on "Home Science Education (HSE) for Rural Women in Uttarakhand", Archana Shah has advocated the need of bringing changes in the existing curricula for making Home Science a tool of empowerment for the women of the rural areas of Uttarakhand. She feels that if the discipline of Home Science is to be extended beyond imparting skills in home-making and serving as a tool for achieving sustainable development and woman empowerment in rural areas of Uttarakhand, then the curricula requires restructuring and reformulation to suit the needs of the rural women of Uttarakhand. The objective of this reformulation shall be to create a cadre of home economists, who are sensitive to the agricultural and rural developmental needs of their respective areas and who can communicate effectively about a wide range of environmental issues that affect rural households. In her view, conservation and sustainable development are mutually dependent and the dependency of rural (and urban) families on the natural resources is direct and immediate which must be conserved to improve the living standards. She feels that as Home Science has a long history of teaching conservation of household resources, therefore, teaching of sustainable Home Economics shall be a movement from consumption to conservation and sustainability. There is a major convergence of interest between environmentally sound and sustainable development and the development of women; therefore, such education and training would be beneficial for the rural women. She has also advocated the need of rural orientation and self-employment, as it is critically important to provide sustainable rural livelihoods for the present and future generations. In view of this, she feels that Home Science curricula should guide the reorientation of information and technologies, for the sustainable use of land and water, and conservation of other natural resources at the household level.

B.C., Upreti, in his paper, "Role of Women in Environmental Conservation and Management in Uttarakhand", has discussed the issue of women's relationship with the environment in Uttarakhand. He feels that gender sensitive approach, to environmental conservation and management, has acquired an important dimension because it has been seen that women are equally and in certain respects more then men, have been affected by environmental degeneration and degradation. In view of women's interest and sensitivity towards environmental conservation, it becomes necessary that women are also included in determining policies and strategies for environmental conservation and management so that they can also play a fruitful and vital role in environmental management and conservation. He has argued that though, the women of Uttarakhand have learned the need and importance of environmental conservation and management; however, the women's participation is still low in environmental protection, management, planning and execution of environment policies. He has opined that as this region is ecologically highly sensitive and environmental protection is very vital for the sustainability of the region, therefore, the under representation of the women in research and training and lack of gender sensitive policies cannot be considered a good sign for this important issue.

Upreti has highlighted that though the women of Uttarakhand have taken a lead in certain areas, such as, saving the forest resources and reforestation and launching the Beej Bachao Andolan, which emphasizes the need to go back to indigenous cropping system, they have also taken significant initiatives towards conservation of forests, bio-diversity and water management but there is still a need to strengthening and broadening these efforts throughout the region. He has also advocated the need for empowering women through training programmes in environmental conservation which should be launched at the local level in a decentralised manner and the participation of women should be ensured in these. Besides, this women can also play a vital role in the development of ecotourism as large scale tourism is creating lots of environmental hazards. There is a need to streamline and broaden the role of women in environmental conservation and management in a planned way. He has emphasized that for decentralised and sustainable approach to environmental conservation in Uttarakhand, the women need to have a share in policy formulation, research and training related to environmental conservation and management. There is also a need to understand the local context, local socio-physical relationship, priorities and constraints, in order to envisage strategies for environmental sustenance. There is a need to develop environmentally sound technologies to strengthen sustainable development in the hills as well as promote traditional subsistence methods to cultivation and natural resource utilisation which are adaptive to local environmental conditions.

Jyoti Tiwari in her paper on "The Changing Status and Role of women in India" has opinied that women in India are becoming more and more aware about their rights and demanding equal status as men. Over the last few decades, there has been a tremendous change in the laws, attitudes and norms affecting women's status, roles and development in India. As a result, many women are looking beyond the traditional role of wife and mother and seeking employment outside the home and are actively participating in the national economy. Women workforce constitutes an integral part of total workforce in India. However, she has observed that there are fewer women in the paid workforce and there is serious underestimation of women's contribution. Since women's participation in workforce is increasing all over the world, therefore, this has resulted in transformation of gender roles and it has also raised concerns about psychological well- being of women and family conflicts. In India there is a wide disparity between the affluent and the poor. As a result, on the one hand, we can see women as business executives and diplomats and on other top positions but, on the other, we find that there are millions of women who are illiterate, malnourished and live in extreme poverty and ill health.

She has highlighted the changes, which have taken place in the status and role of Indian women with the advent of globalisation and liberalisation. This has transformed the gender roles; women are now becoming more self-oriented than being oriented by others. Today many women are educated and not only working in all the sectors but also competing with men. But in India, a general assessment of the status of women is not an easy task, because of the presence of different religions, castes, classes, educational levels and occupations. As a result of these variations, there are many women who are still deprived of the basic necessities, like food, shelter and clothing, while others have freedom to make choices and lead their lives accordingly. The elite and the upper class women have gained the exposure to global network, access to new technology and have more chances of entering into non-traditional fields and opportunities to prove themselves. The invisible Indian woman has suddenly become visible in almost all the fields. However, the exclusion of poor, unequal distribution of benefits, marketisation of women, exhibitionism and rise in abuse against women, the marketisation of women, exhibitionism and rise in abuse against women have deprived a large section of women to take advantage of globalisation and development.

She has observed that economic independence of women has no doubt helped in their empowerment, as it improves their confidence, self esteem and enhances their ability to take part in the decision, making process. But the wage-earning activity increases the workload of women, which can only be reduced, if the men also agree to share the domestic work. Woman has to make most of the adjustments, because our patriarchal society demands more adjustments, from the women. Married working women find it especially difficult to work and as a consequence sometimes they have to forego prestigious career placements. Actually, the modern adult working women have to perform the additional roles of wives, mothers, and housekeepers; therefore, the pressure of dual work often results in family conflicts. Due to this dilemma, many women are delaying marriage and motherhood. For removing these disparities, there is a need to changing the mindset and redefining and reinterpreting the social roles assigned to males and females.

The last paper of this section by Denise Benoit Scott on the "United States Government: Limitations and Opportunities for Women's Empowerment" provides a very different and interesting prespective of women empowerment in the most powerful state of the world. She has discussed the problems of political empowerment of women in the United States of America; however, the similarities of the problems faced by the women in America and India clearly indicate the biased attitude of the society, even in a developed country and make it a very interesting paper. While mentioning the three waves of feminism due to which the identities of the women are no longer derived solely from their roles in the family and community, Scott has highlighted that women outnumber men in the paid workplace and are making headway in high-paying administrative and managerial positions, comprising almost 40 percent of all managers. Women are also increasingly found in the professions, constituting 32 percent of lawyers and 30 percent of physicians. In comparative terms, the proportion of women, in managerial and administrative positions outside government, far exceeds that for other countries. In fact, the United States is at the top of the list, ahead of all 15 countries in the European Union and just about all of the nations of the world. In addition, the U.S. has hundreds of active feminist organisations and has passed such landmark legislation which guarantee women's equality in employment and education. Culturally, women have also gained status and power. They are confident and comfortable in the public realm and are no longer silent with regard to their capabilities and interests. As a result of women's increased independence, marriage is becoming "deinstitutionalised," as many of the social norms and functions of marriage are now being met elsewhere. When women do marry, they are marrying at a later age than in the past. The average age at first marriage which was 23 in 1900 and 20 during the "golden era" of the 50s, now stands at 25. Women are also giving birth to their first child at a later age and have comparatively fewer children. Despite these impressive figures about women's independence and power in the realms of work and family, Scott however, has stressed that women are strikingly underrepresented in positions of power in the U.S. Government, particularly at the federal level. Women though constitute over half of the population, yet in 2011 they comprised only 17 percent of the Senate (17 out of 100) and 16 percent (88 out of 435 seats) of Congressional seats. On account of this, United States ranks 84th among countries around the world with regard to the percentage of women in national legislatures. She feels that dominant ideologies asserting that women are better at domestic tasks and mothering have had major effects on women in and out of the home and due to this women are concentrated in jobs and careers that are "feminised" and correspond with definitions of womanhood. As such, they are devalued, paid less and not seen as important to male dominated occupations. Moreover, the idea, that women have natural talent or ability for housework and childcare, places an enormous burden on them. These ideologies, and the intense focus on the home and children rather than their own lives, explains why women's primary identities are wrapped up in their roles within the family. Men, in contrast, not only have more leisure time than women, but continue to think of themselves first as men, whose identities are primarily connected with their jobs and secondly with their roles within the family. This leads to a power imbalance and explains why men are more likely than women to have extramarital affairs. She feels that for increasing women's political representation, they need to be told that that they too are entitled to power, to think for them, take risks, and make independent decisions. Women also need to be supported in their attempts to rise to leadership positions and there is also a need to critically examine the systems and structures that turn little boys into men and little girls into women and provide opportunities to them.

The third and last section of this book attempts to present a situational ananlysis of the realities of the decentralised governance, regional development and women empowerment through the case studies, conducted mainly in different areas of Uttarakhand. The first paper of this section by Annpurna Nautiyal on "Women's Participation in Decentralised Governance in Garhwal Himalayas: A Case Study of Uttarakshi District" highlights that the hill women's experience, of working amidst severe geographical and physical hardships, allows them to develop a better understanding of the issues and problems; hence, they take a keen interest in the resolution of the socio-political problems and social welfare. Women's participation in various movements, like *Chipko Movement, Anti Liquor Movement* and *Uttarakhand State Movement* stands as testimony to this. However, women's high work burden, lack of awareness and knowledge, poor socio and economic status hampers their continuous activism and participation in the socio-political and developmental process. She has observed that although, the reservation of seats in the Panchayati Raj Institutions have allowed the entry of the women in the political arena in large numbers and making them part of the decision-making process but the lack of awareness and knowledge about their rights and duties and social and financial independence is still not permitting them to show their full potential and caliber. More so, as these provisions have also facilitated the entry of ignorant or totally illiterate women, who remian completely dependent on their husbands, sons or male relatives for performing their duties in these bodies therefore, in some cases the real authority is still being enjoyed by the men, because the women are just acting as rubber stamp or people's representative for name sake. Such women are humiliated and devalued in the panchayats on account of their ignorance and illiteracy and they not only lack self esteem but also feel demoralised. With the result, despite potential, they remain unable to deliver the results. Women's ignorance, illiteracy, lack of awareness, superstitions, gender disparity, coupled with the unfavourable attitude and unwanted interference by the male members of family make the position of the women representatives pathetic in these institutions. Sometimes, women are also found to be suffering from the conservativeness and complexes of considering themselves inferior to men and at times the husbands also aspire to fulfill their own agenda through their wives due to this reason even after winning the election the women representatives' husbands can be found dictating terms in many places. This scenario presents an interesting contradiction about the women of the Garhwal Himalayas, as on the one hand, they are found to be eager to work for the welfare of the family, people and society, but on the other, the social set-up always places them at the receiving end. However, it is also true that women are naturally inclined to work on fundamental issues like making provisions for drinking water, because women generally look after the management of water in their homes. Therefore, they are capable of handling the small and basic issues and focus their attention towards creating the basic facilities like roads, schools etc. than on high-flying projects. Therefore, the involvement of women in large numbers into decision making bodies at the local/village level is likely to change and improve the working of these bodies and fulfill the aim of the real village and regional development. But for achieving these objectives education among the women urgently needs to be promoted, because only the educated women possess the capacity of making a difference in the situation through their working and understanding capacity. Nautiyal has emphasised that as women's empowerment and activism is interrelated, therefore, if women are aware about their rights, it becomes easier for them to actively participate in the political or social decision-making process and also in the elected bodies. Nautiyal has also stressed that women usually try to perform their roles very sincerely as they always remain under the scanner of the society. Therefore, whenever they are given any leadership or decision-making role, they try to leave their mark behind and this quality provides a strong basis for more activism of the women in the political process. Women also believe in creating a healthy and caring atmosphere for learning and their leadership styles not only reflect their feminine values, behaviour, natural instincts, welfare concerns and characteristics but also their attempts to encourage other women to be self-confident. These qualities certainly advocate for more participation and involvement of women in leadership roles, so that the best decisions for the welfare of the society and community could be taken.

She also feels that despite various arguments in favour of women's working styles and concerns as well as provisions, women's participation and leadership role in the political arena is still not as significant as it should have been in comparison their population with, because the implementation part of such measures always lacks commitment. Through this case study, conducted in a few villages of Uttarakashi district of Garhwal Mandal, reality about the problems, perception, vision of the women about the village and regional development, emerging leadership trends and prospects of women's participation have been analysed. She feels that it is still a challenge for the rural women to prove their potential in a conservative and male dominated society where most of the time they have always to undergo a social micro scrutiny. The watchful eyes of the male members on occasions unnerve the women. But as the women share a better idea of the developmental needs of the village like schools, facilities for children, drinking water, community halls and footpaths etc. therefore for there is need promoting good workers among the women. They also need to be provided information and proper training about their duties, so that they are able to fulfill their given task without any difficulty. This would ensure a balanced regional development for the far flung and remotely situated villages of the Garhwal Himalayas.

The next paper of this section by R.K. Maikhuri and Shalini Dhyani focuses on , " Empowering Hill Women for Sustainable Livelihoods and Natural Resources Management: A Case Study of Opportunities and Issues of Governance in Garhwal Himalayas". In this paper, a detailed overview of problems has been provided and also some cost-effective solutions for overcoming the hurdles and pressures on the hill women and also on the forests of Garhwal. The findings and conclusion of the paper is based on the research and development work of more than six years conducted in Upper Kedar valley. The authors feel that if implemented properly, the suggestions shall be helpful in improving the existing forest and conservation policy dialogues and also to addressing the gender concerns and issues in Garhwal Himalayas. Maikhuri and Dhyani has observed that though gender mainstreaming, with its promise of gender transformation, equality and empowerment, has become a central pillar of development discourse, policy and practice. Yet the implementation of these promises has been largely disappointing. While the gap between policy and practice is well, known, proposed 'solutions' bring little new to the table. Technical fixes does not work, and will not work to address complex gendered issues and inequities. Transforming gender requires staying on the edge of what we know, questioning our own certainties and through that, creating openness to risk that allows 'another way of knowing and of living in the world' that expands 'our capacity to imagine the human'. There is need to provide detailed information to the women about the rural development programmes/activities (being executed by the state/central governments and their line departments) and make them empowered through education and awareness programme. Education needs to be encouraged as a means of empowering women from grass-root level. Educational and awareness programmes for women need to incorporate capacity building and skill developmental activities in the field of rural development and livelihood, formal decision-making processes, leadership and strategic planning skills as well as confidence building, role in decision-making in the local level governance etc. Policies that support the mainstream gender issues and acknowledge that women are not only capable to managing their families but also acquiring knowledge of managing their resources and environment need to be formulated. Thus, hill women need to be involved in various programmes and activities that improve their capacities in addressing the issues relevant to rural development. Besides, women also need to be involved in policy-making at local, regional and national level and given equal opportunities to participate in decision-making and selection of appropriate programme/activities for rural development.

Prashant Kandari in his paper "Role and Significance of Women Representatives in Panchayats in Garhwal Himalayas: A Case Study " observes that women, though reflecting a strong presence in the current socio-economic scenario of the hill areas, are still million miles away from attaining the equal status as men. Despite several policy decisions taken by the government to revive the condition of the women of these areas, much perceptible change is not visible. The reservation for women in the Panchayats is one of such policy actions which aim to ensure women's presence in the decision-making bodies at the grass-root level. Although in many studies, a negative assessment of women's role as representative in Panchayats has been portrayed, considering them as mere dummies or functioning as proxy candidates under the close supervision of their guardians. The use of *'pati pradhans'* has therefore become quite common in the hill areas. Kandari, through a study conducted at the micro level in Pauri district of Uttarakhand, examines the problems, the hill women face in the Panchayats, not only from their family but also from the society and also the impact of increasing participation of women in local governance. The study also scrutinises the role of women in the decision making process and their contribution in the developmental process. He has concluded that despite problems the women leaders in the Panchayati Raj system are transforming local governance by sensitising the state authorities about the issues of poverty, inequality and gender injustice and through PRI, they are attempting to tackle the issues which were previously ignored, like scarcity of drinking water, alcohol abuse, education, health and domestic violence. The need of the hour is to encourage the participation of these women and provide necessary training to play the leadership role; this would go a long way, in not only empowering women in a real sense but also help in controlling and reducing corruption. This would provide a right atmosphere for an effective development of the rural areas.

R.R. Nautiyal and R. Datta, in their paper "Decentralised Governance, Empowerment of Women and Village Development: the Road Ahead" present an analysis of community development programmes and people's participation in it. The authors feel that the community development programme needs to be taken as the first expression of people's participation. Through this people can make plans and involve themselves in the development process in various sectors like education, health, infrastructure etc. The authors have examined the experience of such participation in anchayats with women 'Pradhans' with particular reference to the Mahatma Gandhi National Rural Employment Guarantee Act (MGNREGA), the largest single rights –based social protection initiatives in the world, through a case study in the Kirtinagar block of Tehri district of Uttarakhand. Through this they have tried to find out whether decentralised governance has helped in promoting efficiency in poverty alleviation and employment generation programmes? Has it helped in looking after the interest of women. Has decentralisation helped in increasing professionalism among the village women? How far such programmes under the decentralised regime have affected the lives of rural women through village development? Or how far the village women have really contributed to village development? The authors have observed that the level of awareness and right kind of perceptions about the decentralised governance and participation of the people are essential for achieving better development. Without this, the aim of village development or decentralisation cannot be achieved. In this study, the level of awareness and perception of women was found to be encouraging, but the withholding of information, intentionally to minimise the complexities of official work, had adverse affect on their performance. In view of this they feel that more awareness and literacy among the rural women needs to be promoted, so that they can become responsive to their rights and duties. They have also observed that as Gram Panchayat and Gram Sabha meetings are the prime mechanisms of obtaining inputs for planning and implementation, therefore, meetings at regular intervals and unbiased decisions regarding village development is of prime importance for a successful planning process. Accountability and transparency are also viewed as the most important pillars of the decentralised governance, as these ensure the successful delivery of the services at the grass-root level. This is a necessary condition for democratic institution and their smooth functioning, like planning, monitoring and evaluating public services. In view of this, more powers to the Pradhans with proper accountability and transparency is required. Awareness needs to be gererated among the people about decentralised governance by frequent training programmes. It has been highlighted that for the effective implementation of MNREGA many safeguards for transparency and accountability were built like the guidelines of MNREGA require 'muster rolls' to be made available at the worksites, displayed at the Panchayat Bhawan, and submitted to the Gram Sabhas for public scrutiny and social audit, but unfortunately these are not made so transparent in most of the Gram Sabhas. If this could be really done, it could go a long way in preventing corruption in wage payments. However, despite the loopholes and shortcomings, their study suggests that decentralised governance is helpful in women empowerment as well as village development, because, it helps in attaining efficiency in the face of different local preferences for local public goods. It also promotes good governance, people's participation and women empowerment as women can now also voice their concerns. The data-on man-days generated-reveal that though male population is higher in all villages but man-days generated by women is more. This shows the contribution of women in village development as well as their empowerment. It has also helped the growth of social organizations within the village, which promotes coordination and cooperation among the people, local officials and office bearers.

Jaya Pande in her paper "Role of Mahila Samakhya in Empowerment of Women: A Case Study of Uttarakhand" has evaluated the role of Mahila Samakhya in empowering women. The paper deals with three important aspects of women empowerment: upliftment of women in providing information, knowledge and skill in the political, economic and social points of view; developing rational and logical attitude in women: building a positive attitude about women in society and changing the patriarchal mindset and values. Pande in her case study has highlighted that the women representatives who participated in the wprkshops and training programme organised by Mahila Samakhya, were more aware, informed and had a positive attitude. They also attended Panchayat meetings regularly, confident about opposing illegal activities and more sensitive to women issues as well. She has advocated the need to launch more such programmes for promoting qualitative participation of the women in the regional development process. Inakshi Chaturvedi, in her paper on "Political Participation of Women Legislators: An Experience of Rajasthan State Assembly", discusses the political participation of women legislators in Rajasthan State assembly. She has opined that political participation for women should not mean only electing representatives and governing. It also includes efforts of increasing awareness and changing the unequal system. Though there is no denying the fact that voting is the first step towards assimilating in the political system, but the act of voting itself is not any indicator of gender equality. She has mentioned that though women have achieved suffrage in all democracies and Indian women got adult franchise at the advent of independence, but right to vote does not automatically leads to full political citizenship. An important element of political citizenship is political participation and this participation must be more than a chance to vote 'every few years.' Despite having the rights to vote, women are still under-represented in most parliaments, state legislative assemblies and government's structures world-wide. She has emphasized, that women reservation, which provides for 33 per cent reservation in the parliament and legislative assembalies, should be made an act, because only through it women's entry in respectable number in parliament and state assembalies can be ensured. Althought reservation policy is not an end in itself, but it is also one of the means to achieve gender equality. She feels that women's movement must work for more equality and empowerment of women and recognise collectively and critically the forces that limit their power, and also work collectively and continuously to change the unequal power structures. She has presented an analysis of women's participation, role and involvement in decision-making and execution through a study of the women legislatores' participation in the 11th and 12th State assemblies of Rajasthan state.

In the last paper of this section and the book on "Political Activism of Women in India: Importance and Problems" Rakesh Singh Negi discusses the relevance of women activism in the present political scenario and the limitation and problems for women's activism in the socio-political process. Negi emphasizes that as women not only have compassion but also a feel of the needs of the people and area, therefore, women's active participation in political process can create an atmosphere for speedy implementation of policies and other radical socio-political changes. Women's political activism and equal participation is one of the greatest needs of our times, but by improving women's participation only in urban areas cannot bring good results, rather it needs to be improved in the rural and remote areas of the country also. As the women of the remote and rural areas are even deprived of various facilities necessary for development, therefore, for making a productive contribution and registering their activism, the women of the rural and remote areas need to be given equal opportunities for political participation and say in the mainstream political development. Actually, effective measures and implementation of already existing laws/provisions are needed to boost women's activism, enhanced awareness and participation in the socio-political process. The small ~ber of women's participation in assemblies and parliament points the stark reality of the interplay of money and muscle power ions, due to which mostly the powerful, rich and influential only be successful in politics in today's political scene. The women, the poor and the marginalised sections of the society who lack muscle or money power, mostly remain unable to secure their seats in the elections. As the reservation of 33 percent seats to the women in the Panchayat Raj Institutions have produced very good results and a large of number of women taking advantage of such reservation have entered these institutions and by their participation in the decision-making process of these local bodies are making a difference in the delivery system of the services. In view of the success of women's participation in the local bodies, therefore Negi feels that the reservation of seats for the women in parliament and assemblies could be an answer to the problem of under-representation of women in these bodies.

List of Contributors

Dr. Kumud Sharma
Ex Director and Current Vice-Chairperson
Centre for Women's Development Studies
New Delhi

Prof. I.D. Mishra
Former Professor and Head
Department of Political Science
DDU University, Gorakhpur

Prof. Himanshu Bourai
Department of Political Science
HNB Garhwal University
Srinagar, Garhwal, Uttarakahand

Prof. Abdulrahim P. Vijapur
Professor and Chairman
Department of Political Science
Aligarh Muslim University, Aligarh

Dr. Bijayalaxmi Nanda
Senior Lecturer
Department of Political Science
Miranda House, University of Delhi, Delhi
Campaign Coordinator, Campaign against Pre-birth elimination of Females (CAPF)

Mrs. Archana Shah
Assistant Professor
Department of Home Science
SRT Campus, HNB Garhwal University
Badshahi Thaul, Tehri Garhwal, Uttarakahnd

Prof. B.C. Upreti
Professor and Director
South Asia Studies Centre
University of Rajasthan, Jaipur – 302 055
upretibhuwan@rediffmail.com

Dr. Jyoti Tiwari
Assistant Professor, Department of Home Science
H.N.B. Garhwal University, Srinagar
Garhwal (Uttarakhand)

Prof. Denise Benoit Scott
Professor, Department of Sociology
State University of New York
Geneseo, NY 14454 , U.S.A.

Prof. Annpurna Nautiyal
Professor, Department of Political Science
HNB Garhwal University, Srinagar, Garhwal

Dr. R.K. Maikhuri
G.B. Pant Institute of Himalayan Environment
and Development, Garhwal Unit, Srinagar-Garhwal
Post Box-92, Uttarakhand

Ms. Shalini Dhyani
G.B. Pant Institute of Himalayan Environment
and Development, Garhwal Unit
Srinagar-Garhwal, Post Box-92
Uttarakhand

Dr. Prashant Kandari
Assistant Professor, Department of Economics
BGR Pauri Campus, HNB Garhwal University
Pauri

Prof. R.R. Nautiyal
Professor and head Department of Economics
HNB Garhwal University, Srinagar, Garhwal
rrnautiyal@yahoo.in.

Mrs. R. Datta
Assistant Professor, Department of Economics
Doon University, Dehradun
lakshmi_23vishnu@rediffmail.com

Dr. Jaya Pande
Associate Professor
Department of Political Science
Government P.G. College, Ranikhet

Dr. Inakshi Chaturvedi
Vice Principal, Rajasthan College, Jaipur

Dr. Rakesh Singh Negi
Guest Faculty, Department of Political Science
HNB Garhwal, University, Srinagar, Garhwal
rakeshnegi@yahoo.co.in

SECTION I

CONCEPTUAL FRAMEWORK

1

Framing the Discourse on Decentralised Governance and Women's Empowerment

— Kumud Sharma

The governance debate took off in 1990s with obvious concerns with liberal democracy and the rise of neo-liberalism. The year 1990 was marked by two important developments in the Indian context– economic liberalisation and market-led development model and democratic decentralisation and political reservation for the women in institutions of local self governance. In India the process of democratic decentralisation has coincided with the process of economic restructuring. Women's participation in the political arena has increased with representation in the institutions of local self-governance, and at the same time there are added burdens from shrinking work and livelihood opportunities and the resultant 'welfare gap'. The new economic regimes have resulted in increased conflict over basic resources and livelihood options and have increased the vulnerabilities of certain groups because of their social location. Some scholars believe that decentralisation is 'simply a sweetner for the bitter pill of neo-liberal adjustments and rising in equalities'. In the 1990s, the discourse on human development indices (HDR) and democratic institutions led to the questioning of institutions of governance and its agenda. The shift in debates from government to 'good governance' marked a shift in focus on administrative and managerial aspects of governance.

In a liberal, multi-party democracy, arguments for democratic decentralisation have formed part of the liberal democratic discourse in India. It is argued in the following way.

- It will provide greater efficiency, transparency accountability, responsiveness of local governments and opportunities for people's participation.

- Economic complexities and diversities need decentralised governance to respond to diverse development needs of the region and social groups.
- In a plural and unequal society diversity based on class, caste, ethnicity, religion and gender also reflects problems of inclusion and exclusion and unequal citizenship rights. Demand for decentralisation and political representation is seen as a legitimate means for protecting the interests of the marginalised or excluded group.
- Questioning the presumption that state in a liberal democracy works for the 'common good', it is argued that participation and human agency of the marginalised group is crucial for pushing their concerns on the development agenda.
- Within democracy demand for greater representation is also seen as an instrument for redistribution of power and resources.
- Expected political engagement through representation and participation can introduce new interests and concerns.

Mandatory representation of women in PRIs marked a shift to pro-active politics and possibilities of political engagement of women in public life, opportunity for development of local leadership at the grassroot level and expected to changes of priorities of local governance.

The 73rd and 74th amendments envisaged a significant structural change in the decentralisation of power and development planning at the local level by assigning PRIs.

(a) Preparations of plans for economic and social justice.

(b) Implementation of schemes for economic development and social justice in matters listed in the XIth schedule.

Decentralisation involves restructuring of authority between the institutions of governance at different levels – central, state and local. It means transfer of power, responsibility and resources from Central to State and to local government and brings decisions closer to people. The rationale for decentralisation is linked to the principle of subsidiarity i.e. the lowest level of government can perform functions more efficiently and effectively and therefore, the administration of public resources should be brought closer to people. Decentralisation is also expected to improve, not only efficiency and responsive local government, but also transparency and accountability of local government, local development, reduction in poverty and cost effective and improved public services. It involves devolution, delegation and decentralisation of authority, responsibility, funds and functions. People's Plan Campaign in Kerala attempted to make the process of decentralisation part of popular politics.

Effective decentralisation also needs institutional decentralisation and democratisation of the political system. It is largely an administrative initiative and emphasis is on efficiency rather than equity. There is a difference between decentralisation per se and decentralised governance. Governance is not a techno-managerial concept. The discourse on governance confronts the complex matrix of state, political power, democracy and development. It includes economic governance (development framework); political governance (institutions' representative and transformative framework); administrative governance (legal framework, state agencies) and civil society governance (support groups, networks and institutional building activities).

The concept of governance has undergone significant changes from being state-centre to a structure of democratic decision-making. Local governance has a policy dimension (devolution, delegation of power and resources), institutional dimension and social and economic dimensions. UNDP defines governance as 'complex mechanism, processes, relationships and institutions through which citizens and groups articulate their interests exercise their rights and obligations and mediate their differences'.

Decentralisation does not guarantee expected outcomes, but only opportunities to participate in planning and local governance. Outcomes of decentralisation are shaped by many factors, such as local capacity, political and social histories, local social organisations and social stratification, land and tenurial relations, strength of local power elites and bureaucracy and its commitment to decentralisation; the role of development agencies, civil society organisations and NGOs. Decentralised governance is a political process and there are winners and losers. It also carries the risks of :

- Interest group capture of local government and reinforce existing inequalities
- Consolidate existing alliances with local elites (patronage)
- Corruption
- Politician bureaucratic nexus

Initially there was a lackadaisical response from the central and state governments to devolve funds, power, and functionaries and give them autonomy. Starved of funds, these bodies became extended arm of the government for development work. Vertical programmes of the central government (poverty alleviation schemes) and donor funded programmes run parallel programmes without integrating it in the local plans. PRIs instead of bringing participatory democracy and decentralised governance consolidated local power structures. Governance is about the exercise of power—who participates, whose interests are served through allocative decisions and how far those in authority are held accountable for unfair and exclusionary practices.

Is local governance more just, equitable and inclusive? If it is grafted on to the existing system of privileges, power, political patronage and culture, it can prove as discriminatory as any other unequal system and operate along the fault lines of gender, class and caste. Justified on the grounds of efficiency, effectiveness and responsiveness, is it open to the participation of subordinate groups and accountable to their interests? Democratising political power structures and institutions at local level is seen as the key to addressing development issues and inequalities of the region, as well as participation of the marginalised groups. Local governance is multi-sectoral and multifaceted. It needs both upstream linkages with policies and fiscal management and downstream linkages to local area-based and need-based development and effective delivery of services. Empirically, it is difficult to prove direct relationship between decentralisation and poverty reduction or decentralised governance and women's empowerment. Similerily, poverty reduction does not necessarily reduce gender inequality. Equity outcomes are often not realised. These synergies have to be created and cannot be assumed. Infrastructure for development is a functional necessity of decentralisation of administration. There are other significant developments like RTI Act, NREGA, DV Act which emphasise the centrality of PRI's. Ability of the disadvantaged groups to benefit will depend on the positioning of these issues in the governance agenda and their capacity to negotiate and organise strength.

Is Decentralised Governance the Panacea to Promote Gender Justice and Empowerment of Marginalised Groups?

The challenges that both women and democratic decentralisation face, is the question of representation and participation of traditionally marginalised groups and power dynamics at the local level. Issues of gendered governance and gender equitable governance have expanded the debate on democratisation of institutions of governance and search for new institutional mechanisms. Arguments, for greater representation of women in decision-making processes, rest on the possibilities of political engagement of women with democratic institutions using the political space to transform the agenda of governance. The democratic public space in India is marked by competing group interests; conflicts and tensions due to imbalances in power, access to resources and citizenship entitlements. Representation of women, in PRIs as means for redistributing political power, is inadequate to challenge established hierarchies.

Assuming that, women benefit from decentralisation of power to local decision-making bodies, due to the possibility of their greater involvement, greater participation of women will not automatically engender institutional changes, given the male bias of government institutions and structural barriers to addressing gender interests. It is at the institutional level where entitlements are decided, resources allocated and markets regulated. Exclusion of individuals in the political arena also transfers to their exclusion in other institutions. Poor women are more dependent on public services (health care, social security) which often target women in their gender roles. Gendered interests are not considered as 'common good' and have the effect of depoliticising women's interests and failing to acknowledge power issues. Patriarchal structures may be just as strong at local level and may well be combined with non-accountable customary or informal bodies and community relationships which make it harder for women to exert meaningful influence.

Local government is seen as a nursery for developing local leadership among the women. The eligibility criteria for contesting elections are less stringent. The local government is closer to women's sphere of life and it is easier for women to combine domestic responsibilities. The two constitutional amendments have created expanded opportunities for women in public life, especially resource poor women whose dependence is much greater on state for accessing resources.

The entry of more than one million women in PRIs – has it transformed the content and style of local politics? Women had a formidable task of not only representing women's interests but also create agency and negotiate power. Do numerical goals provide take off points? Has it become an investment of social mobilisation of women? Do women constitute an interest group despite differences and plurality of interest?

The first generation of EWR had to continuously struggle to cope with societal structures, conscious targeting by those opposed to the idea, disbelief in their capacities, and resistance to their leadership role. Contestations within domestic sphere took different forms than women's encounters with the development bureaucracies and the local power elites. Many women bruised male egos by becoming head of the local council. The patriarchal family, bureaucracies and other traditional village institutions moved in to contain the potential of women's entry into local politics. A majority of women had to fight for their legitimate spaces within PRIs. Another set of strategies were adopted by local elites like 'proxy politics', consensus candidates, fielding women candidates from the family to keep the seat warm till it was de-reserved in the next election, no confidence motions, misinformation campaigns. Initially they had to deal with not only their own lack of experience but additional barriers posed by patriarchal household, caste, class and local power elites.

The larger framework of representative democracy and the public political space is not a pre-given consensual space upholding the ideals of 'common good' or equity and justice. It is a site of contestation over needs, interests and priorities of various groups. Conflicts and contestations are often tied up to other forms of power struggles and women often face the dilemma in gender and caste based identities. In the latter their negotiating power is minimal. Besides the institutions of local self-governance, there are community based, non-state parallel systems of justice and dispute resolving mechanisms – caste and ethnic councils disciplining those transgressing community norms. These are constantly challenged by people's struggle through alternative language of economic and political empowerment which has become part of the narrative of local governance.

Social transformation is not only dependent upon policy commitments and actions of political parties and government institutions but by organised pressure of civil society groups. There are a number of examples of women having successfully mobilised around the issues of water, village commons, fodder and fuel but were unable to take women's issues like domestic violence, rape and dowry. Some women have shown marked initiative but most have stuck to the standard development concerns such as school, ICDS Centre, roads etc. Does focussing on development benefits, empower women without changing women's traditional status and power structures?

Several studies have focussed on the interlinkages between the unequal power relations within the private domain and the possibilities and limits to the exercise of power in the public sphere of political decision-making and governance. Local governments are often more or equally hierarchical as they are embedded into the local power structure.

- Affirmative action (political quotas for women) which determines terms of inclusion, often creates tensions and conflicts as it directly challenges power configurations.
- Role of traditional authority at village level (caste panchayats, customary institutions)–patriarchal structures combined with non-accountable customary or informal bodies and community (mechanisms) relationship put formidable barrier to women's participation.
- Women as a group are expected to represent women's interest in local institutions of governance. The argument ignores other social divisions and identities at local level.
- Access to assets and entitlements are widely governed by power relations which have political dimensions.
- Women have different degree of access to public spaces and different degrees of participation and control. Their ability to participate in decision-making and capacity to exercise their rights are determined by gender roles (limit their time and leverage in politics) and unequal relations of power.
- Gender equity issues do not enjoy a wide support within the community and women's issues often lack strong social support and legitimacy (dowry, domestic violence, alcoholism). This has a depoliticising effect.
- Gender inequalities often undermine the value of their consent or voice in politics.

Representation does not *ipso facto* lead to women's empowerment, though political representation is universally hailed as 'political empowerment' of women. Too exclusive a focus on representation and visibility alone, without addressing structural barriers, does not make it an effective instrument for women's empowerment or inclusion of their needs, interests and issues.

'Empowerment' has become a catchphrase and a magic bullet that can fast track the process of social transformation. Representation is a key element in empowerment as it entails a voice in public policy decisions. Empowerment is a complex concept and its interpretations vary according to ideological perspectives. It has become part of the governance and development discourse as well as grassroot organisation's strategy to mobilise women on specific issues and their active involvement in decision-making process. Empowerment has been defined 'as the process of increasing the capacity of individuals or groups to make choices and to transform these choices into desired actions and outcomes' (UNDP). World Bank defines it as 'the expansion of assets and capabilities of poor people to participate in, negotiate with, influence, control and hold accountable institutions that affect their lives'. The term empowerment contains the agenda of social change – in terms of both collective and individual self assertion.

Empowerment is a political process, as the critical operating concept within empowerment is 'power'. Empowerment is all about shifts in social, economic and political power between and across individual and social groups. Women's empowerment is more a political and transforming idea for struggle that challenges not only patriarchy but the mediating structures of class, caste, ethnicity and religion.

Notion of women's 'political empowerment' is caught in conflicting agendas. Political institutions and electoral processes, which influence women's access to spheres of power, remain male dominated. Greater representation of women may not actually challenge existing hierarchies of power. There is this temptation to either run down their achievements or romanticise the heroism of few women. Hailed by some as a 'silent revolution', it is denigrated by others for bringing in 'proxy women'. Representation does make an impact on local self-governance, but not necessarily on policy decisions.

Women's empowerment approach is not a grand narrative and it is difficult to approach the issue within the conventional category of political analysis. It is a concept which focuses on everyday resistance and struggle of women, who contest the power configuration in day to day life, claim spaces dominated by developmentalist state and patriarchal structures; create spaces to negotiate and emphasise collective agency of women. Gender accountability of institutions of local governance does not flow from increased representation of women. There is a link between strong political representation and high incidence of female poverty. While women's empowerment issues need to be discussed in the context of power and capabilities of PRIs, there is a need to strengthen the institutional framework with adequate resources and sensitivity to women's issues backed by capacity building, sensitisation, poverty resource monitoring and gender audits. Unless budgetary allocations for health, education and support systems for women are earmarked, an increasing number of women will drift into poverty. Social scientists oppose a depoliticised approach as there is no prior reason why local form of governance should be more democratic and accountable.

Gender accountability of decentralised governance systems, does not flow from the increased representation of women. Institutional norms and practices play an important role in determining women's entitlements and participation. Gender and governance issues need to be discussed in the context of power and capabilities of PRIs. In Kerala, a main strategy of strengthening the role of EWRs revolved around neighbourhood groups for sustaining the gram sabha ethos and take on the task of encouraging participation and social audit. Another trajectory, that needs to be explored, is expanding or contracting spaces of civil society organisations, local women's groups and networks as support mechanisms, user groups (water and forest committees, SHGs etc.) and ideologically grounded programmes like Mahila Samakhya. Are these more concerned with state defined reforms agenda or do they have the potential to mobilise women around their concerns, build their capacities to effectively participate in local planning, implementation and monitoring of programmes? Do community based organisations (CBOs) influence allocation of resources and local development priorities? Do they enhance women's voice and capacities to participate in local government? Political mobilisation has to go with economic mobilisation and advocacy. The central issue remains as to how to strengthen the negotiating spaces for women in the present paradigm of state, market and civil society.

2

Democracy Accentuates Decentralisation

— *I.D. Mishra*

Decentralisation dissolves the power to flow to its constituents so as to make it meaningful, useful and significant. Decentralised power is the core principle of democracy and development. Cetralised power is neither citizen centric nor democratic. It uses coercive means to achieve its target of retaining the power which is centralised to protect the interests of its holders. Power holders are the power enjoyers at the cost of those who are being controlled. Power-holders, to achieve and protect their desired interests, generally make use of the power which they hold. Power, even if institutionalised in such situations remains much more personalised. Power in this form becomes coercive, and sometimes unlimited and legitimacy of the claims remains dependent upon the holders and not upon those who are being controlled. History presents various examples of movements of the people against the rulers, who held or controlled the power and who had different interests from the interests of the public, or those who were being ruled. The public interests, which constitute the will of the people itself the, "general-will", in Rousseau's terminology, hold the potential power, to cause resentment and resistance to the narrow interests of the holders of power or their rule. It poses potential threat to the body-politic. A situation that may be called conflicting claims to power (Sabine), is susceptible to instability and unsuitable to development whether economic or political.

If the power has to be functional for democracy and its people, it has essentially to be decentralised. In that case, the motivating force to power in its process would be "the willed interests" not the desired interests, as there is no place for desired interests of power-holders in the above situations. In fact, the desired interests and willed interests are contradictory in spirit, unless the former is transformed into an inclusive system of people's participation, governance and benefits. In modern state, this could be ensured only in democracy where responsibilities and benefits (both) are due to people. People are the virtual centre of power, its users and beneficiaries. Therefore, power requires to be channeled from people to people, to their groups and associations and to society, and lastly to state, as the custodian and guarantor of power-process in a decentralised manner, so that it may reach to every individual, every citizen, institutions and regions within the boundary of the state. The Constitution of India makes this arrangement and ensures its implementation.

Decentralisation strengthens the capacity building process of the 'Whole' in general and units in particular. It brings the units to the centre with more vital connectivity and strength to just functioning in delivering goods and justice to all those who constitute, institutionalise and make the whole system functioning. This is the basic principle of the state with democratic 'modus operandi'. India as 'Union of States' (federal system) provides a major constitutional framework for decentralisation and federal system is itself an indicator of the decentralisation of power. It recognises the units as constituents of the Union and as such, holders of their autonomy which is defined as jurisdiction of their power to act. Power to act, in turn, includes enactment, execution, and adjudication; the latter one, however, as part of the integrated judicial system is neither subduing nor super-imposing the decentralised power system but to monitor whether there is any violation of constitutionally provided jurisdictions and its autonomy. Hence, whenever there has been demand for more autonomy from the states, it is voiced for keeping their constitutionally decentralised powers intact and non-interfered. There have been several instances of unexpected intervention by the Centre on the internal and autonomous functioning of the states under the constitutionally decentralised power structure on reasons and justifications given by the center itself. The trend, of imposing centre's will and intervening in states' jurisdiction, has weakened in the era of coalition- politics. Every individual in the state is an essential component of decentralisation to which the power should flow for capacity building and enrichment.

Centralised power in a democracy is almost kinetic, non-functional and, therefore, not useful. It destroys itself as it looses its support base of functionality through its component units. Think of a tree with its stem cells, branches and leaves. If these are ill-nourished or destroyed, can a tree remain standing and functional? Thus, any system, like tree which gets its nourishment from its surroundings in which it is situated through its functionaries/units, may hardly function effectively, if the power centre fails to allocate its power or make the power flow to its functionaries and beneficiaries. Democracy is a system of people, it belongs to people and people belong to the system. People, as the makers of the system, run it through the mechanism of their governance. From decision-making to its implementation, the role of people can be found every where. It ensures, people's participation as a basic necessity (Mishra, 1985), as the investors and beneficiaries both are the people. Their participation, therefore, is the pre-condition to install democracy. Since, every individual is a necessary unit of democracy, therefore, if the Indian democracy has to be really functional, it has to empower the people as well as all the democratic institutions. This is possible only through decentralisation and people's participation. Ancient India had a rich experience of people's participation. Amartya Sen argues that even 'the ink-cloud of the Ancient Indians', is not entirely imaginary, since there have been, in fact, several experiments in local democracy in ancient India (more those presently) (Sen, 2009). Democracy and participation, in fact, survives by each-other and the former exclusively depends on the latter. Hence, it is correct to say that democracy virtually depends on participation; by this criterion we could know the movement of the world towards democracy. There is a justification in accepting Amartya Sen's (2009) argument that "in understanding the roots of democracy in the world, we have to take an interest in the history of people's participation and public reasoning in different parts of the world. Democracy, therefore, neither belongs to only the Europeans nor merely to the Americans, but to the world at large and particularly India's significant contribution to the democratic practices and evolution could hardly remain unreckoned with. Amartya Sen reasonably emphasizes this line of argument. According to him, "We have to look beyond thinking of democracy, only in terms of European and American evolutions. We would fail to understand the pervasive demands for participatory living, on which Aristotle spoke with far-reaching insight, if we take democracy to be a kind of specialised cultural product of the west" (Sen, 2009). Besides India as Union of States, the power has been further decentralised through the 73rd Constitutional Amendments, so as to involve people in governance and development at various levels of Zila Parishads, Municipalities and Panchayats. Thus, this has made Article 40 effective.

Functional power is in fact a plural concept. Since every society is almost a plural in structure, therefore its structural units of different varieties and character to become functional need power. For example, even social units are of different varieties based on the various needs and principles, which may be further divided into sub units. Similarly, there are political, economic, cultural, territorial, regional,. rural and urban, professional and occupational and many more other units and sub-units like industrial and technical units. These, are need-and value-based, and require no intervention from the outside of their peripheries, except in the irksome situations that may cause obstructions to the smooth functioning of the system as a whole. Hence, these structural units and sub units require power which is derived from the system's source and need to be retained by them without any central or external restraints. This brings autonomy of jurisdictions (power allocated to them under decentralised governance) among the structural components and sub-components. This is how democracy functions through accentualising decentralisation. Society is institutionalised by familial and group behavioural relations based on their needs. These needs are both simple and complex in nature. Simple needs are the basic needs of individuals and family both. As these needs enter into groups and social relations, the nature of needs and their behavioural relations accordingly changes and acquires complexities. However, as far as these complexities retain cordial relations, power decentralised between them remains a necessity, otherwise, it becomes difficult for them to exist and develop and fulfill their motives.

Now, think of a state system which includes all systems, viz, social, economic, political, religious, cultural and likewise many others (which may be called sub systems as well) and possesses a more complex structure as these are institutionalised within the state system and therefore, remain their protégée. These become the functionaries of the State System in a broad sense and these functionaries need power and autonomy, on the one hand, to secure and promote their identities and, on the other, to help secure and promote state's interests. The causes, of decline of state in the pages of history, whether under monarchy, tyranny, aristocracy, oligarchy or democracy, may be traced in the excessive centralisation of power in the hands of the rulers and its arbitrary use in their own interests. It is why democracy is the most welcome system to ensure the restraint upon the government's domain of power. But even the restrained power of the government is not sufficient for functional democracy.

Against this backdrop, the Indian Constitution adopted provisions for decentralisation of powers which has been made at many layers. A look at the Preamble of the Constitution and other provisions provides an example of this. The Preamble is in fact an indicator of the source of authority of the Constitution and precisely puts its objectives that need to be promoted. It begins with "We", (the totality of individuals and nationals) as the creator of constitution which means all of us have a supreme constitution and under it the system of governance and its institutions as provider of services and benefits to the people. It signifies people as the core of the Constitution. This, however, is impossible without involving the people in the process of governance meaning thereby self governance, self-rule and self development. From this perspective of the objectives of Preamble democracy and decentralisation have to be adjudged and valued. These have been institutionalised under the two important chapters of the Indian Constitution; viz, the Fundamental Rights and the Directive Principles of State Policy. Actualising these would help democratic functioning in the true sense. These are two accessories to democracy, and connecting chains of relations between individuals and society, on the one hand, and individuals and state, on the other hand, as well as the relations between society and state as sine-qua-non. But sometimes we miss in our understanding these relations and their significance for individuals, society and state. Owing to these reasons we fail to put Fundamental Rights and Directive Principles at par and equally significant to each other, both for democracy and state. It is why Fundamental Rights are considered sometimes superior to Directive Principles and sometimes the latter one is considered to be superior. Constitutional protection of fundamental rights has led the judiciary to come to their rescue against the governmental interventions by law/or promulgations of ordinances and it makes fundamental rights superior. This privilege is not available to Directive Principles of State Policy. However, Constitutional Amendments have made some of the principles incorporated in Constitution as inviolable and non-accessible by the court on the petitions related to violation of fundamental rights. And this situation adds more significance to the directive principles than the fundamental rights. "Article 31C accepts the view that there may be situations in which there may be conflict between a Fundamental Right and a Directive Principle. It lays down that if a law is enacted to implement the principles contained in Part IV of the Constitution, then it shall not be open to attack on the ground that it is inconsistent with the Fundamental Right. The law will prevail over the Fundamental Right. Thus Article 31C gives primacy to all laws implementing the DP over the FRs" (Sharma, 2002). In Champakam case, the Supreme Court's observation, that 'the Directive Principles have to conform to and run subsidiary to the Chapter on Fundamental Rights', is of much significance in the context of understanding the broad frame work of decentralisation. Now, such paradigm of superiority and inferiority is unacceptable to relations and also averse to institulising the process of democracy and the state. Two principles against 'superiority' of either of these (i.e. FRs and DPs) endorsed by the Supreme Court in Keshavanand Bharati Case could be cited in this context. First, 'both the FRs and DPs are equally fundamental, though DPs are not directly enforceable by the courts. Second, FRs and DPs are supplementary to each other' (Keshavanand Bharati Case). Analogous view, such as 'harmonious interpretation rule in 1959' adopted by the Supreme Court in the Kerala Education Bill, underlines the principle of harmonious construction in order to make effective to both FRs and DPs (Tripathi, 1972). "In Minerva Mills (1980) the Court reiterated that harmony and balance between FRs and DPs is an essential feature of the basic structure of the Constitution."

Thus democracy and decentralisation are inclusive. Democracy as plurality becomes functional and autonomous, when the' Public reasoning' (Sen, 2009) is developed and accepted as authority and becomes functional in a decentralised way. In fact, Public reasoning demands decentralisation to justify plurality so as to make democracy plurally functional. This could also be used as an approach to social justice. Decentralisation as a framework of democracy, not only ensures plurality, but also strengthens the root of social justice as well. Decentralisation of means of livelihood is the precondition and, to guarantee the right to life to everyone in the system, as its natural member, is a must for a democracy. It is under this notion that the Constitution of India wished the decentralisation of means of production so as to ensure that the wealth should not be concentrated in one or few hands. (Constitution of India) Abolition of Privy-purses (26th Amendment) and Nationalization of Banks were a few major steps by the Government of India to ensure decentralisation of wealth for public purposes. This could be treated as the 'public reasoning' of the then Prime Minister Indira Gandhi, which could be transformed into ordinances/Acts and later on, into constitutional amendments. These steps were to ensure the means of livelihood to the masses at the grass-root level. Planning Commission is another powerful institution which can strengthen the institution of decentralised economy. However, it could not be marked with credit as it could not fulfill the expectation of economic growth for plural and rural India at large. After all, Planning Commission is itself a Central body and hence, can't escape central influence. Deleting the right to property from the fundamental rights section is another major movement towards fulfilling the objectives of decentralisation. However, emergence of corporate sectors as powerful institutions of economic development bears the testimony both from the pockets of centralisation and decentralisation. This new trend is developing as the process of liberalisation, globalisation and privatisation has been augmenting. Consequently, both the trends of centralisation and decentralisation are on increase, in one way or the other. Liberalisation enhances flexibility in the state economy through allowing the people to enter into the market, virtually the corporate houses and multinationals, which means strengthening the economy of the corporate houses in the private sectors. Competition and monopoly, both are seen as a landmark development in the growth of these houses, with a common feature of wealth and capitals being centralised. The areas of market have been widened from national to global, marked by competition and co-operation, for the purpose of selling the products and earn money. As a result, the global market players are engaged in hob-knobbing with the members to find their major areas of interests and benefits. In between them are the institutions like the World Trade Organisation, World Bank, International Monetary Fund etc. which are working to enhance globalisation and strengthen global marketers. In a nutshell, the purpose of decentralisation of securing every individual economically, politically and socially in the Indian plural society is being intrigued under the process of liberalisation, globalisation and privatisation as marked inequality in growth, while severe deprivation could hardly be left unnoticed. People's political and social status in general is still far from the decentralised standard. Their political and social freedom are misshaped and misconstrued by the market leverage as market defines its meaning, frames policy and implements it through the mechanism of governance by the state. Decentralisation is hanged up in this process and its purpose is defeated.

Now, the question is how to make "decentralisation" functional for the plural democratic society and to nourish decentralising capability to neutralise the centralizing tendency of globalization? The slogan 'think globally and act locally' is being used to justify decentralisation through globalisation. But how global can be transformed into local' is yet to be discovered. How global and local could be accommodated is yet to be devised. Is global democracy and local democracy one and the same? Could it be possible to develop a theory of global democracy or single pattern of democracy? Again making a single form or one pattern is to generate violence in freedom of choice inherent in democratic decentralising movement. It would precipitate aberration in the purpose of decentralisation and its theory. Plural empowerment as one of the basic agenda of democratic movement would then remain unfinished. Thus slogan to act locally in the plural world appears to be unrealistic amidst forces augmenting centralisation and globalisation. One burning example is : Why even after so many years and India's economic growth, India is not allowed to enter the UN Security Council as a permanent member? Why only the 5 permanent members have the monopoly over the powers of the Council and the rest of the UN members have to look for their mercy. This structure of the Security Council is a rare example of the legitimate centralised power at the world level. Unfortunately, these powers are the champions of democracy and decentralisation at the global level. Except the Peoples' Republic of China, which is already a case of centralisation of power, the rest four, UK, USA, France, and Russia, the strong supporters of democracy and democratization, have done little to forward the movement of decentralisation nationally and globally (World Bank Reports). And, therefore, their concern of democracy appears to be motivated by no other reason than their self interest.

Conclusively, decentralisation is the living centre of democracy. It integrates individual and their groups to the democratic system and its institutions with their full autonomy and participation for growth and development. Plurality remains intact with minimal chances of intervention and eruption of disharmony provided that the culture of plural co-existence is promoted and nourished. Therefore, if decentralisation ensures many things simultaneously, it demands also many things to get their full expression as well. It ensures individuality and its expression, recognition of groups and society, plurality and plural culture, regionalism and rationality in democratic tune, governance and government with democratic culture; and above all, strengthens state with people's democracy at all levels. But, is it possible where people at large are illiterate and uneducated, poor and deprived with a weak citizenry unable to support and strengthen the state which guarantees their rights and enables them to avail their opportunities? The structural problems that have emerged out of the above situations keep the benefits of decentralisation non-secured in the hands of the masses at the grass-root level. Since decentralisation is multi-fold concept, it needs to be unfolded at policy–making level and due attention to be paid to every field at the level of implementation. In the past, we have fields to uphold the balance of relations between the various filds such as regional and central, rural and urban, social, economic and political at both the above levels. Our urban and economic centric policies have marginalised the social and political objectives of decentralization. The urban centric approach as a model of development can't be justified as a code of development for rural India. The suggestion, at hand, is that the decentralisation should rehabilitate the rural India in its resources and self-reliance. It should neither be anti-urbane nor should be allergic to urbane benefits.

Notes and References

1. The powers are divided between the Centre, 28 States and 7 Union Territories under the constitution of India. Accordingly, the Constitution provides three lists, viz. the Union List, The State List and the Concurrent List which define their jurisdictions of Legislative actions–the broad division of Power as the major guide lines to decentralisation under the federal system.

Even in the unitary democratic system the arrangement of power relations between the central government and the local governments are made through the deconcentration of power by the former to the latter. Under this system, the responsibilities are dispersed by the central government to its regional branches and offices. Decentralisation is a complex concept and it has a different meaning. However, the three relational conceptual terms, associated with decentralisation, are looked upon to explore its meaning. First, 'deconcentration', second 'delegation'; which means the transfer of authority to local government and the third 'devolution' which means transfer of authority for 'decision-making, finance, and management to quasi-units of local government (see Rondnelli, Denis (1981). "Government Decentralisation in Comparative Perspectives: Theory and Practice in Developing Countries", International Review of Administrative Services 47(2) : pp. 135-144). Decentralisation includes three processes: fiscal decentralisation, political decentralisation, and administrative decentralisation. (For details, see Jennie llene Litavac, Junaid Ahmad and Richard Miller Bird (2007) and Inman, Robert P and Daniel L Rubinfeld, : (1997). "Rethinking Federalism: Journal of Economic Perspectives 11(4). pp. 44-63. The political decisions, to devolve powers from central government, can only be translated into actual powers, if sub national governments have the fiscal, political and administrative capacity to manage this responsibility. The developed countries have their own experience of decentralisation—economically, socially, politically and strategically and similarly, the developing countries have also their own problems and prospects. Hence, the emerging nations with democratic systems are modeling and remodeling decentralisation in their own way to accommodate their needs.

2. See the Preamble of the Constitution of India.

3. In Golakhnath v State of Punjab, the Supreme Court, which by majority of 7 judges out of 11, had established the non-amendable

character of fundamental rights, reversed its decisions in Keshvanand Bharati case and upheld the 24th Constitutional Amendment.

REFERENCES

Mishra, I.D. (1985). *Understanding A Political System*, Ch. Varanasi, Ch.1.

Sen, Amartya (2009). *The Idea of Justice*, Allen Lane, Penguin Books, pp. 321-22.

Sharma, B.K. (2002). *Introduction to the Constitution of India*, Prentice-Hall of India. New Delhi, p. 113.

State of Madras v Champakam, AIR, 1951, S C. 228.

Keshvanand Bharati v State of Kerala, AIR 1973.

Tripathi, P.K. (1972). *Spotlight on Constitutional Interpretation*. Bombay, pp. 295-320.

Minerva Mills v. Union of India, AIR, 1980. S C. 1789.

Amartya. (Sen, 2009). *The Idea of Justice*, Allen Lane. Penguin Books, pp. 321-326

Constitution of India, Article 39.

The 26 Amendment to the Constitution, 1971.

See, the World Bank Reports; Jennie llene Litavac, Junaid Ahmad, Richard "Miller Bird, Rethinking decentralisation in developing Countries." (2007).

3

Decentralised Governance and Women: Special Reference to Panchayats in India

— Himanshu Bourai

World Bank Publications.

The desire for a more efficient administration has motivated many of the recent constitutional and legislative changes in the countries all over the world and decentralisation has evolved as one of the means for it. Though, experience has shown that central governments are often unable to successfully implement efficiency-building policies and programmes, but better administration is not always an automatic result of decentralisation. Still, if local governments are properly equipped to fulfill their tasks (UNDP, 1993, p. 75), the chances of achieving "better government" through decentralisation increases because "officials who work for centralised governments do not have the necessary knowledge of local conditions to provide efficient government services, because this knowledge is dispersed among the millions of people who comprise the society, and cannot be transmitted to a central planning board" (Kendall, 1991, p. 15). Paddison opines that "in comparison to national governments, local governments are more accessible, more sympathetic and quicker to respond to local needs" (Paddison, 1985, p. 143), and programmes, and services can be more easily adapted to local circumstances and needs. This is so, because local authorities are obviously more knowledgeable about a local situation than the authorities who are far away from the realities at the grass-root level (Gerster, 1987, p. 66). The close relationship between citizens and government at the local level not only fosters accountability but also is prevent governments from abusing their powers (Kendall, 1991, p.10) for, at least, two related reasons. First, it is more difficult to hide corruption among those in authority when the citizens know the officials than in situations where "the Government" is far away and inaccessible. Second, it is easier to hold local officials and elected office-bearers accountable for their actions than it is to impose accountability on politicians at higher levels of government, as members of local governments are often less protected politically than the corresponding officials in the central government (Kendall, 1991, p. 14). Both the availability of information necessary for taking proper actions and the potentially higher degree of accountability will lead to a better use of available resources. This will allow achieving more with limited resources, as an author recently stressed: "Decentralising responsibilities can bring substantial welfare gains. Government resources can be allocated most efficiently, if responsibility for each type of public expenditure is given to the level of government that most closely represents the beneficiaries of these outlays (Minassian, 1997, p.36)." The Human Development Report 1993 has stated the same idea in more general terms: "[If] local people feel that it is their money being spent, they are likely to keep a tighter lid on expenditures and to use resources more efficiently. Local development also opens the opportunity for people to add voluntary contributions to amplify a programme or impact of a project (UNDP, 1993, p. 75)."

Decentralisation removes institutional and legal obstacles to self-help and it encourages innovative forms of solutions for local problems. Thus, empowering local governments "allows diverse solutions to emerge in response to general problems" (Kendall, 1991, p. 25) and officials at local level can be more accessible to the average person – and thus more "human" – than a very distant and mighty central administration can (Gerster, 1987, p. 67). According to Henkin, "It builds a sense of community and permits more meaningful participation in self-government. In many countries, the autonomy granted to local units is designed to assure self-determination and the rights of minorities and their members against abuse by national majorities (Henkin, 1987, p. 392)." Distribution of power at different levels of government and the competition between these levels allows for a system of checks and balances that sets limits on the central government, if it attempts to overstep or abuse its powers. Thus, decentralised governance also constitutes a specific and extended expression of the basic constitutional principle of the separation of powers (Higuchi, 1987, p. 25). A further traditional argument for decentralised government is that it has the potential to protect ethnic and other traditional minorities (Duchacek, 1979, pp. 65-70 and Gan and Ostrom, 1979, pp. 77-81). If minorities inhabit an area with a certain degree of self-government, decentralisation essentially grants them the right to be free as a collective. (Duchacek, 1987, p. 69). Thus, decentralisation offers "... the possibility of combining democratic ideals with guarantees for minorities ... [and thus] ... can provide a means of accommodating problems arising from ethnic diversity .... By guaranteeing local autonomy, especially to questions considered important to ethnic identity, the potential for conflict within the national political arena is reduced" (Paddison, 1985, p. 127).

However, the coin has two sides, as the local government often remains unable to perform even the very limited tasks, delegated to it. An analysis of such situations usually reveals many peculiarities stemming from the particular political, historical, legal, and socio-economic traditions of a specific country. Nevertheless, it is possible to list some common problems which are generally confronted by the local governments as under:

Lack of resources: Though the local governments have some powers to levy local taxes and fees, but the collection of revenue is not always easy and often remains insufficient to fulfill the tasks assigned to them. Local authorities often lack qualified and well trained staff and, therefore, are unable to deliver services properly even if money is available. Lack of resources takes on dramatic forms, if local governments are granted large powers that have been shifted from the center. On account of non delivery by the local government, the center gets fair opportunity to blame the local levels for such failure.

Lack of or overlapping powers: Sometimes, the powers of local governments are too limited to respond to the expectations of the population. On the other hand, quite often, though the local governments possess broad powers, but the central government offices have also power to carry out such activities at the regional or local level. This leads to an unclear division of powers and overlapping of activities. With the result, the problems are not solved at either level, and the people lose faith in both their local authorities and the central government.

Lack of transparency and accountability: Corruption at the local level also affects the governance at the local level. In view of the difficulties to prove it in places, where government accounts are not accessible to the public and/or when there is no legislation that clarifies the powers and duties of the different bodies involved in local governance issues. On the other hand, if local officials are accountable to several authorities, it also creates confusion and insecurity at the lower level and hampers efficient administration even more. More so, accountability is also reduced when local office-bearers are appointed rather than elected.

Excessive control: A typical problem occurs when the higher levels of government have to approve the budget for the local governments, because not only the approval is often delayed and the process is used to impose conditions on the proposals' acceptance but also it delays the execution of the plans and utilisation of the total funds allocated. In some countries, planning procedures are very complicated and slow, leaving local authorities with no opportunity to decide where to set priorities. Often, local governments must get prior approval for all expenditures above a certain (usually minimal) level. Finally, a very effective control can be exercised through threats to dismiss the local body for not performing "properly" (i.e., according to the wishes of the center). Such control mechanisms ensures that local authorities are constantly supervised by the central government officials. This not only slows the progress of local activities, but also cripples local initiative.

Conditions for Successful Decentralisation

How can the goal of empowering local governments to act as efficient providers of services and as agents of local development be achieved? Practical experience as well as scholarly studies indicate several conditions, necessary for successful decentralisation.

1. ***Secured existence:*** A first necessary condition for strong local government is security of existence. Obviously, local governments cannot perform properly, if their existence remains in jeopardy by the power of the authorities at higher levels of the government, to dissolve them easily or to change their territories (e.g., merge them with neighboring areas).

2. ***Resources and autonomy:*** The success of decentralisation depends, to a very large extent, on the availability of sufficient resources and the possibility of using these resources autonomously. This requires, *inter alia*, the right of local governments to collect local taxes and fees, to get funds from the central government necessary for the execution of the tasks transferred to them; right to spend this money without excessive control by the higher levels of government; right to take decisions on local activities including local development projects; appointing sufficient and well-qualified local staff and the right to dismissal of such staff without undue interference by national planning authorities and line ministries.

3. ***Accountability and transparency:*** In every administrative organisation, it is of paramount importance to introduce a clear concept of accountability. Such accountability has two dimensions: making local governments and their members *accountable to the people* meaning that the citizens can elect those who rule them and assess

their performance at the time of reelection. This requires transparency of governmental actions and access to relevant information such as budgets, accounts, plans, etc. Citizens must also know that office-bearers, who have violated the law, will be punished in all cases. Local governments are also *accountable to the higher levels of government.* Accountability to several authorities might create confusion and insecurity at the lower levels that would be detrimental to the idea of efficient administration. Only well-defined responsibilities provide for the degree of transparency and security needed by authorities, at lower levels, who have to make certain decisions on their own. Therefore, a high degree of transparency, in the relations between local governments and the supervising authorities, is necessary. For example, local bodies must know, in advance, what criteria will be applied, while approving decisions or denying approval. There is also a need for transparency regarding all financial matters. Supervising authorities should exercise a tight control, but such control should have a retrospective (*expost*) character and those, who have violated the law, should be punished.

4. Political will and partnership: Experience has shown that the success of decentralisation efforts depends, to a large extent, on a clear vision regarding the position and function of local governments and on a strong political will to implement that vision. It also depends on the willingness of both the central and the local level to see each other as partners in an ongoing process. Such a partnership implies a willingness by the central government and its regional representatives to exercise self-restraint in supervising local governments. Laws and directives should be framed and applied in ways that encourage initiative and do not curtail local self-government. It also requires a readiness to consult local governments on all matters regarding them and to take their opinion into account while making decisions. For their part, actors at the local level must be ready to assume responsibility for their activities and to take initiatives on their own to foster development, instead of waiting for the central government to act or seeking approval where not needed. Local interest groups and the local population as a whole must support the process of shifting powers and responsibilities from the center to the local level. Finally, structures should be created for facilitating a dialogue between the different levels of government. In many countries, there have been good experiences demonstrating that if efforts are made to encourage local-central discussions and exchanges of ideas, the association of the mayors and other heads of local governments on policy questions could bring good results.

5. ***Strong legal framework:*** Another aspect of successful decentralisation is the need for *strong legal framework*, setting out the powers, rights and duties of local governments clearly. Without such a framework, it is often impossible to know who is responsible for what. This allows central authorities to interfere easily with local affairs and leaves the local authorities with no possibility of stopping such interference. Legal norms must, however, be adapted to local needs and to the circumstances of the local area. Norms imposed from somowhere if imposed, may not be used in practice or may be unsuitable and, therefore, may lose much of their impact.

However, the top-down approach has often failed to promote development and reduce poverty. Disappointment has been particularly high with rural development programmes, many of which were initiated, designed and executed by the central government representatives, with little or no input, from communities. There are a number of reasons why the centralised approach has not worked well, for example, the central government representatives too often remain ignorant of the local preferences, priorities and feelings of the local people feel about the ownership of projects therefore most of the plans fail to promote a sense of belonging among the local people. The decentralisation of power, responsibilities, decision-making and resources to intermediate and local governments, to communities and the private sector gained ground throughout the world during the 1980s, because of the belief that it can improve the efficiency, effectiveness and equity of government programmes, because it empowers underrepresented groups, such as local entrepreneurs to be politically active. It gives communities control over resources to invest in projects they care for, like education, health, rural infrastructure and other growth-promoting activities and it also creates conditions for competition and bargaining among different groups, by improving their efficiency.

Forms of Decentralisation: Before we turn to other expectations, let us briefly reflect on the various forms of decentralisation. In some studies, the following distinctions are usually made:

Deconcentration: Selected functions are taken over by the field officers of central state hierarchy. Examples include field officers, of governmental departments, who at the request of the central government, seize the opportunity to assume control of certain assignments, remote to the central office.

Delegation: Defined responsibilities are transferred to regional or national, usually semi-autonomous, governmental units. This is a frequent practice in the energy, telecommuni-cations and transportation sectors. Decentralisation / "Devolution" means the transfer of certain powers and resources to legitimate local governments, such as, partial states, provinces, districts or municipalities, whiel are obligated to act based on national policies.

Economic Decentralisation: This refers to the deregulation of centralised state control, the pursuit of strategies to strengthen the private sector and the promotion of partnerships between state offices and private actors.

More than one, of the above forms, are usually found in the actual decentralisation processes. Their success depends largely on the combination of selected measures, the chosen sequence as well as historical opportunity.

The decentralisation argument: The major objectives/values, put forward by the case for decentralisation, could be summarised as follows:

(a) increase of democracy (grass-root democracy),

(b) protection of freedom and human rights (vertical check-and-balance),

(c) increase of efficiency through delegation of responsibility,

(d) higher quality of services,

(e) enhancement of social and economic development.

Decentralised Governance in India: An Early History

During the time of the *Rig-Veda* (1200 BC), self-governing village bodies called *'sabhas'* existed. With the passage of time, these bodies became panchayats (council of five persons) which were functional institutions of grassroot governance in almost every village. The Village Panchayat or elected council had large powers, both executive and judicial. From the distribution of land to the collection of taxes of the produce and paying the government's share on behalf of the village, were considered the functions of the village Panchayats. Above a certain number of these village councils, there used to be a larger panchayat or council to supervise and interfere, if necessary (Jawaharlal Nehru, 1964, p. 288). However, casteism and feudalistic system of governance, under the Mughal rule in the medieval period, slowly eroded the self-government in villages and a new class, of feudal chiefs and revenue collectors (*zamindars*), emerged, with which began the stagnation and decline of self-government institutions in the villages. During the British rule, the autonomy of panchayats further declined with the establishment of local civil and criminal courts, revenue and police organisations, the increase in communications, the growth of individualism and the operation of the individual *Ryotwari* '(landholder-wise) system against the *Mahalwari* or village tenure system. The panchayat had never been the priority of the British rulers. The rulers were interested in the creation of 'controlled' local bodiess which could help them in their trading interests by collecting taxes for them. When the colonial administration came under severe financial pressure after the 1857 uprising, the remedy sought was decentralisation in terms of transferring responsibility for road and public works to local bodies. However, this kind of 'compelled' decentralisation focused only on municipal administration.

The panchayat system, was destroyed by the East India Company when, it was granted the office of Diwan, in 1765 by the Mughal Emperor, as part of reparation after, his defeat at Buxar. With this the East India Company abolished the village land record office and created a company official, called Patwari, who became the official record keeper for a number of villages. The Company also created the office of magistrate who carried out policing functions through the *darogha* who had always been a state functionary under the *faujdar* and abolished the system of village police. The primary purpose of these measures was the collection of land revenue. The depredations of the *patwari* and the *darogha* system are part of our folklore and it also led to the worst famine in Bengal. These two measures completely disempowered the village community and destroyed the panchayats. After 1857, the British tried to restore the panchayat system by giving it powers to try minor offences and to resolve village disputes. But these measures were too little to restore the lost powers of the village community. Viceroy Lord Mayo's Resolution of 1870, (for decentralisation of power to bring about administrative efficiency in meeting people's demand and to add to the finances of colonial regime) provided the much needed impetus to the development of local institutions. It was a landmark resolution in the evolution of colonial policy towards local government. The real benchmark of the government policy on decentralisation can, however, be attributed to Lord Ripon, who in his famous resolution on local self-government of May 18, 1882, recognised the twin considerations of local government: (i) administrative efficiency and (ii) political education. The 'Ripon Resolution', which focused on towns, provided for local bodies consisting of a large majority of elected non-official members and presided over by a non-official chairperson. This resolution met with resistance from colonial administrators. The progress of local self-government was tardy with only half-hearted steps taken in setting up municipal bodies. Rural decentralisation remained a neglected area of administrative reform.

The Royal Commission, on Decentralisation (1907) under the chairmanship of Hobhouse, recognised the importance of panchayats at village level. The commission recommended that "it is the most desirable, alike in the interests of decentralisation and in order to associate the people with the local tasks of administration that an attempt should be made to constitute and develop village panchayats for the administration of local village affairs." (Report of the Royal Commission, 1907). But the Montagu-Chelmsford Reforms (1919) brought local self-government as a provincial transferred subject, under the domain of Indian ministers in the provinces. Due to organisational and fiscal constraints, the reform was unable to make panchayat institutions truly democratic and vibrant. However, the most significant development of this period was the 'establishment of village panchayats in a number of provinces, that were no longer mere ad hoc judicial tribunals, but representative institutions symbolising the corporate character of the village and having a wide jurisdiction in respect of civic matters'. By 1925, eight provinces had passed panchayat acts and by 1926, six native states had also passed panchayat laws.

The provincial autonomy under the Government of India Act, 1935, actually marked the evolution of panchayats in India. Popularly elected governments in provinces enacted legislations to further democratize institutions of local self-government. But the system of responsible government at the grassroot' level was least responsible. D.P. Mishra, the then minister for local self-government under the Government of India Act of 1935 in Central Provinces, was of the view that "the working of our local bodies . . . in our province and perhaps in the whole country presents a tragic picture. . . 'Inefficiency' and 'local body' has become synonymous terms. . ." (Vankatarangaiya and Pattabhiram, 1969). Inspite of various committees, such as the Royal Commission on Decentralization (1907), the report of Montague and Chelmsford on constitutional reform (1919), the Government of India Resolution (1918) etc., a hierarchical administrative structure was based on supervision and control, evolved. The administrator became the focal point of rural governance. The British were not concerned with decentralized democracy but were aiming at colonial objectives.

As the Indian National Congress, from the 1920s to 1947, emphasized the issue of all-India Swaraj, and organised movements for Independence under the leadership of Mahatma Gandh. Therefore, the task of preparing a blueprint for the local level was neglected. There was no consensus among the top leaders regarding the status and role of rural local self-government. On the one end, Gandhi favoured Village

Swaraj and strengthening of the village panchayat to the fullest extent and, on the other, B.R. Ambedkar opposed this idea. He believed that the villages represented a regressive India, as well as a source of oppression. Therefore, the model state needed to build safeguards against social oppression through the adoption of the parliamentary model of politics. During the drafting of the Constitution of India, Panchayati Raj Institutions were placed in the non-justifiable part of the Constitution, the Directive Principles of State Policy, as Article 40 which provided that the state shall take steps to organise village panchayats and endow them with such powers and authority as may be necessary to enable them to function as units of self-government. However, no worthwhile legislation was enacted either at the national or state level to implement it. In four decades, since the adoption of the Constitution, panchayat-raj institutions have travelled from the non-justifiable part of the Constitution to one where, through a separate amendment, a whole new status has been added to their history (World Bank, 2000, p.18).

Post- Independence Period

Panchayati Raj had to go through various stages. The first Five Year Plan failed to bring about active participation and involvement of the people in the plan processes, which included plan formulation, implementation and monitoring. The second Five Year Plan attempted to cover the entire countryside with National Extensive Service Blocks through the institutions of Block Development Officers, Assistant Development Officers, Village Level Workers, in addition to nominated representatives of village panchayats of that area and some other popular organisations, like co-operative societies. But the plan failed to satisfactorily accomplish decentralisation. Hence, committees were constituted by various authorities to advise the Centre on different aspects of decentralisation (Bajpai and Verma, 1995, p. 3).

The Balwantrai Mehta Committee (1957)

In 1957, Balwantrai Mehta Committee studied the Community Development Projects and the National Extension Service and assessed the extent to which the movement had succeeded in utilising local initiatives and in creating institutions to ensure continuity in the process of improving economic and social conditions in rural areas. The Committee held that community development could be deep and enduring only when the community was involved in the planning, decision-making and implementation process (Govt. of India, 1957). The suggestions were as follows (Kashyap, 1989, p. 109):

- an early establishment of elected local bodies and devolution to them of necessary resources, power and authority,
- the basic unit of democratic decentralisation was at the block/ *samiti* level, since the area of jurisdiction of the local body should neither be too large nor too small. The block was large enough for the efficiency and economy of administration, and small enough for sustaining a sense of involvement among the citizens;
- such body must not be constrained by too much control by the government or government agencies;
- the body must be constituted for five years by indirect elections from among the village panchayats;
- its functions should cover the development of agriculture in all aspects, the promotion of local industries and others;
- it should also take care of services, such as drinking water, road building, etc. and;
- the higher level body, *Zilla Parishad*, would play an advisory role.
- The PRI structure could not develop the requisite democratic momentum and failed to cater to the needs of rural development. The reasons for such an outcome were political and bureaucratic resistance at the state level to share power and resources with local level institutions, domination of local elites over the major share of the benefits of welfare schemes, lack of capability at the local level and lack of political will.

SK Dey : the First Minister for Panchayati Raj in India

Late Mr. S. K. Dey (1905–1989) piloted and steered, the course of community development and Panchayati Raj in the challenging, formative period of India's independence, as Cabinet Minister of Cooperation and Panchayati Raj under the Prime Minister Jawaharlal Nehru. After Nehru's death, he took leave from Ministerial responsibilities to dedicate himself fully to the cause of Panchayati Raj as long as he lived.

K. Santhanam Committee (1963)

One of the prime areas, of concern in this long debate on panchayati raj institutions, was fiscal decentralisation. The K. Santhanam Committee was appointed to look solely at the issue of PRI finance, in 1963. The fiscal capacity of PRIs tends to be limited, as rich resources of revenue are pre-empted by higher levels of government, and the issue is still debated today. The Committee was asked, to determine issues related to sanctioning of grants to PRIs, by the state governments, evolving mutual financial relations between the three tiers of PRIs, gifts and donation, handing over revenue in full or part to PRIs.The Committee recommended the following steps for improving the structure of Panchayats (Rai, *et al.*, 2001, p. 9):

- panchayats should have special powers to levy special tax on land revenues and home taxes;
- people should not be burdened with too many demands (taxes);
- all grants at the state level should be mobilised and sent in a consolidated form to various PRIs;
- A Panchayati Raj Finance Corporation should be set up to look into the financial resource of PRIs at all levels, provide loans and financial assistance to these grassroot level governments and also provide non-financial requirements of the villages.

These issues have been debated over the last three decades and have been taken up by the State Finance Commissions which are required to select taxes for assignment and sharing, identifying the principles for such sharing and assignment, determine the level of grants and recommend the final distribution of state's transfers to local authorities.

Ashok Mehta Committee: Main Article (1978)

With the coming of the Janata Party into power at the Centre in 1977, a serious view was taken of the weaknesses in the functioning of panchayati raj. It was decided to appoint a high-level committee under the chairmanship of Ashok Mehta to examine and suggest measures to strengthen PRIs. The Committee had to evolve an effective decentralised system of development for PRIs. The committee made the following recommendations (Kashyap, 1989, p. 112):

- the district is a viable administrative unit for which planning, co-ordination and resource allocation are feasible and technical expertise available;
- the PRIs constitute a two-tier system, with Mandal Panchayat at the base and Zilla Parishad at the top;
- the PRIs are capable of planning for themselves with the resources available to them;
- district planning should take care of the urban-rural continuum;
- representation of SCs and STs in the election to PRIs on the basis of their population;

- four-year term of PRIs;
- participation of political parties in elections;
- any financial devolution should be committed to accepting that much of the developmental functions at the district level would be played by the panchayats.

The states of Karnataka, Andhra Pradesh and West Bengal passed new legislation based on this report. However, the flux, in politics at the state level, did not allow these institutions to develop their own political dynamics.

G.V.K. Rao Committee (1985)

The G.V. K. Rao Committee was appointed to look, once again, at various aspects of PRIs. The Committee was of the opinion that a total view of rural development must be taken into account in which PRIs must play a central role in handling people's problems. It recommended the following steps for improving the status of the Panchayat Raj Institutions (World Bank, 2000, p. 21):

- The PRIs have to be activated and provided with all the required support to become effective organisations;
- PRIs the at the district level and below, should be assigned the work of planning, implementation and monitoring of rural development programmes; and
- the block development office should be the spinal cord of the rural development process.

L.M. Singhvi Committee (1986)

The L.M. Singhvi Committee observed that the *Gram Sabha* was considered as the base of a decentralised democracy, and PRIs, were viewed as institutions of self-governance, which would actually facilitate the participation of the people in the process of planning and development. It recommended the following steps (Rai, et al., 2001, p. 9):

- the local self-government should be constitutionally recognised, protected and preserved by the inclusion of new chapter in the Constitution; and
- political parties should not be involved in panchayat elections.

The suggestion, of giving panchayats constitutional status, was opposed by the Sarkaria Commission. The idea, however, gained momentum in late 1980s, because of the endorsement by the late Prime

Minister Rajiv Gandhi, who introduced the 64th Constitutional Amendment Bill in the lower house of parliament in 1989. But it got defeated in the Rajya Sabha as non-convincing and he lost the general elections. In 1989, the National Front introduced the 74th Constitutional Amendment Bill, but it also could not become an Act because of the dissolution of the Ninth Lok Sabha. However, all the suggestions and recommendations about strengthening the PRIs were considered while formulating the new Constitutional Amendment Act.

The 73rd Constitutional Amendment Act

The idea, that produced the 73rd Constitution Amendment Act, was not the result of the pressure from the grassroot, but an increasing recognition that the institutional initiatives of the preceding decade could not do much to remove the rural poverty, eradication of which required overhauling of the existing structure of government. It is interesting to note that this idea evolved from the Centre and it was a political drive to see PRIs as a solution to the governmental crises that India was experiencing. The Constitutional (73rd Amendment) Act, which was passed in 1992 by the Narsimha Rao government, came into force on April 24, 1993. It was meant to provide constitutional sanction to establish "democracy at the grassroot level." Following are the main features of this constitutional amendment act (Thoman Isaac, 2000, p. 19):

- The Gram Sabha or village assembly, as a deliberative body to decentralised governance, has been envisaged as the foundation of the Panchayati Raj System.
- There should be a uniform three-tier structure of panchayats at village (Gram Panchayat—GP), intermediate or block (Panchayat Samiti—PS) and district (Zilla Parishad—ZP) levels.
- All the seats, in a panchayat at every level, are to be filled by elections from respective territorial constituencies.
- Not less than one-third of the total seats, for membership as well as office of chairpersons of each tier should be reserved for women.
- Reservation for weaker castes and tribes (SCs and STs) has to be provided at all levels in proportion to their population in the panchayats.
- To supervise, direct and control the regular and smooth elections to panchayats, a State Election Commission has to be constituted in every State and UT.

- The Act also ensures the constitution of a State Finance Commission in every State/UT, for every five years, to suggest measures to strengthen finances of PRIs.
- To promote bottom-up-planning, the District Planning Committee (DPC) in every district has been accorded constitutional status.
- An indicative list of 29 items has been given in the Eleventh Schedule of the Constitution. Panchayats are expected to play an effective role in planning and implementation of works related to these 29 items.

Present Scenario

At present, there are about 3 million elected representatives at all levels of the panchayat and one-third of which are women. These members represent more than 2.4 lakh Gram Panchayats, about 6,000 intermediate level tiers and more than 500 district panchayats. Spread over the length and breadth of the country, the new panchayats cover about 96 percent of India's more than 5.8 lakh villages and nearly 99.6 percent of rural population. This is the largest experiment in the decentralisation of governance in the history of humanity.

The Constitution visualises panchayats as institutions of self-governance. However, giving due consideration to the federal structure of our polity, most of the financial powers and authorities, to be endowed on panchayats, have been left at the discretion of the concerned state legislatures. Consequently, the powers and functions vested in PRIs vary from state to state. These provisions combine representative and direct democracy into a synergy and are expected to result in an extension and deepening of democracy in India. Hence, panchayats have journeyed from an institution within the culture of India to attain constitutional status.

Panchayat or Panchayati Raj, is a system of governance in which, Gram panchayats are the basic units of administration and operates at three levels: village, block and district. The term 'panchayat raj' which originated during the British Administration is relatively new. 'Raj' literally means governance or government. Mahatma Gandhi advocated *Panchayati Raj*, as a decentralised form of Government to be the foundation of India's political system in which each village ought to be responsible for its own affairs. The he used for such a vision, was "Gram Swaraj" (Village Self-governance). It was adopted by the state governments during the 1950s and 60s as laws were passed to establish

Panchayats in various states. It also found backing in the Indian Constitution, with the 73rd Amendment in 1992 which contains provision for devolution of powers and responsibilities to the panchayats for the preparation of plans for economic development and social justice as well as for the implementation of the twenty-nine subjects listed in the eleventh schedule of the constitution. The panchayats receive funds from three sources: (i) local body grants, as recommended by the Central Finance Commission, (ii) funds for implementation of Centre-sponsored schemes, and (iii) funds released by the state governments on the recommendations of the State Finance Commissions.

On 24 April 1993, in the history of Panchayati Raj system in India, the 73rd Constitutional Amendment Act 1992 came into force to provide constitutional status to the Panchayati Raj institutions. This Act was also extended to Panchayats in the tribal areas of eight states, namely, Andhra Pradesh, Gujarat, Himachal Pradesh, Maharashtra, Madhya Pradesh, Orissa and Rajasthan from 24 December 1996 onwards. Now panchayati Raj system exists in all the states except Nagaland, Meghalaya and Mizoram, and also in all the Union Territories except Delhi. The Act aims to provide three-tier system of Panchayati Raj for the all states having population of over 2 million, to hold Panchayat elections regularly every 5 years, to provide reservation of seats for Scheduled Castes and Women, to appoint State Finance Commission to make recommendations for grants to the Panchayats and to constitute District Planning Committee to prepare draft development plan for the district. The following powers and responsibilities are delegated to Panchayats at the appropriate level:

- Preparation of the plan for economic development and social justice.
- Implementation of the schemes for economic development and social justice in relation to 29 subjects given in the Eleventh Schedule of the Constitution.
- To levy, collect and appropriate taxes, duties, tolls and fees.

At the district level of the panchayati raj system, we have '*Zilla Parishad*', that is, the District Council which looks after the administration of the rural areas within a district and its office is located at the district headquarters. It is headed by the District Collector, or the District Magistrate, or the Deputy Commissioner and provides a link between the State Government and the Panchayat Samiti (local government at the block level).

Constitution

Members of the Zilla Parishad are elected from the district on the basis of adult franchise for a term of five years. Zilla Parishad has minimum of 50 and maximum of 75 members and seats are also reserved for Scheduled Castes, Scheduled Tribes, Backward Classes and women. Zilla Parishad is constituted by the Chairmen of all the Panchayat Samitis and it is headed by a President and a Vice-President. The functions attributed to the Zilla Parishad include:

- providing essential services and facilities to the rural population, planning and execution of the development programmes for the district;
- supplying improved seeds to farmers, informing them of new techniques of training, construction of small-scale irrigation projects, tanks and maintaining pastures and grazing lands;
- setting up and running schools in villages, executing programmes for adult literacy;
- starting Primary Health Centers and hospitals in villages along with mobile hospitals for hamlets, vaccination drives against epidemics and family welfare campaigns;
- construction of bridges and roads, executing plans for the development of the scheduled castes and tribes, running *ashramshalas* for *adivasi* children and setting up free hostels for scheduled caste students, and
- encouraging entrepreneurs to start small-scale industries like cottage industries, handicraft, agricultural products, processing mills, dairy farms, and implementing rural employment schemes.

Sources of Income

1. Taxes on water, pilgrimage, markets, etc.
2. Fixed grant from the State Government in proportion with the land revenue and money for works and schemes assigned to the Parishad.

Panchayati Raj (Rule of Village Committee) is a three-tier system with elected bodies at the village and district levels. It ensures greater participation of people and more effective implementation of rural development programmes. The Gram Panchayat looks after the interests of a village or a group of villages and the Zilla Panchayat at the district level. India has a chequered history of Panchayti Raj institutions, starting from self-sufficient and self-governing village communities that survived the rise and fall of the empires, in the past to the modern legalised three-tier institutions of governance.

In India the Ministry of Panchayati Raj, created in May 2004, headed by a minister of cabinet rank, looks into all matters related to Panchayati Raj and Panchayati Raj Institutions. The ministry is responsible for looking after the process of decentralisation and the three-tier local governance in the states. Since, in a federal set-up, the powers and functions of the government are divided between the union and state governments, but with the passage of 73rd and 74th Amendment Act of the Constitution of India in 1993, more powers and functions have been trickled down to the Local Self Governments, Panchayats at Village level and Municipalities and Municipal Corporations in towns and large cities.

Ministry of Panchayati Raj is also responsible for advocacy, monitoring and implementation of 73rd Constitutional Amendment Act. The State Governments/Union Territory Administrations, at present, are at varying degrees of the implementation of the 73rd and 74th Constitutional Amendment Acts. The Ministry ensures that, they hold timely elections, set up State Finance Commissions and implement their recommendations, constitute District Planning Committees and empower them suitably to ensure grass-root level planning, so that they are able to provide inputs for the state and central level planning effectively. One major task of the Ministry is to ensure that the state governments/UT Administrations devolve funds, functions and functionaries on the Panchayati Raj Institutions in the spirit of the Constitutional provisions. The Ministry of Panchayati Raj is also responsible for the formulation and implementation of an Action Plan for PRIs, to emerge as the real "Institutions of Local-Self Government" as well as securing economic development and social justice in their respective areas.

The goal of empowerment of *Gram Sabhas* can be achieved by holding regular meetings and social audit. The states and Union Territories are also empowered, to institute *Ward Sabhas* and *Mahila Sabhas* and make them functional on the basis of the local situation. The Ministry attaches great importance to the capacity building of the elected representatives and officials of PRIs as well as functionaries involved in the Rural Development Programmes. The Ministry also funds research studies, workshops and seminars for the development of Panchayats. "National Award for the best Panchayat" has also been instituted to encourage the PRI Institutions in discharging their role of "Institutions of Self-government".

Decentralised Governance and Women's Role: Prospects and Constraints

One of the major impacts of the implementation of the 73rd and 74th amendment acts can be seen in the form of the increased presence of the women in the local self governing bodies at all levels. The quantitative change, in the increased participation of women, is acknowledged in the official documents of the Government of India. Unfortunately, the quantitative leap, in women's participation in local bodies, has mostly failed to bring about a qualitative change, because many of the elected women representatives act as a proxy to their husbands or other male relatives or their role is used by *'Pradhanpatis'*. As they are accused for lack of interest, competence and awareness, they are neither being seen as an asset for the community development, nor the harbingers of community change. The illiteracy, poverty, lack of resources, socio-cultural factors, such as patriarchy and caste system, lack of political experience, the negative role of political parties, and the ever, increasing role of money and muscle power in politics at grassroot level, create problems for the women and effects their qualitative participation in these bodies. In a study on the women's participation in the PRIs, Prabhjot Kaur Kahlon has observed that poverty and illiteracy (Kahlon, 2004, p.174) together are responsible for women's dependence on men folk, as illiterate women, due to their ignorance, are not equipped to actively play their role in the PRIs and they have to depend on their male family members, even though some of them might wish to act independently. Keeping this problem in view at both the levels — government as well as non-governmental organisations — several training programmes are organised from time to time to enable and train women to discharge their duties efficiently. But there are instances where women are discouraged or even stopped from attending these training programmes /workshops by their family men who are perhaps not yet ready to accept women as independent decision makers at the community level (Shanta, 2004, p. 163). Women too are not in a position to resist the patriarchal opposition, because of their socio-economic dependence on their male counterparts. Another important factor, responsible for the inequity in the feudal social setup in India, is the prevailing caste system. The Indian political system has been largely dominated by the upper castes at all the levels. The caste dynamics is more at play in rural areas as compared to the metros or urban areas, because the urban and metro areas are somewhat influenced by cosmopolitanism, while the rural areas are still deeply bogged down by the caste politics. With regard to the participation of women in the PRIs, it has been noted that before 73rd Constitutional Amendment the women representatives elected to PRIs were largely from, the upper caste (Gopal Singh, 2002, p. 164). However, with the reservation of seats for women under 73rd Constitutional Amendment Act, the number of women, from the lower and backward castes, has also increased, although there have been instances of non-acceptance or resistance against the lower caste (dalit) *sarpanchas* from the upper castes. Moreover, the patriarchal notions about the family honours also prevents the younger and unmarried women (who ironically are more capable of discharging their duties, as women representatives at the PRIs, as they have more energy and time on account of light domestic responsibilities as well as better education than the older women) from contesting election. The growing use of 'muscle' and 'money' power in the election process also discourages women's participation in politics.

Theoretically speaking, the elections to the PRIs should be conducted strictly on a political ground, meaning thereby that political parties should keep away from these elections; however, the ground reality is different. The ISS Studies of PRI elections in Karnataka (1987-90) revealed that 60 percent elected women members were from dominant castes, supported by the political parties, who on account of possessing a biased attitude towards the women, did not encourage the common women to contest elections. Their choice of candidates is generally dictated by class, caste and gender bias; however, the compulsion of applying 33 percent reservations of seats for women candidates, to some extent, has emerged as a means of diluting the impact of these biases. But, despite the criticism about women's role in the PRIs, particularly in the post 73rd Amendment period, there are many success stories pointing to political empowerment of women as well as their constructive role for community development. The 33 percent representation has not only increased women's participation in politics at the grassroot level but also enhanced political awareness, self esteem, prestige, and better political orientation among them. (*The Hindu*, 30 April 2010). Their growing involvement in the community development work is also leading towards the better management of it.

There are several examples of successful women panchayat chiefs, who have contributed to the development of their areas and have become the role models. The initiatives taken by Nishika Sabitri, Gram Pradhan of a remote tribal area of Orissa, to augment the income of panchayat by leasing out the ponds and mango orchards, stands as testimony to this phenomenon. Besides working to ensure the basic needs of the rural people such as providing hygienic facilities for toilets and bath, she also focused on the social welfare schemes, like eradication of poverty, widows' pension, old age pension, low-cost housing, public distribution system etc. In another case Meena Rani Bahera, an SC woman Gram Pradhan took up the cudgel against the corrupt practices of the panchayats in the distribution of money for low cost housing. (Rajendra and Prabhu, (*The Hindu*, 30 April 2010). There are examples of strong leadership by women in other states as well. In Karnataka women have proved their leadership qualities, in Andhra Pradesh the presence of women in PRIs has paved the way for the development of social identities and political awareness. (Bidyut Mohanty, web). In Punjab also this has made a significant difference both qualitatively as well as quantitatively, but if constraints (like domestic responsibilities, caste and gender biases etc.) are removed, women would be able to contribute more and show leadership qualities. Norwegian Embassy Delegation interacted with the elected women representatives of PRIs in Rajasthan (Jaipur and Tonk districts). The delegation observed that women had developed the abilities to articulate the priorities of their respective areas and were influencing the decision-making process effectively. (H.M. Hemalatha, 2003, web). In view of this, it can be said that the impact of reservation of seats for women at the PRIs has been a mixed one. As majority of the non-experienced women, constrained by centuriy old factors, have entered the political arena, therefore, miracles cannot be expected. More so corruption and unresponsive bureaucracy also work to women's disadvantage; nevertheless, experience shows that women are capable of providing leadership to the people, if they are given time, support, resources, training, and freedom.

Women's Participation in Panchayats in Uttarakhand

For long, community activism and political aspirations have remained a closely held preserve of the male-dominated society, with the 'weaker sex' involvement in public domain, largely negligible and insignificant. Though by the provisions of the 73rd Constitutional Amendment Act, one-third of the seats were reserved for women in local self-governance, however, the impact of women panchayat members and chiefs (pradhans) on the local bodies remained peripheral for a long time. This has been observed in a number of studies on the functioning of local bodies that have women as chiefs, that the male panchayat members had an upper hand, as they carried out most of the proposals for developmental schemes. Our own experiences and studies, conducted in different villages of Uttarakhand, under the UGC-SAP programme, during the last three years, have revealed that there are cases which present a different scenario, particularly, in

Uttarakhand. Not so long ago women pradhans in Uttarakhand used to be manipulated by the male members of their household to further their own political and personal agenda. Lack of knowledge about the functioning and procedures of panchayats, prevailing traditional system which restricts women from speaking freely in front of elder male relatives, and little experience in attending the male-dominated meetings, affected their effective participation in discussions and decision-making process at the policy level. But gradually, the women, who got elected to the panchayats through reservation, started asserting their rights. As a result of this, local self-governance in the state has received a new direction and thrust. The widespread awareness, created among them about the opportunities of the 73rd Constitutional Amendment, has helped the socio-political empowerment of women. With most of the able-bodied young men migrating from the state, either serving in defence forces or working in other parts of the country, the entire economy of Uttarakhand revolves round the hard work put in by the women. The local bodies, therefore, not only need to work towards addressing their problems of water, fodder and fuel but also are provided effective solutions wher by the Panchayati Raj Institution are turued into an effective instrument of social transformation and rural development.

More importantly, women have been gently nudged by an NGO to change their attitudes and improve their status. Since 1995, *Pragati*, an NGO, with its programme of dealing entirely with the Panchayati Raj, has sought to empower women politically as well as socially, not only in Uttarakhand but also in Himachal Pradesh and Haryana. Its mission is to enhance the status of women through a process aimed at changing the nature and direction of systemic forces that marginalise women and other disadvantaged sections of the society. *Pragati* continues to impart training to women on a regular basis, that is, pre and post election period. Moreover, it also actively encourages and assists women to contest elections to the local bodies, teaches them the mannerism with regard to speech, mobilising support, filing their nominations and other essential requirements for contesting election.

Moreepver, women have been motivated to enhance their leadership skills and problem-solving capability to spur developmental activities at the local level. In particular, women are being encouraged to cultivate qualities of self-esteem, confidence and positive outlook and bid adieu to subordination as well as subjugation. Notwithstanding the hurdles and handicaps, today these very women have proved to be the better task masters, in managing the affairs of local bodies. In fact, a number of women pradhans, hailing from humble social background, have gathered courage to successfully wage a war against "corruption, commission raj, leakage of funds as well as shoddy work which for long has remained an ugly feature of the administration of local bodies". There are many examples of women pradhans managing and implementing developmental activities with honesty and transparency. The case of 45-year-old Radha Devi, the Pradhan of Gram Panchayat Sahaspur, Dehra Dun, can be cited as an example of her determination to bring changes with her outmost dedication to conduct developmental activities. She contested from an unreserved seat on three occasions and won with huge margins, notwithstanding the hurdles put in her way by the well-entrenched male lobby in the village. She took the affairs of the Gram Panchayat as a challenge and proved to be a true leader, ever ready to reach out to the rural folks. To her credit goes the creation of basic amenities, such as drinking water, electricity, public toilets and roads. Radha Devi believes that women can acquire knowledge of any work only when they will cross the boundary of their households. Their participation in every sphere of work, is of paramount importance, no matter whether they are literate or illiterate.

Likewise, 28 year-old Ganga Devi, Gram Pradhan of village Sasolu, Bagehswar district of Uttarakhand, successfully made a beginning and led an agitation which saw the closure of a liquor shop located in the village of Bhakadpant. Another women pradhan, Sunita Devi, a 35-year-old woman of Kashirampur in Garhwal region, pulled off a tremendous feat by winning against eleven male contestants and that too from an open seat. With her leadership, the Gram Sabha has undertaken projects including construction of roads and schools. In particular, she has motivated the parents of school-going children to desist from withdrawing them for the reasons of poverty and family constraints. The women Panchayat members and chiefs regularly exchange views and air their grievances at interface meetings held in Dehradun and Almora, with Government functionaries, so that appropriate solutions can be found for the problems enlisted.

The movement of empowering women has undoubtedly picked up momentum as was reflected at an interface meeting held in Dehradun in November 2010, wherein 900 women Panchyati Raj functionaries from 13 districts of the State participated. The participants were cautioned against the dangers of groupism on caste lines, which could spell doom for the developmental activities. The representatives, from all the three tiers of local self-governance, were firm that they have to work for the removal of the problems in health, hygiene and education sectors with the support of the people. They also expressed that it was equally necessary for them to be acquainted with the existing schemes because the male members were not quite willing to lend a helping hand. The elected women's attempt to ask the "inconvenient" questions regarding work undertaken by the panchayats and the commitment and accountability of the elected members, has helped to focus on the need to create a transparent system for fruitful use of the public funds.

This political as well as social awareness campaign, for an enhanced women's participation in local self-governance, has significantly acted as a catalyst for the formation of women's self-help groups. Issues, concerning local community, are thus discussed with particular emphasis on the government-sponsored schemes. The churning has clearly led to evolving of the concept of micro planning for holistic rural development with women being in the forefront. It would be worthwhile if women in other states would take a cue.

Problems of the Panchyat Raj Institutions

The above scenario suggests that, by and large, PRIs have not delivered the services to rural people even though they are empowered to prepare plans for economic development and social justice. They have not yet become the real institutions of self governance–largely due to (a) lack of people's participation, especially, the women, the poor, and other marginalised groups because of ignorance, poverty and lack of distributive justice; (b) reluctance of the higher tiers of the Government to devolve financial and administrative powers to them as the Line Departments and District Rural Development Agency continue to control the planning and implementation of developmental projects; apathetic attitudes of the bureaucrats and politicians; insufficient capacity of resources of the PRIs (and Gram Sabha) in running their activities effectively; and the lack of organic linkages among the three tiers.

Our studies conducted under SAP programme of the department of Political Science and the review of concerned literature reveal that in almost all villages, a large majority of villagers fail to attend the Gram Sabha (GS) meetings for reasons, such as lack of education, lack of time, lack of interest, lack of information about the meeting, lack of faith in the system, distance from home, etc. The provisions to convening GS meetings regularly in far-flung dwellings, is not followed. Therefore, the villagers, living in far off villages, find it difficult to attend the GS meetings. The daily wage earners and farmers also do not attend the meetings for the fear of loosing wages and many others because of the lack of information about the meeting in advance. Therefore, low attendance and poor participation of women and Scheduled Caste and

Scheduled Tribes (SC/ST) people in Village Panchayat and Gram Sabha in almost all villages becomes a normal phenomenon. Political factionalism in some villages tends to create disputes and disagreements which affect the proceedings of the meeting. It also creates an aversion in the minds of the common man towards attending GS. In interaction with the author during a SAP programme field meeting, the village women showed their annoyance towards the tendencies of selecting the beneficiaries among the privileged class. They also complained that the GS as an institutional mechanism for making complaints or seeking redressal of grievances have remained ineffective; therefore, the GS are held only as a formality and accomplished only on paper. Actually the general lack of interest on the part of rural poor except if some perceptible gain is in sight, the emasculated condition of the GP, paucity of resources, the high opportunity cost of attending the body for labour class, and the lack of specific role, for the ordinary members of the Panchayat in GS, stand in the way of development of the institutions of GS. On account of these reasons, it fails to perform effectively its statutory functions relating to granting approvals to plans and selecting beneficiaries.

It is important to create awareness among the people with regard to their responsibilities, duties and rights in the process. The people need to be motivated to understand that their active participation in GS is crucial to the development of their village as well as to control malpractices, to monitor proper application of guidelines, and to ensure transparency and accountability of Gram Panchayt (GP) to GS. GS could be effective in its role only through its empowerment and capacity building, political education of masses, larger participation in developmental programmes, more effective control over Panchayat leadership, better responsiveness of the administration, better mobilisation of resources, and better care of community/village assets. Thus GS needs to be strengthened by handing over real power; otherwise, it will remain only a shadow of the panchayat and not an independent entity.

The Panchayats at all levels are still dominated by bureaucracy and the middle level bureaucrats are not yet prepared to give powers to the poor and illiterate villagers. For removing these hurdles, the bureaucracy needs to change their mindset. It is also important to *strengthen the internal resources, mobilisation capabilities* of PRIs for functional autonomy. They should also be given *control over natural resources* such as land, water, minor forest produce and minerals. All the groups of users at village which are formed under different developmental programmes, such as watershed committees, water users' groups, forest protection committees, self-help groups, etc. should be linked and brought under the control of GP. The Panchayat should have better control over funds which is possible through *timely release of funds* so that they have enough time to plan and implement the programme and freedom to take up works in response to local imperatives. Further, the special grant, given to the *MP/MLA for local area development, should be allotted to the Panchayats* for making use of it to strengthening local development and poverty alleviation measures.

Decentralisation, which ensures people's participation in planning and governance, is considered an efficient instrument of conveying benefits to the poor with the least cost. Accountability and transparency are expected to ensure good governance, better enforcement of asset acquisition, its retention and maintenance, loan repayment, capital flow back, etc. Since local wisdom and local resources are readily available under decentralised governance, therefore, the local human, animal and physical resources can be effectively utilised for creating employment opportunities and production of goods and services relevant to the needs of the poorer section of society. In order to ensure greater involvement and effective participation of gram sabha and to improve accountability and transparency in the administration, it is necessary that GS should be vested with *Right to Information* and *more powers*. At present, the wide powers, of suspension and dismissal are vested with the bureaucracy, which is a disadvantage for PRI, as it weakens their rights as elected representative bodies. The GS should, therefore, be given power to dismiss the GP. Besides, stringent disciplinary regulations must be adopted for defaulting Government, semi-Government and Panchayat employees. GS should be further empowered with Right to information regarding irregularities committed by any employee of PRI.

Apart from package of devolution of powers, the PRIs also need *qualified and trained technical staff* to help them in day to day transactions at various levels and to advise Gram Panchayat or group of Panchayats in formulation of action plans or assessing technical feasibility of the plans. The technical staff posted at block level may be assigned to work in GP for this purpose. Orientation, training and time to time guidance should be provided to GS/ GP with respect to their day-to-day conduct, regarding financial and administrative matter. Gram Panchayat must be provided with adequate manpower support including technical, and authorised to take up works up to Rs.10, 000/- with the approval of GS, but without seeking approval from Block Development Officer (BDO) and District Rural Development Agency (DRDA). The GP president should be accountable only to GS and no one else. In order to ensure that PRI functions as an instrument of local government, it is important that their functional and financial autonomy is guaranteed and transparency in their functioning is ensured. The role of local people in conducting social audit and fixing responsibility on Panchayat functionaries can be effectively ensured with GS becoming active and empowered. State government's control and intervention over PRI should be minimized and if there is any specific complaint against any Panchayat, it should be referred to a body similar to the 'Ombudsman'. A time-bound and comprehensive training programme for elected representatives of PRI as well as general awareness among the rural people is essential for strengthening the PRI. To enable the Panchayats to function as instrument of Self Governance, it is no longer necessary for the Centre, to route its financial support to the Panchayats through the state government. In a large number of instances, funds for rural development and poverty alleviation are diverted, at least temporarily, leading to inordinate delays and lapsing of funds meant to be spent through PRIs. It is, therefore, suggested that the Central Government must channelize all funds directly to the Panchayats at the appropriate level. There is also a need to clearly demarcate responsibilities for the three tiers and establish a panchayat service, for both administrative and technical functions, on the lines of existing state and central services for effective self-governance. With a view to enhance women's participation in the meeting of GS, a sub-quorum of female attendance should be built into the required quorum. A provision may be made that meetings of GS be preceded by meetings of the Mahila Sabha comprising all adult women voters of the GP, to ensure that gender concerns and preferences get fully reflected in the proceeding of GS (Prasad and S. Harnath, 2004, p. 3). It may be more appropriate for the Panchayats to function only as an institution of "Governance" and not as institution of 'Execution' of projects. The Projects implemented by beneficiary committees, Self-Help Groups or any other group of individuals selected by the GS were found to be more effective than projects directly implemented by the Panchayats themselves. Simple and transparent methods of monitoring projects by people were found to be more efficient as compared to pre-designed official procedure. Constitutional amendment alone cannot be effective if demand for de facto decentralisation does not arise from the grassroots. For this, social mobilisation is required which could be done only through a social movement for greater autonomy of the Panchayats in discharging their responsibilities. The civil societies—NGOs and voluntary actions of all kinds—can play an intermediate and supportive role in their effort to strengthen PRIs and democracy at the grassroot level through various interventions, such as public awareness, information, dissemination, social mobilisation, capacity building efforts, advocacy and campaigning for various issues with a view of working towards a just society, and by enabling local bodies to engage in participatory bottom-up micro-planning processes to determine priorities and programmes, which address locally appropriate the needs of different segments of local society. Infact, the participatory approach needs access to a wide variety of information from the officials as well as the people and civil society and the use of information technology can be helpful in increasing the speed and quality of this process. It can ensure more accountable, responsive and citizen-friendly PRIs. The government civil society interface gets a facelift by increased access to government information and facilitating dialogue and public feedback on government projects and performance. E-panchayat can only be realised by e-gram Sabha which is designed to facilitate interaction between the members of GS and the PRIs. If panchayats have to function as the institution of self-governance at the grassroot level, they have to fulfil three basic conditions, namely, (a) institutional existence in the sense that decisions are taken by 6 committees of GS representatives, (b) institutional capacity in the form of empowering institutions to make their rules independently, and (c) financial viability in terms of sufficiently empowering panchayats in raising resources to meet their responsibilities. In other words, the panchayats should enjoy functional, administrative and financial autonomy.

NOTES

1. The conditions necessary for making local governments service-oriented have been discussed in Part III.
2. Kendall mentions the example in his *The Heart of the Nation* (1991) that "instead of central government attempting to solve the housing shortage with one programme which it imposes on the entire country, various regions and communities act as laboratories for testing numerous ideas, the best of which are then imitated elsewhere."
3. It has to be acknowledged that the advantages of decentralisation for minority, may be ambiguous. Although it has the potential to provide autonomy for traditional religious, political, or linguistic minorities, the empowerment of local governments does not ensure the protection of minority rights. For minorities inside a given minority (minority sub-groups), for instance, local autonomy may cause problems of its own, such as oppression by the local majority.

REFERENCES

Aiyar, Mani Shankar. "Panchayati Raj: The Way Forward." *Economic and Political Weekly*. August 3, 2003, pp. 3293-97.

Kashyap Anirban: *Panchaytiraj: Views of Founding Fathers and Recommendation of Different Committees*. New Delhi: Lancer Books, 1989.

Ashok Mehta Committee. "Government of India, Report of the Committee on Panchayati Raj Institutions, Ministry of Agriculture and Irrigation, Department of Rural Development," New Delhi, 1978.

"Auctioning of several GP seats." *The Hindu*. April 30, 2010.

Bajpai and Verma. *Panchayati Raj in India: A New Thrust*, Vol. I, 1995.

Duchacek, Ivo D. "Federalist Responses to Ethnic Demands: An Overview." Daniel J. Elazar (ed.). *Federalism and Political Integration*. Ramat Gan, 1979, pp. 65-70 and Vincent Ostrom, "Federal Principles of Organisation and Ethnic Communities," in: ibid., p. 77-81.

Fleiner-Gerster, Thomas. "Problems de la souverainete interieure et exterieure." *Federalism and Decentralization*, Vol. 2 Fribourg, 1987.

"Government of India Report of the Team for the Study of Community Projects and National Extension Service." Chairperson, Balvantray Mehta. *Committee on Plan Projects, National Development Council*, New Delhi. 1 (November 1957).

Hemalatha, H.M. "A Hand That Cradles Can Handle The Panchayat", *Kuruuskehtra*, March 2003. Also available on http:/ www. csopartners. org.in/newsletter HYPERLINK "http://www.csopartners.org.in/ newsletter0210" 0210.

Henkin, Louis and Albert Rosenthal, eds. *Constitutionalism and Rights: The Influence of the US Constitution Abroad*. New York/Oxford, 1990.

Higuchi, Yoïchi. "La décision de la decentralisation." *Federalism and Decentralisation*, Vol. 2 Fribourg, 1987, pp. 409-10.

Kahlon, Prabhjot Kaur. "The Impact of 73rd Amendment on Womens' Political Empowerment : A Study of Punjab." *Decentralised Governance in India: Myth and Reality*. Ed. Surat Singh. New Delhi: Deep & Deep Publication Pvt. Ltd., 2004.

Kar, Esther. (2010, May 05) "Transform Rural India through Panchayat Raj." *Jansamchar.net* (online newspaper) Available on www.dalit.eu/india-dalitwomen- in-panchayat=raj.

Kaushal, R. "Governance in India - Myth and Reality" *OIDA: International Journal of Sustainable Development* 01:09. 2010, pp. 90-92.

Kendall, Francis. *The Heart of the Nation: Regional and Community Government in the New South Africa*. Norwood: Amagi Books, 1991.

Louis, Henkin. "Federalism, Decentralisation and Human Rights," *Federalism and Decentralisation*, Vol. 2. Fribourg 1987.

Mathew, George, ed. *Status of Panchayati Raj in the States and Union Territories of India*. Delhi: Concept for Institute of Social Sciences, 2000.

Rai, Mahoj *et al. The State of Panchayats: A Participatory Perspective*. New Delhi: Smscriti, 2001.

Mohanty, Bidyut. "The daughters of the 73rd amendment." http://www.onlinewomeninpolitics.org/india/bidyutHYPERLINK "http://www.onlinewomeninpolitics.org/india/bidyut7"7 3rd.pdf.

Nehru, Jawaharlal. *The Discovery of India*. Calcutta: Signet Press, 1964.

Paddison, Ronan. *The Fragmented State*. Oxford: Blackwell, 1985.

Pal, Mahi. "Panchayati Raj and Rural Governance." *Economic and Political Weekly*. Vol. 39, 2004, pp. 137-42.

Prasad B., Devi and S. Harnath. "Participation of Women and Dalits in Gram-panahcyat." *Journal of Rural Development*, 23.3, 2004.

Rajendra, S. and Nagesh Prabhu. "Politics Creeps into Gram-panchayat Elections." *The Hindu*. April 24, 2010.

Report of the Royal-Commission on Decentralisation, 1907.

Shanta, E. K. "Political Participation of Women in Pacnahayti Raj. In Surat Singh Ed." *Decentralised Governance*. New Delhi: Anamika Publishers & Distributors, 2002.

Singh, Gopal. "Social and Political Background of Women Leadership in Panchayat Raj Institutions of Haryana. In Surat Singh Ed." *Decentralised Governance*. New Delhi: Anamika Publishers & Distributors, 2002

Singh, D.P. "Impact of 73rd Amendment Act on Women's Leadership in the Punjab." *International Journal of Rural Studies* (*IJRS*) 15.1, April 2008.

Ter-Minassian, Teresa Ter-Minassian. "Decentralising Government, Finance and Development." September, 1997.www.terra-space.com/Teresa/cv.html.

"The Constitution (Seventy-Third Amendment) Act, 1992." *The Gazette of India*, Ministry of Law, Justice and Company Affairs, New Delhi, 1993.

Issac T.M. Thomas, and Richard Franke. *Local Democracy and Development: Peoples Campaign for Decentralized Planning in Kerala*. New Delhi: Leftword Books, 2000.

UNDP, *Human Development Report* 1993.

Venkatarangaiah, M. and M. Pattabhiram. *Local Government in India: Selected Readings*. New Delhi: Allied Publishers, 1969.

"Women Empowerment Impresses Norwegian Delegation." *The Hindu*. May 3, 2010.

World Bank,:"*Overview of Rural Decentralisation in India*" 3, 2000, 18.

World Bank: "*Overview of Rural Decentralisation in India*." 3, 2000, 21.

SECTION II

DIVERSE ISSUES

4

Gender Equality in Islam and Muslim Women in India: An Agenda for Reforms

— *Abdulrahim P. Vijapur*

Islam is one of the great religions of the world, whose followers are found in every country and continent. As an egalitarian belief system, it introduced the concepts of universal brotherhood and non-discrimination among the Muslims on the ground of sex or race. Islam gave the women fundamental rights and championed all movements to improve the status of women, at a time when societies were overtly traditional and socially underdeveloped. This paper attempts to examine the following questions: Does Islam provide for gender equality? To what extent this equality of sexes is found in practice in Islamic societies? Are there any deviations from the scriptural precepts of gender equality? What reformative measures have been undertaken in Muslim countries to improve the status of women by enacting laws? What has been the picture of India in this regard? Answers to these and related questions are explored in this paper.

Islamic Ideals and Precepts

Both the Quran and the Prophetic traditions elevated the status of woman and gave her human, civil, social and economic rights, never previously given by any religious system. The Muslim woman has an independent personality, equal to man in religious duties, in the right to education, in reward for her deeds as well as in defending her beliefs. She has complete independence and total control over her possessions. Islam gave her equal legal capacity with man. This means that she has the ability to enter into all kinds of contractual arrangement and to conduct business on her own, without the need for her husband's consent. Such a legal right, given in the 7th century, is yet to be achieved by the married woman in some contemporary societies where the husband has a certain right to oversee his wife's affairs. French women did not achieve this legal right until 1965. In inheritance, the woman, as a daughter, gets half of her brother's share, but under other circumstances, she gets as much as or even more than other men in the family. Women's share in property varies depending on the circumstances. In Chapter 4, Verse 7 of the Quran identifies four circumstances:

1. ***Higher share for males***: the son takes twice as much as his sister, if the deceased is their father.
2. ***Equal shares for males and females***: "The female takes an equal share to that of the male if the deceased is their son who has children of his own: 'And to parents (of the deceased) a sixth each of the inheritance, if he has children.'"
3. ***Equal shares*** are given to males and females (brother and sister) who are distant heirs: 'to each of them twin (the brother and sister) the sixth'.
4. ***Higher shares for the females than men***: The female who is the daughter (with no siblings) of the deceased takes half and his father takes one sixth. And if there be only one (daughter) then the half, and to the parents of the deceased a sixth each.

Thus Quranic prescription is based on the principle of equity. Higher shares are usually given to those whose needs are greater, so that they may discharge their financial responsibility. A woman as a daughter is under the care / responsibility of her father, as a sister under the care of brother, as a wife under the care of her husband. The often made criticism that Islam does not treat women equal to men in the matters of inheritance is unjustified. Critics always base their remarks looking at the first situation and ignore the three other situations where she gets as much as or even more than males. Many critics are either unaware of the other situations or are biased. Moreover, it should be noted that Islam gave right to property to women twelve centuries before England adopted it legally. Hindu women got this right only in 1955-56 when Hindu Code Bill (comprising four Acts – the Hindu Marriage Act, 1955, the Hindu Succession Act, 1956, the Hindu Minority and Guardianship Act, 1956 and the Hindu Adoptions and Maintenance Act, 1956) was adopted by Parliament.

Muslim woman has other rights too. She cannot be forced into marriage by her family or guardian; she has to give her consent. If the marriage was solemnised during childhood she can repudiate it on reaching puberty. She can retain her maiden name after marriage, if she so wishes. She has the right to demand the power of divorce plus the power at the time of the marriage contract to disallow polygamy by her husband. Muslim woman was also given equality in the principle of jihad (religious war). Many women participated in battles during the time of the Prophet Mohammad. One Muslim woman, Nasiba bint Ka'b, defended the Prophet with her sword and arrows in the battle of 'Uhad'. Another example of brave woman can be found in Umayyati bint al-Gafariyya, whose courage at the battle of Khaibar was praised by the Prophet. After the victory, the Prophet presented her with a necklace, as a counterpart of the military decorations of our day. She wore it throughout her life, and it was buried with her in accordance with her will. In the Prophet's wars of conquest, women generally worked alongwith men and succoured the wounded. It is also interesting to note that until the third century of Islam and even later, women enjoyed with men the right to pray in the mosques. Khaliph Omar is said to have appointed a reader of Quran especially for them at public worship.

In sum, woman in Islamic teachings/theory enjoys a higher status in comparison to her counterparts in other religious traditions and systems. The Prophet declared many times that "Paradise lies under the feet of the mother." In his last public address, he advised Muslims to "treat their women well and be kind to them".

Varying Practices and Modern Reforms

Throughout the Islamic world, there has been a considerable gap between scriptural dictates and actual practice. As a result, we find many discriminatory practices toward women. Due to these discriminatory practices, Islam has been criticised on the ground of polygamy, divorce laws, veiling and seclusion of women and the generally prevailing unequal treatment of women as compared to men. Moreover, there are varying practices of applying gender equality in different regions of India. In fact, we find divergent practices in different countries and different schools of Islamic law (Shariah). These discriminatory practices can be removed by reforming and reinterpreting Shariah in the light of contemporary socio-political thought and the huge corpus of international human rights law.

Though Islam does permit plurality of wives, not exceeding four, it is only on the condition of strict equality of treatment among them. But the practice shows that this condition is not followed universally by majority of Muslims in the world. God warns in the Quran that "If you fear you will not be able to deal justly with them, then marry only one" (Chapter 4, Verse 4). In another place, He cautions: "You are never able to be fair and just between women, even if it is your ardent desire" (Chapter 4, Verses 3 and 129). Polygamy is not a general rule, it is only a necessary and emerging provision for the preservation and fostering of high social values (involving marriages of widows or orphans) and for safeguarding society against promiscuity. This permission has undoubtedly been abused, but many Muslim States are seeking to eradicate such abuse through legal regulation of the institution of marriage. For instance, Egypt changed its marriage laws in 1920, 1923, 1929 and in 1956 it abrogated the Shariah courts. In 1931 Egypt restricted the solemnisation of child marriages by precluding the court from hearing any claim of marriage whatever if the husband had not reached the age of 18 and the bride the age of 16 at the time of litigation. Furthermore, the court could not hear any disputed claim of marriage, unless that marriage contract had been registered. Earlier, in 1923, it had made a criminal offence for a Registrar to register a marriage in a case where the bride was not above 16 and the bridegroom above 18. Similarly, Tunisia, Morocco, Algeria, Iraq and South Yemen have enacted new provisions governing personal laws. Syria, Morocco, Pakistan and Iran have also severely restricted polygamy noting the impossibility of fulfilling the Quranic injunction that multiple wives be treated equally. Tunisia and Turkey have gone the farthest in directly outlawing polygamous marriages. In Lebanon, Jordan, Egypt and Morocco, the woman can insert in her marriage contract the right to divorce if her husband should take a second wife. Regrettably, no serious attempts have been initiated in India to reform family laws with a view to improving the status of women. Such initiatives should come from the leaders, theologians and cross-section of people of the Muslim community. Government initiative will be misconceived by the community as a step towards Uniform Civil Code.

Though the Quran commands that the wife alone shall receive the dower (mahr) payable by the husband, which was paid in pre-Islamic period to her father, in many cases in India, it is hardly paid in practice. Originally, divorce laws were fair. Out of three kinds of divorce, two were to be initiated by women. First, a wife may seek from a court a **judicial separation** on grounds of deficiency, mischief, fear of temptation arising due to long absence of the husband or inadequate maintenance. Second, a wife can seek divorce by redemption (Khul) on the ground of deep-seated animosity. But the most commonly practised system is divorce by the husband – independently of the intervention of his wife or of court – leading to misuse. In the majority of divorce cases, husband plays a dominant role. The tightening of divorce laws were the later developments. Moreover, the Quran prescribes that this kind of divorce will not be effective until the "waiting period" (*Idda*) is over. Prior to Islamic era, a husband could discard his wife at a moment's notice. The Quran now virtually suspended the effect of the divorce until the expiry of *idda*, which was to last until the wife had completed three menstrual cycles or, if she proved pregnant, until the delivery of the child. This period is primarily designed, according to the express terms of the Quran itself, to provide an opportunity for reconciliation, and during it, the wife is entitled to receive maintenance from the husband. In fact, the husband is required to pronounce *talaq* (divorce) thrice to his wife with a gap of one month each between these utterances. The practice of triple *talaq* in one breath, which prevails in India and other Muslim countries, goes against this Quranic precept.

The basis of discrimination against women is generally attributed to Quranic injunctions / verses. A literal or restrictive interpretation of these verses reduces women to a lower status. Let us cite these verses: "*Men stand superior to women* in that God has preferred the one over the other, they have authority over the other, they have authority over women *because they spend their wealth to maintain them*. Good women are obedient.... As for those from whom you fear disobedience, admonish them and send them to beds apart and *beat them*, but if they obey you, take no further action against them [italics added]" (Quran, 4:34). Veiling of women is supported through verses 30-31 of Chapter 24, and verses 53 and 59 of Chapter 33.

In the 7th century Arabia and other places, women were economically dependent on men for their survival and security. In such a social and historical context, the Quranic pronouncement of men's superiority was rationalised. Women were then considered as wards of men. Applying his evolutionary principle of interpretation, Ustadh Mahmood Taha, the leader of reformist movement in Sudan, who was executed by former Sudanese President Numeri, says that now the male guardianship over women should be terminated as women are no longer economically dependent on men, these days. This Quranic verse (i.e., 4:34) should be set aside as having served its purpose and should not be applied to the contemporary societies.

As regards the veiling, it should be said that it was a pre-Islamic practice in many societies – from Greece to Persia and the Byzantine Empire. One verse of the Quran (24:30-31) tells women to veil their bosom and hide their ornaments. "Ornaments" was later taken (by the early interpreters of Quran from Persia) to mean everything except the hands, feet, and perhaps the face, though this interpretation makes no logical or linguistic sense. In addition, if everything was to be veiled, there would be no point in ordering bosoms veiled separately. Another verse tells them to draw their cloaks tightly round them so that they may be recognised and not annoyed. And these are the only words taken to refer to veiling. Thus, it appears that the veiling and the harem system were later developments that arose in certain Muslim countries as a result of social conditions and local traditions. Whatever are the causes of their developments, such practices have nothing to do with the principles of Islam. The gap between precepts and practices is quite glaring with respect to women's inheritance rights. It must be noted that except for the Arab populations, which was responsible to develop Shariah under the guidance of the Prophet, for other peoples (who became Muslims later) Shariah posed serious problems, because its basic concepts were often wholly alien to the traditional structure of their societies. Despite being Muslims, they could not strictly adhere to Shariah. Local customs determined the inheritance rights of woman. For instance, the Berber community of North Africa does not provide inheritance to women. Berber customary law of this nature is applied to almost half of the Muslim population of Morocco in all civil matters. In Java and Sumatra, inheritance rights continued to be regulated by the customary matriarchal law. In western Nigeria, Shariah is scarcely applied. It is interesting to note that certain Arab tribes of the Yemen never relinquished their established customary law under which, inter alia, women did not enjoy any property rights.

In the Indian sub-continent, the Ismailite Khojas, the Bohoras and the Kutchi Memons continued, after their conversion to Islam from Hinduism, to be governed by the Hindu law of succession, and thus retain the power, in contravention of Shariah, to will awy the whole of their estates. In almost every region of India customarily Muslim women were not given share in landed property. It was a prerogative of males only. Muslim males resented when attempts were made to enforce Shariah rules on giving inheritance rights to women. When the Federal Assembly was debating the adoption of Muslim Personal Law (Shariah) Application Act, 1937, there was strong opposition to it from the landowning classes of Punjab on the ground that the bill would ruin agriculturists. Though the Act was passed, this abrogated prevailing customs or usage concerning inheritance rights, among others, it explicitly excluded from its purview agricultural land, the devolution of which would continue to be governed by local customs. While the Act meant to extend women's property rights, it hardly served that purpose. Thus the Act served the political purpose of affirming Muslim identity, without antagonising the powerful Punjabi landlords.

After India's independence, legal reforms were initiated in the subcontinent. The Pakistani Parliament initially passed the West Punjab Muslim Personal Law (Shariat) Application Act of 1948, which included agricultural land in its purview. In 1962, it passed the West Pakistan Muslim Personal Law (Shariat) Application Act, which was applicable to the whole of West Pakistan, except the "Tribal Areas" in North West Frontier Province. It made women legally entitled to inherit agricultural property as full owners. The Bangladeshi (formerly East Pakistani) Muslims were not affected by legal reforms in West Pakistan. Here the 1937 Act of India was in force. Here despite the absence of subsequent amendments (or even before the passage of 1937 Act), Shariah applied also to agricultural land.

In India too, the 1937 Act has continued to be applicable even after independence. It is gratifying to note that in Tamil Nadu and Andhra Pradesh the Act was amended in 1949 to include agricultural land, in 1963, Kerala did the same. In Assam, Maharashra, Gujarat, and West Bengal, there was no strong preference of custom even before the Act was passed; hence, in these states, the Shariah rules could be applied to agricultural land as well. But in several states of north-west India such as Uttar Pradesh (which included till recently Uttrakhand region too), Punjab, Himachal Pradesh and Haryana, the Act has not been amended to include agricultural land. Despite the land reform laws, customary laws still govern the succession of such land. Thus, in these states severe gender inequalities still persist as far as succession of landed property among the Muslims is concerned. Muslim intelligentia and leaders (both political and theological) should mobilise public support to amend/reform the 1937 Shariah Act to remove gender inequality.

Empowerment of Muslim Women: Towards Reforming Muslim Personal Law

Mahatma Gandhi once said, "one step for women, ten steps for nation." "Human Development, unless engendered, is endangered," proclaimed the 1995 UNDP's *Human Development Report*, which was released on the eve of Fourth World Conference on Women: Action for Equality, Development and Peace, held at Beijing, China. These two profound statements highlight the importance of women's empowerment. Empowerment means to give somebody the power or authority to act. Therefore, empowerment of women means that the women have the power or capacity to regulate their day-to-day lives in the social, economic and political fields. This will enable them to move from the periphery to the centre stage. The main motive behind women's empowerment is to protect their rights, to enrich their quality of life and involve them in decision-making process at all levels, particularly in those decisions, which are related to their lives and families. Empowerment of Muslim women involves: higher literacy level and education, better health care for them and their children, awareness about their reproductive rights, implementation of Shariah law to give inheritance rights, abolition of triple talaq, a practice followed in India in contradiction of Quranic dictum, punishing those demanding dowry (as it is against Shariah), ensuring the payment of Mehar (dower) to women at the time of marriage, encouraging their participation in local and urban governments as elected representatives.

Some of the reforms / measures, suggested above, require the reforms of Muslim Personal Law. Initiatives in this regard should come from the Muslim community itself. If the Government, a political party or Supreme Court advocates such modest reforms, it will be taken by the community leaders, both religious and political, as interference in their personal laws and threat to their identities, which are protected by the constitution. Moderate Muslim intellectuals and women's groups, from the Muslim community, should initiate debate and discussion in this direction. The Women's NGOs and Hindu women's organisations should not insist on the need of drafting Uniform Civil Code, rather the approach of all should be to advocate reforms in all personal laws of different communities, so as to make them gender just. Changes made in all family laws, as a result of the initiatives of the respective communities to reform their personal laws, will be more acceptable to them than the uniform laws which may threaten their distinct cultural identities.

REFERENCES

The Quran: Chapter 4, Verse 7

The Quran: Chapter 4, Verse 4

The Quran: Chapter 4, Verses 3 and 129

The Quran: Chapter 4 Verse 34

The Quran: Chapter 24 Verses 30-31

Human Development Report, UNDP, 1995

FURTHER READINGS

Agnes, Flavia. *Law and Gender Inequality: The Politics of Women's Rights in India* (New Delhi: Oxford University Press, 1999).

Ahmed, Anees. "Reforming Muslim Personal Law". *Economic and Political Weekly*. 24 February 2001.

Ahmed, L. *Women and Gender in Islam Historical Roots of a Modern Debate* (New Haven: Yale University Press, 1992).

Ali, Shaheen Sardar. *Gender and Human Rights in Islam and International Law – Equal Before Allah, Unequal Before Man?* (The Hague: Kluwer Law International, 2000).

An-Na'im, Abdullahi Ahmed. *Toward an Islamic Reformation: Civil Liberties, Human Rights, and International Law* (New York: Syracuse University Press, 1990).

Ansari, Iqbal A. "Muslim Personal Law in India". *Journal of Muslim Minority Affairs*, Vol. 1, No. 2, 1979, pp. 86-96.

Chavan, Nandini and Kidwai, Qutub Jahan. *Personal Law Reforms and Gender Empowerment: A Debate on Uniform Civil Code* (New Delhi: Hope India, 2006).

Choudhury, Cyra Anila. "(Mis) Appropriated Liberty: Identity, Gender Justice and Muslim Personal Law Reform in India", *Columbia Journal of Gender and Law*, Vol. 17, 2008 (Also can be accessed at: www.ssrn.com).

Derrett, J. Duncan M. *Religion, Law and the State in India* (London: 1968).

Esposito, J. L. *Women in Muslim Family Law* (Syracuse: Syracuse University Press, 1983).

Fayzee, A. A, *Outlines of Mohammedian Law*, 4th edition (Oxford University Press, 2003).

Hassan, Riffat. "Are Human Rights Compatible with Islam? The Issue of the Rights of Women in Muslim Communities">www.

Jaising, Indira (ed.). *Justice for Women – Personal Laws, Women's Rights and Law Reform* (Mapusa, Goa: The Other India Press, 1996).

Jones, Justin. "'Signs of Churning': Muslim Personal Law and Public Contestation in twenty-first Century India." *Modern Asian Studies*, Vol. 44, No. 1, 2010, pp. 175-200.

Kazi, S. *Muslim Women in India* (London: Minority Rights Group International, 1999).

Larson, G.L. (ed.), *Religion and Personal Law in Secular India: A Call to Judgment* (Indiana University Press, 2001).

Mahmood, Tahir. *Muslim Law of India* (New Delhi: Lexis Nexis Butterworths, 2002).

Menski, Werner. "The Uniform Civil Code Debate in Indian Law: New Developments and Changing Agenda". *German Law Review*, Vol. 9, No. 3, 2008.

Metcalf, Barbara. "Puting Muslim Personal Law in Perspective". Center of Advanced Studies on India, University of Pennsylvania, 2007. (This paper can be accessed at: www.casi.ssc.upenn.edu/iit/bmetcaff.)

Parashar, Archna, *Women and Family Law Reform in India: Uniform Civil Code and Gender Equality* (New Delhi: Sage Publications, 1992).

Rahman, Fazalur. "Status of Women in the *Quran*". In G. Nashat (ed.), *Women and Revolution in India* (Boulder: Westview Press, 1983).

Subramanian, N. "Legal Pluralism, Legal Change and Gender Inequality: Changes in Muslim Family Law in India". www.profs-polisci.mcgill.ca\subramanian\papers

Upadhyay, R., "Muslim Law: Should it be Politicised?"< www.saag.org.papers7\paper666.html> Vijapur. Abdulrahim P. "The Shariah is not as Immutable as it Seems". *Indian Express*, October 31, 1993.

......., "Is Shariah Immutable or Dynamic? – The Scope for Reformation", *21st Century Trust News* (London), January 1994. Also published in *The Muslim World League Journal* (Makka, Saudi Arabia), Vol. 21, No. 9, March 1994 and an extended version in *New Quest* (Poona), No. 104, March-April 1994.

World Bank, *Engendering Development: Through Gender Equality in Rights, Resources, and Voices* (New York: Oxford University Press, 2001).

5

Gender Concerns and Development Debates

— Bijayalaxmi Nanda

Development as a global issue became prominent after the World War II. The gender bias in development indicates that women are particularly disadvantaged with respect to access to health care, education, political and labour force and other forms of participation. Voices, for the inclusion of women in the development, emerged in the 1970s. Over the past two decades, ideas, about how to effectively include women in development, have shifted through three distinct phases – women in development, women and development and gender and development. It has been realised that development can be achieved only, if women get equal share and opportunity to participate in all the spheres of development. In this context, this papers attempts to critically examine the strategies adopted under the national policies in India, for women's empowerment and their development.

Thinking about 'Development' goes back to classical political economy of the 18th Century, while Development theory, as a special field of study with is intimately linked to economics and emerged after the World War II. The essential thesis of development theory was: (i) That development meant an increase in the quantity and range of goods and services. (ii) This was best achieved through industrialisation and technology. (iii) It required increasing capital (resources used for future production). (iv) Such capital has to come from savings. (v) If domestic savings are inadequate, then the emphasis is to be on borrowing. (vi) The state has to play a critical role – either 'total command', 'guide', intervene in critical sectors or a mix (Krishnaraj and Pore 1996).

The earliest model was known as the Harrod Domar Model. Though much sophistication and elaboration has since taken place, in substance, the underlying assumption of all models is the same. It believes that promoting economic growth will benefit developing countries and eventually the developed nations as well. Development, thus, consisted of conscious planning and intervention by which resources, techniques and expertise are assembled and invested in developing countries, so as to improve the rates of economic growth (Kabeer, 1994). The United States was a significant player in administrating foreign expertise and technology as well as monetary aids to the developing world, through its role in the United Nations, International Monetary Fund, the World Bank and other similar agencies (Mitra 2003). However, despite careful planning and channelising of funds, the gap between the rich and the poor has widened in the developing countries. There were many instances of strong economic growth but the "trickle down" effect failed to reach the majority of the poor (Visvanathan, 1997:2). By the 1970s, the former colonies were calling for a New International Economic Order, where there would be greater equity in the distribution of wealth.

Women and Development – Debates and Concerns

It was realised that the decades of 60s and 70s had brought about little real development. It was at this time that voices were calling for the inclusion of women in the development process as there were negative impacts in various development projects (Visvanathan 1997). Feminist Theory entered these debates at this stage and the focus of feminist theory has since gone through various phases. The distinct theoretical perspectives include Women in Development (WID), Women and Development (WAD) to Gender and Development (GAD). These perspectives indicate the need to envisage the relationship of women and men and the resulting inequalities as well as recognising the multiple role played by women in reproductive and community management work (Mikkelson 1995; Kabeer 1994; Visvanathan 1997).

The first intervention is arguably Esther Boserup's pioneering work which was published in the late 1950s and was picked up by international agencies in the 70s. In her work, based mainly on Africa, she pointed to the impact of development on women's lives and livelihood, and by development planners and policy makers to integrate women into development as workers and producers. An amendment, introduced in the UN General Assembly in 1974 through the U.S. Senator Percy, launched the discourse of 'Women in Development'. The WID perspective has close similarities to liberal feminism. It did the pioneering task of exposing sexual inequality in the development process and amassed considerable evidence from all over the third world that women were not getting the 'fruits' of development (Krishnaraj & Pore 1996).

The WID discourse sets the stage for inclusion of women by the development agencies. However, it ignores the structural and socio-economic factors that form the basis for gender inequalities.

The Women and Development (WAD) perspective, stems from the Marxist feminist studies, that contends liberation of men and women is not possible within the capitalistic system and the creation of a socialist economy is a pre-condition for it. It sees capitalism and patriarchy as mutually reinforcing and argues that sexual inequality is structurally and dialectically related to social class, uneven and unequal development. This kind of approach worked within a broadly Marxist framework with deviations that ranged from the overtly mechanistic approach to the issue of women's subordination, inhering in its relation to capital. The changing roles of women in capitalism is determined by a number of factors, such as the way the sexual division of labour in production and reproduction is actually expressed in local class structures and the articulation of specific regions and sectors of production within national economies and the international economy. Within this debate, the Third World feminism has emerged which has made its distinct contribution. It rejects both Western feminist theory and development theory as reductionist, Eurocentric and racist. It rejects the generalisation and universalisation of 'development model' as another form of discursive colonisation (Krishnaraj & Pore 1996). WAD analysis includes the structuralist perspective, as exemplified by the Marxist and dependency theorists, goes well beyond the traditional Marxist framework (Kabeer 1994; Visvanathan 1997).

The detailed examination of the structural perspectives on Women and Development does reveal certain limitations. It gives very sketchy attention to the domain of reproduction and household level relations between men and women (Kabeer 1994; Visvanathan 1997). Kabeer also points out that the overemphasis on the structural basis of production for exchange, actually de-emphasizes the role of men in subordinating women. The 1980s saw the emergence of a more holistic perspective. The limitations posed by WID and WAD did not figure in the new perspective which is referred to as the Gender and Development perspective. Its main emphasis is on the social relations between men and women, in the work place as well as in other settings. It also considered gender relations in both labour force and in the reproductive sector. This approach views development as a complex process subjected to the social and economic factors. The category of analysis is not restricted to women but rather on the social relations between men and women, where men are viewed as potential supporters of women

(Visvanathan 1997). While the GAD model differs from the WID and WAD perspectives, there remains considerable overlap between the three approaches (Young, 1997).

Since the focus in GAD is on diverse relationships that men and women share as part of their everyday lives, the interaction of relationships within the existing social structures, i.e., the household or the workplace are central to their analysis. The other factors that are considered along with this are the effects of specific regional and global forces which have an overall impact on the relationships considered. The GAD approach does not isolate any factor and considers all factors as integrated and interrelated. Young points out to the basic elements of this approach which distinguish it from the earlier approaches. The primary distinguishing factor of this approach is that women are considered as active participants in the overall decision-making process and not mere beneficiaries of development. The approach is based on the understanding that men are not necessarily responsible for the patriarchal order of society and the subordination and exploitation of women. Women are not always aware of the social bases of their subordination.

Young also outlines systematically the holistic nature of the GAD model:

1. It regards societal development as an integrated whole and sees welfare, anti-poverty or equity approaches as interconnected issues.
2. The model urges involvement of the State in the local, regional and central levels, particularly, in the emancipation of women.
3. It regards the sustainability of development as a shared concern and not just individual responsibility.
4. The GAD model encourages support and the involvement of local communities in women's empowerment. Since, families and kinship groups can directly or indirectly pose constraints on women's emancipation. GAD emphasises the bases of support that can be found within these social structures and the resistance to it.

The development paradigm has undergone much change in the recent years with the emphasis on human rights. The UNDP in the Human Development Report 1991 says: "Development must be participatory and for this people must have the opportunity to participate and to invest in the development of their capabilities. They also must have the opportunities to put their capabilities to use, to be fully involved in all aspects of life, to express them freely and collectively." Amartya Sen and Jean Dreze have interpreted development in terms of enhancement of freedom and elimination of illiteracy, ill-health and other deprivations. The Beijing Conference in 1995, raised questions, whether women have access to build their capabilities and to enjoy opportunities as the men. The two indices constructed were Gender Related Index (GRI) and Gender Empowerment Measures (GEM). The GEM reflects the opportunities available rather their capabilities. It captures gender inequalities in the economic and political life of the country. Thus, while a State may have appeared to have achieved a high level of human development, women in the State may still face discrimination in building their capabilities and gaining access to economic and political participation. These concerns in the international arena influenced and were influenced by the feminist approaches to development. (Verma, 2003)

Policy Approaches in India

Unfortunately, gender and development practice in India evolved without firm roots in either gender studies or in the Indian women's movement. In opposition to the analytical category of gender relations, simplified notions of gender, as socially constructed differences between women and men were popularised by some of the aid agencies, government departments and non-government organisations in India in the 1990s. This definition does not grapple with the power elations underlying the construction of difference between women and men and between different groups of women (Murthy, 2001). This liberal notion of gender does not even challenge the paradigm of unfettered economic growth that benefited from the construction of these differences. Several internationally developed gender planning frameworks are provided as the solution to the gender blindness of time bound development projects, but have very little to say on the complex process of women's subordination or empowerment (Murthy 1994, Kabeer 1994 and Bhasin 1997).

Until the report of the Committee on the Status of Women in India in the mid-70s, the neglect of the women's question was invisible to policy makers. The perspective on women that actually got incorporated after independence was that of keeper of the family, and their role in the household and community (Banerjee 1998). The planned economy had a definite emphasis on nation-building and matters of distributive justice were not given any priority.

The first Five Year Plan (1951-56) focused on the need to provide adequate services for women's welfare. In 1953 the Central Social Welfare Board was established which symbolised the welfare approach to women's problems and subsequent establishment of State Social Welfare Advisory Boards to promote and assist voluntary organisations in the field of welfare of women and children.

The Second Five Year Plan (1956-60) emphasised the need for special attention to the problems of women workers. Recognising that they were less organised, these women were organised into Mahila Mandals, to act as focal points at the grass-root level for the development of women. The Plan stated that women should be protected against injurious work and it also suggested speedy implementation of the principle of equal pay for equal work, provision of facilities for training to enable women to compete for higher jobs and expansion of opportunities for part-time employment and to provide the facilities of crèches. The Maternity Benefits Act, 1961, was enacted at the end of this Plan.

The emphasis of the Third Five Year Plan (1960-66) was on the expansion of girl's education, which continued in the Fourth Year Plan (1969-74). Crash Schemes for Rural Employment, Food for Work Programme, Draught Prone Areas Programme, and Dessert Development Programmes were initiated, aiming at strengthening the rural base of the economy. Though these schemes seemed to be gender-neutral, they were male-biased. They were targeted at men as the heads/earners of the families, with the assumption that benefits to men will trickle down to the rest of the family members. The Committee on the Status of Women in India (CSWI) was appointed by the Government of India in 1971, having a three-fold objective: (a) to evaluate the changes that had taken place in the status of women as the result of the constitutional, legal and administrative measures adopted since independence, (b) to examine the impact of the complex processes of social change on the various sections of Indian women and (c) to suggest measures which would enable women to play their full and proper role in building up the nation (Ministry of Education and Social Welfare, 1974).

The Fifth Five Year Plan (1974-79) showed a shift from welfare to development. This was largely because of the influence of the International Women's Year (1975) and International Women's Decade (1975-85). The new approach aimed at an integration of welfare with developmental services. A Report of the Committee on the Status of Women in India (CSWI) called 'Towards Equality' was published by the Department of Social Welfare in 1974. In order to operationalise the recommendations of the report, a Blueprint of Action Points and National Plan of Action for Women were formulated in 1976. The Plan emphasised the need to train women in need of income and protection. In spite of Directive Principles of State Policy up to the Fifth Plan, there was no effort to see women as human or productive entities. "The statistical 'purdha' concealed the full extent of their participation in these sectors and their contribution to the national domestic product, and this made them invisible persons to the policy planners." (Bandyopadhyay, 2000).

For the first time, the Sixth Five Year Plan (1980-85) introduced a separate chapter on women. This plan adopted a multi-disciplinary approach with a three pronged thrust on health, education and employment. It stressed on economic independence, giving of joint titles to husband and wife in all asset transfers, including land, house sites and other economic units, a public policy package that included ownership rights and enforcement of wage laws. The Department of Rural Development announced a 30 percent quota for women in all anti-poverty programmes for the rural areas and a special programme called 'Development of Women and Children in Rural Areas' was introduced providing for collective action by rural women. The department also sensitised public servants on gender issues.

The main thrust of the Seventh Five Year Plan (1986-90) was in making women to realise their role in the process of development. The developmental programmes for women continued with the major objectives of raising economic and social status and to bring them into the mainstream of national development. A significant step in this direction was the identification and promotion of beneficiary oriented programmes for women. The Seventh Plan also had a separate chapter on women this time, titled 'Socio-Economic Program for Women'. It focused on the concept of equality and empowerment of women which was expressed by the International Decade for Women. During this period a number of policies and programmes focused on mainstreaming women's issues. The National Policy on Education which was released in 1986, had a chapter on 'Education for Women's Equality', which in fact began the women's empowerment phase in India. The Twenty-Point Programme against poverty, adopted in 1986 also included a point on equality for women. The National Perspective Plan for Women 1988-2000 was published by a Core Group set up by the Detachment of Women and Child Development under the Chairperson, Mrs. Margaret Alva, providing government leadership. In the same year the National Commission on Self-Employed women published 'Shramshakti', which is a comprehensive study of the working and living conditions of the poor women in rural and urban areas.

These efforts influenced the Eighth Five Year Plan (1992-97) which shifted the focus from development to empowerment. In 1990 the National Commission for Women Act was enacted and two years later the National Commission for Women was set up as a national apex statutory level body to review the Constitutional and legal safeguards for women which recommends remedial legislative measures, facilitates redressal of grievances and advises the government on all policy matters affecting women. In 1991 a National Plan of Action for the SAARC Decade of the Girl Child (1991-2000) was formulated by the Department of Women and Child Development. In 1996 the Draft of the National Policy for the Empowerment of Women was finalised.

As a follow-up of the Fourth World Conference at Beijing, "Growth with Equity" was adopted as the theme of the Ninth Five Year Plan (1997-2002) and the following were the main objectives: (a) Generation of adequate productive employment and eradication of poverty. (b) Provision for basic minimum services of safe drinking water, primary health care facilities, universal "primary education, shelter and connectivity to all villages in a time-bound manner: (c) Promoting and developing people's participation through Panchayati Raj institutions, Cooperative and Self-Help Groups and (d) Empowerment of women.

The approach of the Tenth Plan (2002-2007) to empower women is to continue with the major strategy of 'Empowering Women' as Agents of Social Change and Development. This is to be done by adopting a Sector-specific 3-Fold Strategy for empowering women, based on the prescriptions of the National Policy for Empowerment of Women.

They include:

- **Social Empowerment** - To create an enabling environment through various affirmative developmental policies and programmes for development of women, besides providing them easy and equal access to all the basic minimum services, so as to enable them to realise their full potentials.
- **Economic Empowerment** - To ensure provision of training, employment and income-generation activities with both 'forward' and 'backward' linkages with the ultimate objective of making all potential women economically independent and self-reliant.
- **Gender Justice** - To eliminate all forms of gender discrimination and thus, allow women to enjoy not only the de-jure, but also the de-facto rights and fundamental freedom on par with men in all spheres, viz. political, economic, social, civil, cultural etc.

An analysis of all the five year plan efforts for development of women reveals gaps between rhetoric and reality. Literacy levels, morbidity and mortality levels, participation levels, all show us that the status of women in India remains abysmally low. The 1990s economic reforms and the process of liberalisation and economic globalisation, that followed, have affected women and vulnerable sectors adversely. Faster economic growth does not necessarily lead to more secure employment and reduction of poverty. What need to be addressed are the interconnections between poverty, education, cultural inhibitions and gender factors. The vision of the Beijing Conference 'Growth with Equality' can only be realised by a consideration of these factors and a set of multiple strategies where the State is involved. Women have to be integrated at all levels in the mainstream of development and economic activities. At the same time, the status of women can be enhanced by removing social and cultural barriers that impede progress and increase women's vulnerability. Development today should be visualised as empowerment through participation. The hurdles in the path of participation need to be removed. Only then, the gap, between the rhetoric of women's development and the reality of their development, can be bridged. Only then women will not just endure but finally triumph.

Acknowledgement

I would like to acknowledge the inputs of Dr. Babita Verma in the formulation and structuring of this paper.

REFERENCES

Bandarage A. "Women in Development: Liberalism, Marxism and Marxist Feminism". *Development and Change*. 15. pp. 495-515, 1984.

Mitra, Kaumari. "Gender, Development and Women's Health in India". *Indian Journal of Social Development*, Vol. 1. Number-1. June 2003. pp. 74-83, 2003.

Meena Rao B. & S. Uma Devi. "Gender Justice: A Study of Policy Approaches". *Indian Journal of Social Development*. Vol. 1. Number-2. December 2001, pp. 251-255.

Kabeer, Naila. *Reversed Realities: Gender Hierarchies in Development Thought*. London. Verso. 1994.

Visvanathan & Lynn Duggan. "Theories of Women, Gender and Development: Introduction to Part I". In *The Women Gender and Development Reader*. Visvanathan & Lynn Duggan. Laurie Nisonoff and Nan Wiegersma, eds. Halifax. Nova Scotia. Fernwood Publishing Ltd. 1997.

Verma, Babita. *Implications of Women's Representation in Panchayats for the Role of Bureaucracy: Selected Case studies in Uttar Pradesh*. thesis submitted to the University of Delhi for the degree of Ph.D in Political Science, 2003.

Young, Kate. "Gender and Development". In *The Women Gender and Development Reader*, Visvanathan & Lynn Duggan; Laurie Nisonoff and Nan Wiegersma, eds. Halifax. Nova Scotia. Fernwood Publishing Ltd. 1997.

Krishnaraj, Maitreyi & Kumud Pore. "Gender Concerns in New Economic Policy". *Concepts in Feminist Theory II.* Women's Studies Centre, Department of Sociology, University of Pune. 1996.

6

Home Science Education (HSE) for Rural Women in Uttarakhand

— *Archana Shah*

Home Science is the art of managing resources efficiently and the science of achieving a healthier, happier home and a successful career. It is the only academic discipline which prepares young learners for the two supremely important goals in their lives – one, looking after their home and family and achieving and maintaining their welfare and well-being in an ever changing society and two, preparing for a career or vocation in life. The author in the present paper aims to discuss certain pertinent issues surrounding Home Science, chiefly, its relevance to the rural Himalayan women in Uttarakhand in the context of its proposed role in bringing about domestic preparation as well as in addressing larger issues of development, such as sustainable development and women empowerment. Keeping all these factors in mind, the present paper attempts to highlight the scope of Home Science as a tool for improving the status of the rural Himalayan women of Uttarakhand.

Home Science Education as the Art of Home-Making

According to Rajmal Devdas "Home Science is the service of the home and is concerned with the maintenance and enrichment of human relationships through the development and judicious use of all available human and material resources to achieve a maximal satisfying life for all the members of the family and the community" (Malviya, 2007). As a field of study, Home Science draws from a range of disciplines (such as chemistry, physics, physiology, biology, hygiene, economics, rural development, child development, sociology and family relations, community living, art, food, nutrition, clothing, textiles and home management) to achieve optimal and sustainable living for individuals, families and communities in an ever changing society through management of resources and utilisation of decision-making skills. It enables people to tackle increasingly complex challenges including those related to human development and relationships, and the provision of commodities such as food, clothing and shelter. The historical origins place Home Science in the context of the home and household, and this is extended in the 21st century to include the wider living environments, ranging from the household, to the local and also the global community. Concerned with the empowerment and well-being of individuals, families and communities, the discipline aims at enhancing personal and family growth and development, including a sense of personal identity; making decisions about entering into new relationships and responsibilities, establishing and maintaining relationships, and dealing with the pressures that threaten relationships; developing a society that fosters family harmony, gender equity and ecological sustainability.

Popularly known as Home Science in Third-World or emerging countries, the preferred terminology for the same sort of training in developed countries is Home Economics. In India, Home Science has been a part of female education since the early 1930s (Hancock, 2001). Interest in Home Science existed in British India and in the Princely States from the turn of the twentieth century. In 1932, Lady Irwin College became the pioneer in Home Science Education (HSE) for women when it was first opened in Delhi with eleven students and was the only institution of higher education in India at that time that was dedicated exclusively to that subject. The nomenclature 'Home Science' was adopted by the Home Science Association of India in 1952.

Relating Home Science to Sustainable Development

Sustainable development entails maintaining a delicate balance between the human need to improve lifestyles and feeling of well-being and preserving natural resources and ecosystems, on which the present and future generations depend. It involves establishing equilibrium between the fulfillment of human needs and the protection of the natural environment so that these needs can be met not only in the present, but in the indefinite future as well. The essence of this form of development is the creation of a stable relationship between human activities and the natural world. Conservation and sustainable development are mutually dependent. The dependency of rural (and urban) families on the natural resources is direct and immediate which must be conserved to improve living standards. Home Science celebrates a long history of teaching conservation of household resources in the near environment. In an article, Grover and Goldey cite Margaret Khalakdina who states that "sustainable home economics is a movement from one of consumption to one of conservation and sustainability". It is, therefore, logical to conclude that the Home Science curricula should on the one hand, encourage the conservation of natural resources at the household level and, on the other hand, guide the reorientation of information and technologies for the sustainable use of natural resources, such as land and water.

Home Science Education for Empowerment of Women

The UN definition of women empowerment encompasses five components: women's sense of self-worth; their right to have and to determine choices; their right to have access to opportunities and resources; their right to have the power to control their own lives, both within and outside the home; and their ability to influence the direction of social change to create a more just social and economic order, nationally and internationally. Empowerment of women, therefore, covers several realms: personal, familial, economic, social, environmental and political. The World Bank defines empowerment in its broadest sense as, the expansion of freedom of choice and action'. Since the 1990's, women have been recognised as the key agents of sustainable development. The issues of equality and empowerment of women are regarded as central to a more holistic approach towards establishing new but sustainable patterns and processes of development. By virtue of its interdisciplinary nature, its wide ranging content and comprehensive practical component, Home Science as an academic discipline, naturally promotes empowerment.

Rural Women in Uttarakhand

Women in the rural areas of Uttarakhand, especially in the mountainous regions of Garhwal and Kumaon, assume multiple and crucial roles in day-to-day life. For instance, in their productive role, women carry out domestic chores such as fetching water, fuel and fodder; food production, storage, processing and preparation; washing and repairing clothes; assisting in building, maintaining and cleaning the house etc. In their reproductive role, women are involved with responsibilities of childbearing, child care and child rearing as well as family upbringing and care of sick family members. Corresponding with their multiple roles are the basic needs of the rural women, such as, those of food, shelter, water, health and education and financial resources to procure the basic necessities of the household.

Uttarakhand itself stands out as one of the few States in India, where an overwhelming number of women have been part of the active work force, since times immemorial. This is because 76 percent of the women live in rural areas who are engaged with agriculture, forest protection, and animal husbandry. Women here are thus the backbone of the rural economy. Since most of the men migrate to towns in search of salaried jobs, women end up undertaking 75 percent of the workload in the villages. Even where the men continue to reside in the villages, it is the women and girls who look after agriculture and live-stock. It is estimated that the women, here, contribute to 98.54 percent of the total work of cultivation and animal care. They live in close harmony with nature and environment and help to preserve the agricultural traditions of Uttarakhand and quality of life. While the decisions regarding the agricultural operations lie with the women and they look after all of them (except preparing the field for sowing), the involvement of men in these activities is limited to ploughing of the land. Dependent mostly on the rain-water in the high altitudes, the mountain women labour over fragmented lands all through the year, just to produce enough for survival. Additionally, the rural women have to trek daily long distances in search of fuel, fodder and water.

Rethinking the Home Science Curricula

At the Lake Placid Conference of 1908, Home Economics was defined as "the study of laws, conditions, principles and ideals concerned with man's immediate physical environment and his nature as a social being, and especially the relationship between the two for the purpose of "improving the quality of his daily life". However, in practice, the discipline has placed a disproportionate emphasis on training for the productive and reproductive roles of women such as baking, embroidery, child care and household technologies. The field of Home Science is a borrowed concept from the West with predominant influence of British and North American models. This is cogently expressed by P. Sundaram who notes that "in our country Home Scientists have been sidetracked, making a peripheral existence, probably, as the model adopted is not suitable to our needs" (Grover and Goldey, 2002). Not surprisingly, many professionals and higher education administrators hold the view that the role of HSE is to impart knowledge of western life styles to women students.

In the Indian context, meaningful regional development through empowerment of women in Garhwal is feasible, only, if the western model of Home Science that is inappropriate to the needs and realities of the rural living is replaced with one that addresses their pressing needs, is culturally appropriate and equips the rural women with skills that will help them fulfill their roles in development. This can be achieved through training in HSE which enables them to increase agricultural productivity, to use natural resources in a sustainable manner, to acquire new industrial and administrative skills, and to develop leadership qualities. Therefore, the Home Science curricula should be carefully designed so as to meet the needs of rural women (and their families) with regard to agricultural production, processing, preservation, storage, exchange, and environmental management and conservation.

This viewpoint calls for a focused effort on restructuring the Home Science curriculum. Redefining Home Economics and its general goals, contextualising the content of home economics, describing the skills and competencies that are required to do extension work and training and retraining home economists and agricultural home economists involved in rural development would serve rural women better (Mtshali, 1999). Home Science curriculum needs revision giving due weightage to newer topics and areas, such as, population and family welfare, economic empowerment, governance, capacity building and leadership, entrepreneurial development, agro processing, women and agricultural development, legal literacy, women and environmental issues, technology assessment and refinement etc (Grover and Goldey, 2002). Redesigning of Home Science and agricultural curricula at the training institutions would enable extension workers to provide appropriate need-based advice and training to rural women farmers. The training and extension methods, approaches, and curricula should be structured to enable rural women to improve productivity, deal effectively with environmental change, and improve their well-being. Alongside, due attention must also be paid to other pressing problems that touch the lives of the rural women, such as, those of family planning, family nutrition, education, alternative employment strategies, health, sanitation, and migration.

Extension services are a key link to increasing food production and to transforming rural household economic activities that contribute to livelihood security (Mtshali, 1999). In the rural areas, although the migration of men to urban areas to seek employment leaves the women as *de facto* heads who are solely responsible for the family and the agricultural fields, their access to agricultural information and extension services is meagre. Also, Home Science extension services extended to rural women frequently involves teaching of skills that are not traditional to rural living such as sewing, embroidery and others which do not address their pressing needs, are unrealistic and hold little relevance to the rural women who lack the resources to attend these skill-building classes namely, time, money and motivation. Presently, Home Science as an academic discipline has an urban bias and a western ideology, as a result, its elitist content and methodology has little to offer to the rural women of Uttarakhand. Therefore, to fulfill the needs of rural society the curricula taught in schools, universities and colleges in the State of Uttarakhand needs redesigning, for mainstreaming rural women and young girls. Agriculture, animal husbandry, nutrition and household resources management must be included in Home Science curricula, and gender issues should be considered in agricultural in-service training. This way, the Home Science extension professionals will be better equipped to counsel, advice and train rural farmers – especially the women and also impart knowledge of business management, environmental and health education.

Rural women would gain immensely from training in appropriate technology to improve their quality of life, such as, labour-saving equipment for water collection, food processing and alternative energy sources. The reoriented Home Science curricula should therefore, include, imparting training to the Home Scientists in making appropriate technology accessible to the rural women and in producing simple but powerful extension messages and technologies that increase productivity and incomes, and mitigate drudgery by saving time and energy and reducing waste. In the words of Tej Verma, rural orientation and self-employment need to be kept in sharp focus, as it is critically important to provide sustainable rural livelihoods for the present and future generations (Grover and Goldey, 2002). Improving women's purchasing power will enhance the prospect of meeting basic needs of the household, namely, food, clothing, shelter, health and education adequately and in supporting their efforts to increase food production. Research in Africa, Asia and Latin America has established that improvements in household food security and nutrition are associated with women's access to income and their role in household decisions on expenditure. They tend to spend a significantly higher proportion of their income than men, on food for the family. Therefore, with the aim of increasing participation of rural women in market production and other income generating ventures, the reoriented Home Science curricula should include knowledge about means of generating, building and sustaining resources that enhance economic condition such as: establishing a successful small enterprise that includes inculcation of a range of technical and business skills such as bookkeeping, marketing and promotion skills; ways of seeking accurate information of markets as well as business management, policies, credit organisations and arrangements, quality-control procedures and suitability of equipment and suppliers; and various income-generating activities which are built on the rural women's traditional skills and indigenous knowledge systems of handicrafts, agriculture, livestock or technologies.

Women have a critical role to play in upholding standards in household nutrition and food security as they are responsible for food production and provision in the family. Therefore the reoriented Home Science curricula should include, new approaches and strategies of training rural women in appropriate food storage, processing and preservation so as to effectively reduce food losses as well as provide them with a source of income and employment; skills in food processing and preservation by employing improved technologies for drying fruit, vegetable and root crops.

Rural women are the collectors and managers of agricultural produce, water, forestry and energy resources. Rural women and children are the most affected by environmental degradation. For instance, depletion of forests and natural water resources increases their burden and affects their health when they have to work harder and longer to procure food, fodder and drinking water. The revised curriculum should provide training to the Home Science students in supporting and educating the rural women in caring for the environment who are the repositories of traditional knowledge; and inculcate skills of natural resource management that can be built upon. Training of such nature given to rural women will naturally extend to their children as well since they are the primary care-givers and, therefore, can play a significant role in inculcating positive attitudes toward the environment in children. Not only should the Home Scientists have sufficient knowledge and an understanding of the natural environment, causes of its deterioration, ways of improving environmental quality; conservation and methods appropriate to rural environments; and sustainable use of natural resources; they should also be skilled in communicating this information to the rural women they interact with.

In a rural extension, delivery system alongside promotion of messages on production and consumption of food are needed in a balanced diet and general principles of good health and hygiene to rural women. Home Scientists, therefore, can play a critical role in preventive health care, if they receive appropriate in-service training.

To conclude, the objective of reorienting Home Science curricula should be to widen the scope of the discipline and besides imparting skills in home-making, it should also serve as a tool for achieving sustainable development and woman empowerment in rural areas of Uttarakhand.

REFERENCES

Grover Indu and Patricia Goldey: *Restructuring Home Science Education for Empowerment of Women in Empowerment of Women,* in Grover Indu and Deepak Grover (Edt.) Empowerment of Women, Agrotech, 2002, pp. 356-368.

Hancock Mary. Home Science and the Nationalisation of Domesticity in Colonial India. *Modern Asian Studies.* Volume 35, Part 4, October 2001, pp. 871-903.

Mtshali M Sazile. Training and in-service training of home economics extension professionals in rural areas of Kwazulu-Natal. *Journal of Family Ecology and Consumer Sciences.* Vol. 27, No. 2, 1999.

7

Role of Women in Environmental Conservation and Management in Uttarakhand

— *B.C. Upreti*

The environmental conservation and management has become a crucial issue due to the growing menace of environmental degeneration. It has indeed become a global issue and both the developed and the developing countries are concerned about the challenges of climate change. Since the Reo-Earth summit up to the Copenhagen summit in 2009, a lot of thinking has been given to the causes and effects of climate changes and the mitigation and adaptation strategies that can be followed in order to secure the environment. While it has been globally accepted that climate change is taking place all over the world but the threats to environment vary in different regions and countries in-terms of nature and intensity. Therefore, even as the global concerns and strategies for environmental protection are significant, the regional context is equally important.

In recent years, much has been said regarding the gender sensitive approach to environmental conservation and management. This poses a question as to why the issue of gender is being raised in the context of environmental management or why a correlation between gender and environment is being considered important. It has been now widely accepted that women are equally and in certain respects more than men, affected by environmental degeneration. Therefore, it is necessary that women are also included in determining policies and strategies for environmental conservation and management. It is in this perspective that women become a vital aspect of environmental management and conservation.

Climate Change and its Implications for the Environment

Climate change has become a global issue in recent years and it has become a matter of global concern (Lodha, 1992,). It is considered to be a major non-military security threat to humanity (Gupta and Dutta, 2009.)

The climate change is a problem related to the patterns of energy use and as a consequence increase in the level of carbon dioxide (CO_2) caused by the burning of fossil fuel. How to reduce level of emission of CO_2 has been the focus of the debates being organised to finding means and ensuring the four important aspects considered responsible for environmental degeneration throughout the world:

Concentration of green-house gases in the atmosphere has increased tremendously, since the industrial revolution due to the combustion of coal, gas, oil, etc. and change in land use patterns and activities. The abundance of green-house gases in the atmosphere has reached to its highest stage. For instance, it has been estimated that the concentration of CO_2 was 280 parts per million in the pre industrialization phase, which has now gone to 390 parts per million.

The emission of CO_2 has increased 3.1 per cent a year during the last one decade.

The global-warming with an increase of 0.8°C has reached to a very high level during the last 140 years.

The international panel on climate change in its 2007 report stated that most of the global warming over the last 50 years has been caused due to various human activities. It is also estimated that there would be an increase of 1.5°C to 6°C in temperature till the end of present century. (IPCC Report on Climate Change, 2007) This clearly shows that the course of climate change would be worse in the coming years. It may also be pointed out here that there are countries and areas which are more vulnerable to environmental degeneration due to climate change, because of extreme climatic conditions, poor living conditions and larger dependence of people on natural resources. (Metler and Rainer, 1995)

The impact of climate change is wide ranging and severe. Although the intensity may differ in different countries and regions. However, the severity of the impacts may increase further in years to come, if no appropriate steps are taken towards securing the climate. Following are some of the impacts of climate change on the environment:

- Global warming and melting of glaciers.
- Increase in sea level, thereby posing threat to some costal countries and regions, such as, Maldives, Kuvalu, Kiribati, etc and changes in marine bio-system.

- Oceanic disturbances: Cyclones, Sunami and others.
- Increase in tropical cyclonic intensity.
- Loss of bio-diversity.
- Drying up of water resources, water scarcity and desertification and increase in water borne disease like Malaria, Dengue, Diahorrea, etc.
- Floods and landslides.
- Deforestation and breakdown of the eco-system.
- Migration, displacement of population and refugee problem.
- Decrease in agriculture productivity leading to scarcity of food and forest resources, conflicting situation and increase in poverty and unemployment.

It can be said that the climate change has wide ranging implications for the environment. It is obvious that the developing states and the weaker sections of the society are the worst sufferers of the environmental degeneration. As women, constitute half of the population, belong to the weaker sections of the society and on account of their dependence on natural resources, have to face the fallouts of the environmental.

Women and Environment

It is estimated that in most parts of the world the daily lives of women are affected most, due to environmental degradation. Women are intensively associated with the environmental issues, particularly, in the rural context. In the rural set-up the gender division of labour is such that the responsibility of collecting water, fuel, forest resources, agriculture, live stocking, etc. is shouldered by the women and all these areas are directly and vigorously influenced by the environmental degeneration. As women's lives are affected by the environmental degradation, therefore, women can play a better role in finding means of the sustenance of the environment.

It was only at the First World Conference on Women held at Mexico City in 1975 that the women and environment issues were brought to the focus. During the 1980's, government and various development agencies became actively aware of the need to consider gender issues in the environmental management and natural resource management programmes. It was also gradually being realised that the active participation of women and the integration of gender issues in environmental policies and actions are critical determinants of environmental regeneration. The Beijing Platform for Action (1995), the World Sustainable Development (2002) and the Millennium Development Goals have further emphasized the need for women friendly approach to environmental conservation.

The impact of environmental degeneration is faced by women in the following major areas:

1. Agriculture and Livestock

It is true that men have a larger role to play in agriculture works but there are several areas where women bear a larger responsibility. The general trend is that men are more engaged in cash cropping and large scale agriculture. The women are more responsible for small scale cropping, agriculture labour, managing natural resources, raising livestock, vegetable growing, collection of food, fuel and fodder from the forest and fetching water. In a rural set-up, all these form the essential duties of women. According to some studies in sub-Saharan Africa, women are responsible for 80 per cent of food production. In South East Asia women contibute nearly 90 per cent of the labour in rice cultivation and in South Asia women bear the major burden of agriculture as well as they are also solely responsible for rearing livestock and collecting items of household needs from the forests. As there are instances of acute food scarcity and crisis in South Asia, therefore, in view of women's work and their dependence on natural resources, it is obvious that women are most adversely affected by the impact of climate change on agriculture and natural resources. Decline in crop production, desertification and such other problems are on the increase, due to environmental degeneration.

2. The Water Issues

It is a well established fact that women share a larger responsibility in respect to water uses and water management. The men are generally concerned to the management of water resources for irrigation and such large scale purposes which is not a matter of vital daily needs. But the women are responsible to make arrangement of water for daily household needs and for the livestock. (Fisher, 2008) The drying of water sources, due to environmental impacts, has direct implications, as water is needed every moment for drinking and sanitation and women are primarily responsible for making these arrangements. Thus, environmental degeneration has direct implications for women in respect of water uses. The question of water hygiene is also important. The increased floods also deteriorate water quality and the water borne disease is yet another problem that women have to face the first.

The water scarcity, which is going to be a big issue in future, would definitely add to the familial burdens of women. According to a study by the year 2025, two-third of the world population are likely to face some kind of water related problems. The shortage of water will be a severe problem for a large chunk of the population. (Miza and Ahmad (eds. 2005). In the desert areas, water security has already become a challenging issue and in most of the areas of the world, women have to travel a long distance to fetch water. Due to the paucity of potable water, the conflicts related to water in several countries are making the women victim, as it is their responsibility to make available water for household needs. Like rural areas in the urban areas also, women have to spend a lot of time to fetch water, as there are frequent water supply disruptions and shortage of water.

3. Natural Disasters

Increased natural disasters, both in terms of intensity and frequency, are linked up with the climate change. There are studies which have argued that women and children are much more vulnerable to natural disasters, such as, floods, cyclone, hurricanes, draughts, etc. In the case of Tsunami which was of course not directly related to climate change, the highest number of causalities were those of the women. (Aguilar, 2006) As the women are not equipped with the skill and training which is useful for natural calamities, therefore, they also become victim of natural hazards. Actually due to traditions and social customs in many societies, women do not get the knowledge and training which would save them from such calamities; for instance, the training of swimming could save women in case of floods, but she is hardly equipped with this knowledge. Some studies have shown that in countries like Bangladesh, women did not leave their houses during floods as they were unable to swim (Aguilar, 2006). The women suffer most in the aftermath of the natural disasters, due to displacement of families, rehabilitation, etc.

4. Environmental Degeneration and Conflicts

Environmental degeneration has also been a cause of increased conflicts, particularly, in the resource poor societies. The growing scarcity of water resources, diminishing natural resources on which rural people are particularly dependent for food, fuel and fodder, scarcity of cultivable land, migration and displacement due to natural calamities have given rise to conflicts in various parts of the world. The women are more affected in comparison to men due to these conflicts, as the sources of conflicts are related to women, more in the overall context of division of labour and responsibilities, particularly, in a rural set-up. It is also a fact that migrations and displacements due to natural calamities also result in increased cases of abuses and sexual harassment to women. (Reueveny, 2007)

5. Health Hazards

The changes in the environment are also responsible for a number of health hazards, such as, the increase in water borne diseases, due to contamination of water sources, floods, etc., increase in respiratory and other problems, due to pollution, increased cases of heat strokes due to rise in global-warming and desertification, malnutrition due to food scarcity and so on. The women are more vulnerable to these hazards due to their larger responsibilities of health care, exposure to deceased persons and on the other hand, lack of knowledge about health preventions.

Role of Women in Environmental Conservation in Uttarakhand

Uttarakhand constitutes of hilly region by and large except a small stretch of plains areas. As a part of the Himalayan ranges, it comprises a highly fragile and environmentally sensitive zone. The global warming, causing melting of glaciers in the Himalayas, is a serious threat to ecology of the region. (Khodey, 2007) The development related destructions: construction of high dams, roads, etc., and the excessive dependence of people on natural resources in rural areas and scarcity of alternative means of livelihood have caused several environmental hazards. The problems of deforestation are acute in the hills of Uttarakhand. The depletion of forest has deep impact on the household economy of Uttarakhand. The non-availability of fodder trees have resulted in the decline in animal husbandry. There is a decline of agriculture activities due to heavy reliance on the 'money order economy'. The massive extraction, of natural resources, such as, timber, limestone, magnesium and potassium by the commercial contractors, has caused disruptions of the fragile Himalayan ecology. There are problems of floods, massive landslides, soil erosion, etc. in various parts of Uttarakhand. It clearly indicates the changing eco-balance in the Himalayas. The fast drying of traditional water resources has become a serious problem in the rural hill areas which is the result of the fast depletion of forest and other ecological hazards. As the management of water for the household use is shouldered by the women, therefore, in the absence of the water resources near their home, they have to travel a long distance to fetch drinking water. The alternative means of drinking waters are either not available in the rural areas or they are ill managed and unsuccessful.

In the hill society women constitutes the most vital aspect of family and the household economy. The family, livestock and agriculture labour are her sole responsibilities. On an average, she has to work for 16 hours a day to complete her responsibilities. One important dimension here is that due to large scale migration of men to plains in search of jobs, to carry all the activities, domestic or agriculture, becomes the sole liability of the women. Besides performing her familial responsibilites, she has also to collect fodder and fuel, fetch water, maintain agriculture fields, collect food and raise live stock. In performing these responsibilities, as the women depend immensely on the natural resources, therefore, they always remian the first to be affected by the environmental hazards. The women of Uttarakhand seem to be conscious of this phenomenon, so they have been playing an important role in environmental conservation and management.

Women's Concern for Forest Resources

As forests are a very important source of the well being of the people, particularly, of the women of Uttarakhand, therefore, they have strongly resented against the destruction of forests. The large-scale cutting of trees was objected by women of Rani Village, located in a very far flung and remote corner in Chamoli Garhwal in 1974, under the leadership of a village woman Gaura Devi. In order to save their forests from the axe of the contractors' labourers, the women adopted the strategy of hugging the trees, which later on became famous as *Chipko Andolan* under the guidance of Gaura Devi. The women's protest produced good result and in view of their strong resistance, the contractors and labourers had to leave the forests. In 1977, Bachni Devi, wife of a forest contractor, led village women to save Adwani forests. The *Chipko Movement,* gradually spread in many areas during the eighties, and emerged as a strong grass-root movement. It also became a source of inspiration for many other hill areas in India and Nepal. The women's concerns to save the forest resources have taken many new forms. In many parts of the state women's organisations have been taking interest in plantation works. In some villages, at the time of marriage each bride is given a tree by the villagers which she plants in her maternal home and it is nurtured by her parents. The planting of trees during the time of marriage has given birth to Maitee Movement which reflects people's concern towards the degradation of forest resources and its conservation. Similarly, women are playing active role in *save seed movement* and bio-diversity conservation the activities. The voluntary organisations like Mahila Mangal Dals, Society for Environmental Education and Rural Development (SEERD) have been active in conservation of forests. Women have now been actively taking part to put out the fire in forests. Women are also associated with social forestry programmes.

Water Conservation and Management

The water harvesting is another area where women are playing an important role along with men. It has now been realised that storing of rain waters is necessary in order to maintain the natural water streams. Cleaning and maintenance of traditional sources of drinking water is yet another area where village women organisations are taking a lead. Actually it is the women and the girl child who has to see the management of water in their homes, therefore, they have a better understanding of the problems related to the drinking water in the rural areas.

In view of the water woes, the women of the hill areas of Uttarakhand are also being involved in catchment area treatment programmes. The main objective of such programmes is: to conserve such areas which are denuded due to excessive deforestation, soil conservation in catchment areas and protection of agriculture fields. The uncontrolled grazing by wild and household animals has caused destraction of new forest crops. In many areas, women have taken a lead through Mahila Mandals in controlling free grazing. They decide when to allow grazing and when to control it. Similarly, women can also regulate collection of fuel and fodder from forests so that a balance can be maintained between household needs and the eco system. The women of Uttarakhand have strongly resented and responded radically against the attempts of destroying the land and forest resources of the hills. (Rawat, 1996)

One very important area where women of uttarakhand have taken a lead and which also has indirect implications for the conservation of the environment is curtailing liquor menace. The anti liquor movement has been quite successful and it also indicates towards women's organisational capacity as well as ability to lead a movement. It also signals towards the increased consciousness about the social abuses and the social destruction caused in the hills due to the excessive use of liquor, even on ceremonial occasions.

Conclusion

In the context of Uttarakhand, environmental protection has become a vital issue as the region is ecologically highly sensitive. There is no doubt that the women of Uttarakhand have taken a lead in certain areas, such as, saving the forest resources and reforestation. Similarly, Beej Bachao Andolan emphasizes the need for going back to indigenous cropping system. There is a need to strengthen these efforts to every corner of the state, taking measures towards broadening these activities and imparting training for empowerment of women in environmental conservation, bio-diversity and water management at the local level in a decentralised manner. Women's participation in these programmes needs to be ensured as this is related to livelihood in the hill areas.

Uttarakhand Seva Nidhi Paryavaran Siksha Sansthan, (NGO) is playing an important role in imparting training to women for environmental conservation. Similarly, Mahila Mangal Dals, SEEDS and some other organisations are also active. But there has to be a broader network of such activities, so as to encourage research and training in the local context.

In the context of decentralised and sustainable approach to environmental conservation in Uttarakhand the following aspects appear to be important:

The women need to have a share in policy formulation, research and training relating to environmental conservation and management.

There is a need to understand the local context: the local socio-physical relationship, priorities and constraints in order to envisage strategies for environmental sustenance.

There is a need to develop environmentally sound technologies so as to strengthen sustainable development in the hills.

The traditional subsistence methods, to cultivation and natural resource utilisation that have been adaptive to local environmental conditions, need to be strengthened.

A decentralised and gender friendly approach towards planning, applications, research and training in environmental conservation and management is also needed.

The Beijing Platform for Action emphasized the following aspects regarding women and the environment:

- Gender participation and involvement of women in environmental decision-making.
- Development of gender perspective in environment related activities.
- Increase in women's capabilities in the environmental field.

- Economic empowerment of women in order to ensure their better participation in environmental conservation programmes.

On the whole, it can be said that the women of Uttarakhand have learned the urgency of environmental conservation and management. However, it is ironical that the women still have low participation in environmental protection and management, planning and execution of environment policies. They are also under-represented in research and training and a general lack of gender sensitive policies is found in all the areas. For ensuring maximum participation of the women, there is also a need to follow a gender sensitive approach to environmental management.

REFERENCES

See R.M. Lodha (ed.). *Environmental Ruin and the Crisis of Survival*, Indian Publishing Company. New Delhi. 1992. A Marian Metler and Lynne Rainer, *The Third World in Global Environmental Politics*. Boulder. Colorado. London. 1995.

IPCC Report on *Climate Change 2007*. Cambridge University Press. UK. 2007.

Arvind Gupta and Sujit Dutta. "*Climate Change and Security, Explaining the Link*". In IDSA Working Group, *Security Implications of Climate Change for India*. Academic Foundation. New Delhi. 2009.

Fisher. *For Her It's the Big Issue: Putting Women at the Centre of Water Supply, Sanitation and Hygiene*. WSSCC. Switzerland. 2008. http://wash-cc.org/pdf/publication.

See, MMQ Miza and D.K. Ahmad (eds.). *Climate Change and Water Resources*. A.A. Balkema Publ. Leiden. Netherlands. 2005.

See, L. Aguilar. *Climate Change and Disaster Mitigation, Gender Makes the Difference*. World Conservatin Union. 2006.

R. Reueveny. "Climate Change-Induced Migration and Violent Conflict", *Political Geography* (Netherlands). Vol. 26, 2007, pp. 650-73.

K. Khodey. *Climate Change and the Right to Development: Himalayan Glacial Malting and the Future of Development in the Tibetan Plateau*. UNDP, 2007.

Some studies useful in understanding environmental hazards in Uttarakhand are: *Uttarakhand: Need for a Comprehensive Eco-Strategy, South Asian Dialogue on Ecological Democracy*. New Delhi (n.d.), T. Weber, *Hugging the Trees. The Story of the Chipko Movement*. Viking-Penguin Inc. New York. 1987; B. Dogra, *Forests and People: A Report on the Himalayas*. Bharat Dogra. New Delhi. 1983; S. Dharmadhikary. *Mountains of Concrete, Dam Building in the Himalayas*. Berkeley CA. 2008.

Rijiv Rawat. *Women of Uttarakhand, On the Frontiers of the Environmental Struggle*. May, 1996. http://uttarakhand.prayag.org/chipko.html.

8

The Changing Status and Role of Women in India

— *Jyoti Tiwari*

In most of the traditional societies, the role of women was confined to household chores and child rearing. In rural set-ups, her duties were extended to work in fields and arranging fuel and fodder. But changing social scenario, pressing economic needs and education of women have enabled them to seek employment opportunity. The women in India are becoming more and more aware of their rights and they have also started demanding equal status as men. Over the last few decades, there has been a tremendous change in the laws, attitudes and norms affecting women's status, roles and development in India. As a result many women are looking beyond the traditional role of wife and mother and seeking employment outside the secure confines of their homes and registering their actively participation in the national economy. Women participation in workforce is increasing all over the world and though it also constitutes an integral part of total workforce in India, however not only there are fewer women in the paid workforce but there is also a serious underestimation of women's contribution at workforce. In India there is a wide disparity between the affluent and the poor. As a result, we can see women as business executives and diplomats and on other top positions. This has, on the one hand, led to a transformation of gender roles but, on the other, also raised concerns about psychological and physical well being of women in the urban areas. Then there are millions of women who are still illiterates, malnourished and live in extreme poverty and ill health in the urban, rural and remote areas. The present paper intends to highlight the changes in the status and role of Indian women.

In the past few decades, participation of women in the workforce has increased considerably in India and Indian women can now be seen in many more jobs than was imaginable a few decades ago. They are into jobs which were once considered as men's work like engineers, doctors, scientists, politicians, lawyers, in armed forces, business, sports, art and culture and various other male dominated areas. They have marked their presence in every area and have proven their worth. They have shown that if given opportunity to develop necessary skills and training, they can be at par with men. The condition, of educated Indian women especially in the urban areas, has undoubtedly improved in, last few decades, though it is not enough. It is just a beginning and they have a long way to go. Some of the factors responsible for the change in the status of women are industrialisation, globalisation and urbanisation. According to Swarnkar (1988) the magnitude of female participation in workforce, primarily, depends upon the status the woman enjoys in her family. Economic exigencies, availability of suitable jobs and degree of consciousness to avail the opportunities at hand and claim for their share are necessitating their participation at work. Besides economic necessity other motivating factors, like desire for enhancing their standard of living by earning extra income, personal satisfaction, individual development, making use of one's talents and skills, utilisation and justification of training and education and making use of leisure time have also encouraged the women to veture out for employment and make proper use of their talent and skill.

Participation of Women in Workforce

Indira Nooyi of Pepsico, Kiran Shaw of Biocon and Chanda Kochhar of ICICI are the few representatives of the Indian Corporate women which have encouraged more and more women to enter in the corporate world. There is growing demand for soft skills, such as communication ability, emotional intelligence and sensitivity in the corporate sector since these qualities are associated with women, and hence they are considered as an asset in the organisation. Success stories of many women have proved that with determination and focus, the women can also achieve their goals. Indian women though have come a long way, but this is not enough, because a vast majority of women are still locked in the agriculture and low paid jobs sector. In rural India agriculture and allied industries employ a large number of female workers, however, in urban areas women are primarily employed in unorganised sector, mostly doing low paid work under harsh conditions. According to the statistics, the proportion of women in workforce in 1981 was 19.67 percent which became 22.73 percent in 1991, and 25.68 percent in 2001. In 2005 some 50.16 lakh women were employed in the organised sector (public sector: 58.23 percent, private sector: 41.77 percent). According to the National Commission Enterprises in Unorganised Sector (NCEUS), there were about 362 million workers, out of which 117 millions were women. More than half of all service sector employees are women, mainly concentrated in the community, social and personal service categories, which also include care-giving work. As per the official data, women's employment in the organised sector too has grown. Women's participation in the wage labour sector is also increasing; they represent half of all wage earners in only 17 countries. But unfortunately women still earn less than men in both developed and developing countries with the result they remain the poorest of the poor. Women and children constitute more than two-thirds of one billion people in the world living on less than $ 1 per day. (WHO, 2009) Though rural women in India are extensively involved in agricultural activities, however, the nature and extent of their involvement differs with the variations in agro production systems (Foster, A.D. et. al. 2004).

Women's Employment in the Organised Sector (%):

Year	*1961*	*1971*	*1981*	*1991*	*2001*	*2007*
Figures in %	10.9	11	12.2	14.1	17.8	19.2

Source: Director General of Employment and Training, Ministry of Labour, Government of India: New Delhi.

Percentage of Female Workers in Various Services

Services	*Percentage of Female Employees*	*Percentage females in total workers*
Agriculture, forestry and fishing	77.42	41.63
Mining and Quarrying	0.28	16.52
Manufacturing and Repair services	11.67	31.05
Electricity, gas and water	0.03	4.07
Construction	1.88	10.75
Trade, Hotels and Restaurants	4.11	12.31
Transport, storage and communication	0.4	3.19
Finance, insurance, real estate, Business	0.61	11.72
Community, social and personal services	8.59	33.93
Total	100	32.47

Source: NSSO 2004-05.

Female Literacy Rate in India

As per the provisional totals of the 2011 census, the total literacy rate has increased from 64.83 percent in 2001 to 74.04 percent in 2011, male literacy from 75.26 percent to 82.14 percent and female literacy from 53.67 percent to 65.46 percent, with a reduced gender gap of 16.68 percent which was 18.30 percent in 1951 and 21.59 percent in 2001. The data for literacy rate in India has been shown in the following table:

State	*Percentage of Female literacy*	*State*	*Percentage of Female literacy*
Andhra Pradesh	51.57	Maharashtra	67.51
Arunachal Pradesh	44.24	Manipur	59.70
Assam	56.03	Meghalaya	60.41
Bihar	33.57	Mizoram	86.13
Chattisgarh	52.40	Nagaland	61.92
Delhi	75	Orissa	50.97
Goa	75.51	Punjab	63.55
Gujarat	58.60	Rajasthan	44.34
Haryana	56.31	Sikkim	61.46
Himachal Pradesh	68.08	Tamilnadu	64.55
Jammu & Kashmir	41.82	Tripura	65.41
Jharkhand	39.38	Uttar Pradesh	42.98
Karnataka	57.45	Uttarakhand	60.26
Kerala	87.86	West Bengal	60.22
Madhya Pradesh	50.28		

Source: Census of India 2001.

Female literacy rate in India has increased from 8. 86 percent in 1951 and it became 54.16 percent in 2001 and 74.04 percent in 2011. Though this rate is constantly rising, but as the data shown above indicates that half of the female population is still illiterate. Only two states Kerala and Mizoram have approached universal female literacy rate. As per 2001 census, female literacy rate in Kerala is 87.86 percent and in Mizoram it is 86.13 percent. But there are still certain states like Bihar and Jharkhand where female literacy rate is below 40 percent. Bihar ranks the lowest with 33.57 percent. Among the Union Territories,

Lakshadweep has the highest female literacy rate i.e. 81.56 and the lowest in Dadra & Nagar Haveli i.e. 42.99. In Chandigarh, Andaman & Nicobar, and Pondicherry female literacy rate is 76.65 percent, 75.29 percent and 74.26 percent respectively.

Percentage of Female Literacy Rate in India (1951-2011)

Year	*Female Literacy Rate*
1951	8.86
1961	15.35
1971	21.97
1981	27.76
1991	39.29
2001	54.16
2011	74.04

Source: Census of India 2001 and Provisional Population Total Census of India, 2011.

The data presented in the above table indicates improvement in the female literacy rate but there is still a lot needs to be done. Another positive change is that the growth in access to schooling has been constantly increasing from 5.4 million girls enrolled at primary level in 1950-51 to 61.1 million girls in 2004-05. In the upper primary level, the enrollment increased from 0.5 million girls to 22.7 million girls. Though female literacy rate has increased from about 8 percent at the time of independence to 65 percent now, but still over 200 million people in India are unable to read and write. There are signs of a gradual breakdown of the traditional belief that there is no need of education for women, as they have to remain inside the four walls of house. However, despite changing mindset about the girls' education, it has been found that by the time they are 19 year old, 41 percent girls drop out from the school. As a result, there are just 62 girls for every 100 boys in colleges and universities.

Women in Politics

More women have succeeded in reaching at the top of the power in Asia in the recent years, than in any other part of the world. Sirimao Bandarnaike of Sri Lanka became the world's first female Prime Minister in 1960, followed by female leaders in India, Pakistan and Bangladesh. Although these women leaders were from the politically prominent families and therefore, the rise of these leaders did not reflect any change in the patriarchal society and its mindset in India as well as in other Asian countries. These leaders infact did very little for the causes of women's rights and their welfare. It is very unfortunate that when women reach at the top positions, they become insensitive to the problems of women. It is also seen that those women who reach at the top ladder do not take any interest in giving greater representation to other women in their own organisation or in the political process.

Number of Women Members in Lok Sabha

Year	*Total No. of Seats*	*No. of Female Members*	*Percentage*
1952	499	22	4.4
1957	500	27	5.4
1962	503	34	6.7
1967	523	31	5.9
1971	521	22	4.2
1977	544	20	3.4
1980	544	28	5.5
1984	545	45	8.9
1989	543	28	5.1
1991	536	39	7.2
1996	543	40	7.3
1999	543	49	9.0
2004	539	44	8.16
2009	543	59	10.8

Source: Election Commission of India, Government of India, 2009.

The 15th Lok Sabha has 59 women members raising the percentage of women participation to 10.8, making it the highest percentage since independence. In the present Rajya Sabha there are 22 women members, out of 239 members and for the first time the speaker of 15th Lok Sabha has also become a woman. Although, the women in India have taken active part in various political movements, may it be freedom struggle or any other regional or national movement after the Independence and as voters also they are aware of their political rights and actively participate in the election process; but when it comes to contesting elections, the percentage of their participation is very low as compared to males. The reason behind their reluctance to participate in politics may be the negative attitude of our society towards the women's participation in public life and their own lack of self-confidence. Though women are taking part in politics at the grass-root level and one-third reservation in the seats in the Panchayat Raj Institutions, has already been given to women, but there is serious under-representation of women in politics in India at the higher levels and women are excluded from the decision-making process. Participation of women in the parliaments all over the world is 18.8 percent only. Status of women in America and Europe is still better, where the participation of women in Parliament is nearly 42 percent. In some countries reservation has been given to women to increase their participation in politics, particularly, at the higher level. In Nepal 33 percent, in Pakistan 22 percent and in Bangladesh 14 percent reservation has already been given to women in Parliament. In India also women's reservation bill for 33 percent reservation for women in parliament has been passed by the Rajya Sabha but it has yet come for discussion and consideration of the Lok Sabha. But it is equally true that proper representation of women in legislatures and parliament is imperative for women's empowerment and true democracy.

Effects of Globalisation on Women's Status

In the present era, globalisation has brought many changes in the lives of both men and women who are being forced under the pressures of globalisation to adjust their attitude and life styles according to these changes. This has resulted in transformation of gender roles also. Women are now becoming more self-oriented rather than oriented totally towards others and they have started to think for their own self also. Today many women are educated and besides working in all the sectors, they are also competing with men. But in India assessment of the status of women is not an easy task because women also belong to different religion, castes, classes, educational levels and occupations; therefore, their status cannot be generalised. Due to this, on the one hand, we find that there are many women who are still deprived of the basic necessities, like food, shelter and clothing, while many others have freedom to make choices and lead their lives accordingly. A section of Indian women, the elite and the upper class have gained the exposure to global network, access to new technology and they have more chances of entering into non-traditional fields and availing the opportunities to prove themselves. With the result, the invisible Indian woman has suddenly become more visible everywhere in home, workplaces or politics. However, at the same time, there are also certain ill effects of globalisation process which has promoted marketisation of women, exhibitionism and growing abuse against women. In this process of globalisation the poor are still excluded and they are unable to take the advantages of globalisation and development. This has increased divide between poor and rich in all sections of the society.

National Scenario of Women's Health and Nutrition

Women's health and nutritional status is bound with social, cultural and economic factors that influence all aspects of their lives. This has consequences not only for the women themselves but also for the well-being of their children. Malnutrition continues to be a major health burden in developing countries. It is globally the most important risk factor for illness and death of millions of pregnant women and young children (Muller, O, *et.al.*, 2005). Sharma (2009) has compared the status of Indian women with the European region, and concluded that the gap is enormous. Maternal mortality rate in India is 16.6 times, tuberculosis and HIV positive population is 2.8 times, and mortality rate from non communicable diseases is 1.2 times. Only the incidence of cancer in India is significantly lower than that in Europe. According to Victoria et.al. (2008), the maternal care in India has definitely improved since 1992, but with only 76 percent women accessing any antenatal care and only 40.85 percent of births taking place in health centers; this cannot be considered satisfactory. There is also a clear rural-urban gap in maternal care in India.

Status of Women in Uttarakhand

The status of women in Uttarakhand is a portrait of contradiction. In some areas, like education, agricultural work participation, decision-making and sex ratio, their condition is better than the condition of women in other states of India. However, there are many areas like work load, nutritional and health status, the condition of women is unpleasant than the women in other parts of India. The rural women in this hilly state are overburdened, besides household activities; women's contribution in agriculture is also very significant and their contribution is more than three-fourth of the labour required for agricultural and animal husbandry operations. In a study it has been highlighted that in the Indian Himalayas, a pair of bullocks works 1064 hours, a man 1212 hours and a woman 3485 hours in a year on a one hectare farm, a figure which illustrates women's contribution to agricultural production (Venkateswaran, 1992).

In the rural areas of Kumaon and Garhwal region, women and girls share much of the burden of domestic chores, like collection of fuel and fodder and agricultural operations, besides the sibling care. The poor toilet facility, lack of safe water supply and lack of hospital facilities for the sick make it more difficult and adversely affect their status. (Pande, 1997). Women in Uttarakhand are very disadvantaged in terms of their health and nutritional status. NFHS-3 (National Family Health Survey) states that 41 percent of currently married women had some type of reproductive health problems, almost one-third of women in Uttarakhand are undernourished. Nutritional deficiency is much more prevalent in the women of rural areas, illiterate women and from households with a low standard of living than other women. Overall, 46 percent of women in Uttarakhand have some degree of anaemia, compared with 52 percent in India.

The Dilemmas

Although there is no doubt about the fact that economic independence of women has helped in their empowerment and development. Economic independence is important as it improves their confidence and self esteem and it also enhances their ability to take part in decision-making process. But at the same time, wage-earning activity increases the workload of women immensely. This could be reduced significantly, if their domestic load is equally shred by the men, but this is still a wishful thinking. In fact, women have to make most of the adjustments, because our patriarchal society demands more adjustments to be made by the women than by the men. Married working women find it difficult to leave the place where their husband and family stay (Deitch and Sanderson 1987). As a consequence, they may have to forego prestigious career placements. Viewed from the perspective of the developmental task, for various stages in one's life span, as defined by Havighust (1953), the modern adult women have to perform the additional female roles as wives, mothers, housekeepers on the one hand, and their role as employees on the other. The pressure of dual work often results in family conflicts. Due to this dilemma of dual role, many women are delaying marriage and motherhood. To overcome these problems and allowing women to play their roles smoothly, there is a need to change our mindsets and also a redefining and reinterpretion of the social roles assigned to males and females. The improved working conditions, appreciation and recognition of women's contribution in the economic activity are also required for improving women's status in the society.

REFERENCES

Deitch, C.K. & Sanderson, S.W. "Geographic Constraints on Married Women's Careers". *Women Occupations.* 1987. 14 (4) pp. 616-34.

Ghosh, J. Women in Indian Politics. *Frontline*. Vol. 16. Sept. 25-October, 2008.

Ghosh, L. Mukhopadhyay, I. Chakraborty, S. *Women Across Asia: Issues of Identities*. New Delhi. Gyan Publishing House. 2006.

Havighust, J. *Human Development and Education*. New York. Longman. 1953.

Muller, O. & Krawinkel, M. *Malnutrition and Health in Developing Countries*. CMAJ. 171 (3). pp. 279-293, 2005.

NCEUS 2007. Conditions of Work and Promotion of Livelihood in the Unorganised Sectors, *National Commission for Enterprises in the Unorganized Sector*. Government of India. New Delhi. 2007.

National Family Health Survey. 2005-2006. International Institute of Population Science. Mumbai.

NSSO 2004-05. *Employment-Unemployment Situation in India Round. 61st*, Report No. 515-I and II. National Sample Survey Organisation, Ministry of Statistics and Program Implementation. Government of India. New Delhi.

Sethi, A.M. "Working Women: Dilemma of Dual Roles". In K. Pawar (Ed.) *Women in Indian History: Social, Economic, Political and Cultural Perspective*. Vision and Venture. New Delhi. 1996. pp. 263-66.

Sharma, S. *The EU-India FTA, Critical Considerations in a Time of Crisis*. CENTAD Working Paper No. 11, 2009.

Swarankar, G.P. *Women Participation in Rural Environment*. Allahabad, Chugh Publications. 1988. p. 23.

Verma. S. Shadow Over Venus. *The Times of India*. New Delhi, March 6, 2010.

Victoria, C.G. Adair, L. Fall, C. et. al. Maternal and Child Under Nutrition: Consequences for Adult Health and Human Capital. *The Lancet*. 371. pp. 340-57, 2008.

Women and Health: Today's Evidence Tomorrow's Agenda, WHO press, World Health Organisation. 20 Avenue Appia. 1211. Geneva 27. Switzerland, 2009.

9

United States Government: Limitations and Opportunities for Women's Empowerment

— *Denise Benoit Scott*

Three waves of feminism in the United States have taken women to a place where, for the most part, their identities are no longer derived solely from their roles in the family and community. According to U.S. Labour Department statistics, women outnumbered men in the paid workplace, in January 2010. Thus, seventy-eight percent of women with children between the age group of 6 to 17 are employed, as are 64 percent of women with children under the age of 6 years. By 2010, 67 percent of women, in the labour force, had either attended some college or graduated with a degree. Women are now also making headway in high-paying administrative and managerial positions, comprising almost 40 percent of all managers. Women can also be increasingly found in the professions, constituting 32 percent of lawyers and 30 percent of physicians (Bureau of Labour Statistics, 2011). In comparative terms, the proportion of women, in managerial and administrative positions outside government, far exceeds that in other countries. In fact, the United States is at the top of the list, ahead of all 15 countries in the European Union and just about all of the nations of the world. (Burns, et al. 2001) In addition, the U.S. has hundreds of active feminist organisations and has passed such landmark legislation as Title VII in 1964 and Title IX in 1972, which respectively guarantee women's equality in employment and education.

Culturally, also women have gained status and power. They are confident and comfortable in the public realm and are no longer silent with regard to their capabilities and interests. Compared with the past, women are comfortable expressing their sexuality. Cohabitation, as an alternative to marriage, has become quite common. Between 2009 and 2011 alone, there has been a 13 percent increase in the number of opposite-sex couples cohabiting. In 2011, there were over 7.5 million cohabiting couples in the United States. Partly as a result of women's increased independence, some scholars argue that marriage is becoming "deinstitutionalised," as many of the social norms and functions of marriage are now being met elsewhere (Cherlin, 2011). When women do marry, they are marrying at a later age than that in the past. The average age at the first marriage was 23 in 1900, then dipped to 20 during the "golden era" of the 50s, and now stands at 25. Women are also giving birth to their first child at a later age and have comparatively fewer children. Women have an average of 1.9 children currently in the U.S., compared with 3.1 in 1976. (U.S. Bureau of the Census, Current Population Reports).

Although, women in the United States have achieved a degree of independence and power in the realms of work and family, yet they are strikingly underrepresented in positions of power in the U.S. Government, particularly at the federal level. Women though constitute over half of the population, yet as per the data available they have only 17 percent share in the Senate (17 out of 100) and 16 percent (88 out of 435 seats) seats in the Congress in 2011. The United States ranks a sad 84th among the countries, around the world with regard to the percent of women in national legislatures (Center for American Women in Politics, 2010). This paper will examine the structural and cultural factors that help explain why women have not made more headway in U.S. Government. What are the opportunities and limitations, and how do they might move forward?

Women in the U.S. Government: Where are they and How did they get there?

For most of U.S. history, prior to British colonialism, women had a great deal of status and power in their communities. Native American women sat on tribal councils and even went into battle field with their male counterparts. Gender egalitarianism in the family and in leadership positions was characteristic of many tribes across the country, particularly matrilineal ones. (Coontz 2011, p. 44) When the British settlers arrived, they brought with them dominant ideologies asserting that women were, relative to men, pure, and dependent, which curbed women's independence and empowerment. The British attempted to destroy the Native American kinship system by encouraging Native American men to control their women and Native American women to submit. (Coontz, 2011, p. 47) During the colonial period in the United States, women were generally not involved in the formal political system.

It was not until the early part of 1900s, and especially after 1920, when women won the right to vote, that they began to emerge as public figures. In 1916, Jeannette Rankin of Montana became the first woman to be elected to the U.S. House of Representatives. In 1922, Rebecca Felton of Georgia was appointed to the U.S. Senate to fill a temporary vacancy but as the first woman senator, she got this opportunity to serve just for two days only. In 1925, Nellie Tayloe Ross became the first woman to serve as governor of a state. In the fall of 1924 she was elected to succeed her deceased husband, William Bradford Ross. In 1932, Hattie Wyatt Caraway of Arkansas became the first woman to be elected to the U.S. Senate. In 1933, Frances Perkins was appointed secretary of labour by President Franklin D. Roosevelt, making her the first woman member of a presidential cabinet. (University of Illinois at Urbana-Champaign, 2008) However, most of the early women politicians served as replacements for their husbands or fathers who died while in office, through a practice, called "widow's succession". These women were allowed to hold the vacant positions of their husbands, through election or direct appointment, until the next election. Although, no doubt intelligent and capable, and even achieving some level of political prominence while in office, these women nevertheless had come to politics of their own accord. Today, highly educated, politically astute driven women hold positions in government at the federal, state, and local levels.

The Federal Government in the United States is divided into three parts, the "Legislative," "Executive," and "Judicial". The Legislative Branch consists primarily of the Congress and the Senate. The Executive Branch consists of office of the President, Vice-President, Cabinet, and several administrative offices. The Judicial Branch is made up of The Supreme Court, District Courts, and Territorial Courts. There are also various Departments, falling under the Executive Branch, that provide rules and regulations for various parts of the government and the society at large. The election of Hillary Rodham Clinton to the Senate and her subsequent rise to Secretary of State, a position formerly occupied by another woman, Condeleeza Rice, Sonia Sotomayor as the first Latino woman to the Supreme Court, indicate that women are making some progress at the national level, although the United States has yet to see a woman president.

Like the federal government, state governments in the U.S. have three branches: executive, legislative, and judicial. The chief executive of a state is its popularly elected governor. State governments have the power to make and enforce laws in the areas of education, family, contract, and criminal law. All states, except Nebraska, have a bicameral legislature, with a Senate and a House of Representatives, a House of Delegates, and an Assembly, or something similar. Women make up 21.8 percent of state executive officers and 23.5 percent of state legislators are women. The state with the highest percentage of women legislators is Colorado, with 41 percent.

In addition to the federal government and the 50 state governments, there are 89,500 local governments in the United States. Local governments directly serve the needs of the city, county, or community. They provide everything from police and fire protection to sanitary codes, health regulations, education, public transportation, and housing. Types of city governments vary widely across the United States. Almost all have an elected central executive officer or mayor and a council. The mayor is responsible for appointing heads of city departments and other officials, sometimes with the approval of the council. Mayors have veto power over ordinances (the laws of the city) and preparing the city's budget is also often considered their responsibility. City and town councils have the power to pass city ordinances, fixing the property tax rate and making decisions about the property rights. Women are more involved in the city or municipal level than in the state and federal levels. Scholars theorise that this is because women feel that, at this level, they are able to have the most effect on policy that directly affects the community (Abrahams, 1996). They find that there is less gender bias and role conflict on the local level (Assendelft and Stottlemeyer, 2009). Some women see it as a stepping stone to higher political posts. Given that women are more highly educated than in the past, are a significant part of the workforce, and are becoming more involved in government on the local level. But despite this, a pertinent question can be asked as why are the proportions of women in government at the state and federal levels still so low?

Dominant Family and Gender Ideologies

One of the most significant reasons, why women are less likely than men to occupy high-level political positions in the U.S. government, is because, since the rise of industrial capitalism, the corresponding "dual spheres ideology," which asserts that women's place is in the home and men's in the market, has exerted a strong influence on women's opportunities. Women continue to be viewed as the primary caregivers and homemakers and, in fact, they also spend three times more time on childcare and housework than men. Arlie Hochschild (1989) refers to this as the "second shift". Although women, on the whole, are doing less work in the home, which means that the "leisure gap" is narrower than in the past, it is still the case that women do more than men, even when they have careers (Cherlin, 2009). It should be no surprise, then, that women in public office are less likely than other women to be married and have children. This is true not only in the United States, but elsewhere in the world. As Monique Essed-Fernandes, a presidential candidate in Suriname (2000/2005), states:

"Women, who run for public office, are single, have no children, have grown children or have a support network for childcare. Childcare is an issue which starts before nomination, because in practice, those who have a problem with childcare are either excluded or exclude themselves from the system." (Women's Environment and Development Organisation, 2008, 4)

In addition to the physical labour involved in childcare and housework, there is also mental and emotional labour associated with tasks, such as, making doctor's appointments, keeping track of birthdays, planning for holiday events – and managing the household in general. These activities, like the core tasks of cooking, cleaning, shopping, and so on, are typically done mostly by the women only (DiLeonardo, 1987). These activities are not only problematic as these are not only tasks, and involve mental and emotional labour also but these are not typically seen as "work," which is important– unless of course, these are left undone. As DiLeonardo notes:

"How often should sheets be changed? When should children be toilet trained? Should an aunt send a niece a birthday present? Although this work tends to be unlabeled and relatively unnoticed – until, of course, it is withdrawan – and then we see its tremendous consequences in the form of broken kin ties, feelings of love and closeness, etc." (DiLeonardo 1987, 56)

The expectation that women are better at raising children and keeping the household running smoothly stands in the way of a full commitment to politics. Particularly, at the national level, lawmakers and other government leaders are required to work late into evening and on weekends. Their schedules are impossibly hectic. They are expected to attend dinners, fundraisers, and interact with fellow government officials and heads of business on the golf course and at other social events. Although there are stories of "superwomen" who are able to do it all, in reality, there are not enough hours in the day. In the course of a recent research project, examining women corporate lobbyists in Washington, D.C., the author asked one woman who works as a lobbyist for a major corporation whether she aspired to be a government official in the future. She told the author that her present job as a corporate lobbyist gave her the right "balance" of work and family, and that the "costs", associated with becoming a government official, would be too high – so no, she was not interested.

We could attribute the absence of women in U.S. government to the choices they make to hold back on their political careers for the sake of their homes and children. The rhetoric of choice, however, obscures the ideological and structural conditions that are unsupportive of women's assent to positions of power and in fact pressure them to hold back. Not only do women fall short on time and energy, because of the unequal division of labour in the home, they will not be viewed as good mothers and wives if they give all to their careers at the expense of their families. If their homes are not immaculate, their children appear disheveled - and if they do not worry enough about any of this - they are likely to be criticised and labeled as deviant. A legislative staffer that the auhor interviewed in Washington told me that she and her friends carry "tremendous guilt" about their children's difficulties or deficiencies. (Benoit, 2008, 122) The cleanliness of their homes, the health, welfare, and appearance of their children–are all viewed as a "reflection of women's competence as a wife and mother–but not men's competence as a husband and father" (Bianchi, et al. 2000, 196). The rhetoric of choice keeps us from understanding the structures and mechanisms that prevent women from reaching to the top policy-making positions.

Not only do the expectations in the home present structural obstacles for women who are trying to juggle the high demands of political careers, but they also reflect and maintain gender ideologies that are inconsistent with definitions of a good leader, and thus interfere with women's credibility as politicians. Men are viewed, compared with women, as rational, instrumental, and productive. Women, relative to men, are seen as expressive, soft, passive, and nurturing. These beliefs are reinforced in the media and elsewhere in the social world and are reflected in the way women's and men's jobs are characterised. It should be no surprise that women tend to be concentrated in occupations (e.g. nursing, teaching) characterised in "feminine" ways-expressive, interactive, and nurturing. Men, on the other hand, tend to be concentrated in occupations characterised in masculine ways. The characteristics associated with leadership positions in particular–strength, instrumentality, rationality, productivity –are the ones associated with men and masculinity; hence it should not be surprising that men are disproportionately found in this positions and women are disadvantaged.

Women in leadership positions within government work very hard to maintain their credibility, and they do this by engaging in "masculinised" activities. Golfing and hunting, for example, are ways women penetrate the "ole boys' network" in Washington, D.C. However, they must walk a fine line – if they are too feminine and they are discredited as ineffective, and if too much masculinity is reflected in their personality they may be seen as threatening.

Gendered Policy

The state itself also operates to reinforce dominant ideologies that sometimes work for the disadvantage of the women. Public policy reflects and maintains the interests of the dominant groups, and as such works to disadvantage others and it is not gender neutral. For instance, homicide policy in the U.S. works to the disadvantage of women, because inherent in it are assumptions about masculinity and femininity: "When women commit violence in the private sphere, they are breaking the rules of gender and must be either 'refeminised' or severely sanctioned. When men commit violence in the home, they are in a sense fulfilling the grim assumptions about masculinity. They do not have to be 'remasculinised' to be considered redeemable or 'human'. Instead, judgment turns on whether they took masculinity too far." (Heberle, 1999, 1103). The gendered nature of homicide policy helps explain why women who are convicted of domestic violence receive harsher sentences. Instead of being an engine for equality, the state has become an engine for inequality. (Benoit, 2008, 49)

Women, more than men, tend to be associated with such public policy areas as education, health, welfare, and peace. Some scholars argue that policies representing the "maternal traits" of women locate them not only in the private sphere of the home but also in the public sphere of the state itself. They argue that the result is to increase both the public's view of women as suitable political leaders and the percentage of women actually elected to political office. (McDonagh, 2010) Although it may be the case that making "women's issues" legitimate, public issues places women in a more advantageous position with regard to seeking public office, at the same time, the nature of welfare policy works to hold women down and to maintain their passivity and vulnerability. Women are more likely than any other group in the

United States to be poor. One of the main reasons is because of something, Ann Crittenden calls the "mommy tax". The mommy tax is essentially the costs of caring for children that are uncompensated. And the costs of caring for children, which include wages lost while raising them, are extremely high, especially for those head households. (Crittenden, 2001) Economists estimate the cost of raising a child in a middle class household in the U.S. to be approximately $250,000 – without the cost of a college education (United States Department of Agriculture, 2011). Women who are raising children alone are expected to bear the sole burden of this expense, which means that they must either hold high-paying jobs, in which case they have the added cost of daycare; or they stay home to care for their children, thereby foregoing income. Either way, they are vulnerable to poverty. Welfare policy does not recognise the costs of motherhood; in fact, the TANF Programme that replaced welfare at the federal level essentially forces women to work in low-wage jobs for which they receive no benefits, thus ensuring a life of poverty. Welfare policy in the United States does nothing to empower women but instead reinforces women's unequal status and conditions.

Although welfare, education, and family are policy areas, mostly associated with women's interests, tax policy, traditionally thought of as a "male" policy area, also affects women's interests and maintains their secondary status. Women are full-fledged members of the workforce and yet they are typically thought of as the "secondary earners," when it comes to tax policy. As the secondary earner, the first dollar of her income is taxed at the rate where her has left her; in other words, her income is considered on top of his. Not only does this system encourage families to think in terms of "primary" and "secondary" earners, but it keeps women down by discouraging them from entering, or remaining in, the paid workforce. (Benoit, 2008) Take the example of Earl, who makes $30,000 a year. He pays nothing in tax on the first $20,000, 15 percent on the next $10,000. His wife earns $30,000 as she is more likely than her husband to file as the secondary earner, her first dollar is taxed at 15 percent. Thus, she pays three times the tax her husband does. And her $30,000 triggers $4,500 in tax. (McCafferty 1997) Naca Eissa, an economist at the University of California at Berkeley, says: "..we think the effects of the tax structure are the strongest for married women, who are usually the family's secondary wage earners and are more likely to consider not working outside the home" (Postrel 2000). State policy, then, reflects and reinforces family and gender ideologies that position women as the primary caretakers of the home and children and men as the primary earners. The related assumption is that women are inherently more nurturing, softer, more loving and caring – assumptions that leave women economically vulnerable and work to women's disadvantage when being evaluated for leadership positions that call for more of masculine qualities.

The Incumbency Advantage and the Cost of Elections

The cost of running for office in the United States prohibits most people from entering politics. It is especially prohibitive for women, who have not yet amassed the kind of wealth, or established the degree of connections, needed to mount a successful campaign. Ashley Baker's research (2006, p. 20) corroborates the following:

- The average size, of individual donations to most female candidates, continues to be smaller than the average donation to male candidates.
- The vast majority of large donors to political campaigns are men.
- Female candidates generally depend upon female donors for financial viability and win monetary support from men only as their odds of election approach certainty.
- The small individual contributions received by females suggest that they must attract far greater numbers of individual contributors than their male counterparts, just to equalise the total monetary value of their contributions.
- Women who win raise significantly more money than women who lose, while male winners collect only marginally more money than their losing counterparts.
- Female candidates require more money than men to reach the thresholds of both campaign viability and electoral success; thus, a decline in female candidates' fundraising and/or funding needs to be interpreted as a decline in their ability to participate in the electoral process.

Analysts estimate that it will cost Barack Obama nearly $1 billion dollars to run for the office of President in 2012. The last time he ran in 2008, it cost him only $750 million. (Shear, 2011) It is not unusual for candidates for Congress to spend $2 million and Senate candidate $20 million or more to run for office (Center for Responsive Politics, 2011). Running for state office can be equally as expensive. Meg Whitman, former President and Chief Executive Office of Ebay, raised a total of $173 million and still lost for governor of California. She is the only woman among the top ten self-funded gubernatorial candidates, nationwide; 82 percent of the total raised, $141.6 million, came from her own personal fortune (National Institute on Money in State Politics, 2011). Not only are women less likely to be able to fund themselves, given the fact that women continue to earn less than men in almost every occupational category and are disproportionately burdened by the "mommy tax;" in addition, the number of male donors far outweighs female donors. According to Open Secrets: "While women outnumber men in the general American population and among voters, they are far surpassed by men among political donors. At the federal level, men consistently give more than two-thirds of all itemised donations (over $200) when measured by number of donors and amount of money contributed." (Center for Responsive Politics, 2011)

In federal elections, candidates are chosen not by party officials, but by primary elections. Candidates thus have no chance of winning a seat, if they cannot get on the primary ballot. Compared with other countries, ballot access in the United States is difficult. Each state has its own ballot access laws; what is fairly consistent is that, in most states, excessive filing fees along with a high number of signatures is needed to get on the primary ballot. Once on the ballot, candidates must raise enormous amounts of money, in order to have any chance of making it to the general election. For example, the 2008 presidential primary cost Mitt Romney $110 million. (Shear, 2011) Congressional and Senate primaries can run into the millions. This presents an overwhelming challenge for many women.

One of the significant structural barriers to women is that men presently have the advantage of incumbency (Palmer and Simon 2001). The fact, that most incumbents are men, provides them with a tremendous advantage in getting their message out, raising funds, and mobilising constituents. Incumbency provides name recognition and media coverage, and thus a ready-made opportunity to argue ones positions before a public audience (in other words, campaign) under the guise of simply doing their jobs. Incumbency also provides access to a network of donors and in-house resources at their disposal and that they can mobilise when needed. In order to mount a successful challenge against an incumbent, which involves media coverage, get out the vote campaigns and other grass roots efforts, and various other strategies, candidates must amass significant amounts of money. Some candidates, particularly those who run for the Senate, are wealthy in their own right. Most, however, must rely heavily on campaign contributions. This means that candidates must be well connected to individuals and groups who have the potential to make significant donations. Although ordinary citizens can, and do, contribute to campaigns, the largest contributors are organisations, especially big business. As Susan Estrich notes "..everybody brags about their small donors, but the bulk of the money continues to come in the form of the largest checks, and bragging rights generally go to the candidate with the most rich friends (Estrich 2007)." Women have come a long way in developing fund-raising organisations for promoting women candidates. EMILY's List is such an organisation, "dedicated to electing pro-choice Democratic women to every level of office. EMILY's List members believe that the power of women as candidates, as contributors, as campaign professionals, and as voters can bring about great change in our country." (EMILY's List 2011)

NARAL America, another organisation that supports pro-choice (a.k.a. pro-abortion) women candidates, was described by the top business magazine, *Fortune*, as "one of the top 10 advocacy groups in America" (NARAL 2011). There are also conservative organisations, such as the Susan B. Anthony List, that support pro-life (a.k.a. pro-abortion) candidates. The group has fashioned itself as a sort of conservative answer to Emily's List. The Susan B. Anthony List spent $6 - 12 million to help Republican women candidates it endorsed in the 2010 elections (Hennessey, 2010).

Opportunities for Women's Empowerment

Based on studies of women in local, state, and federal politics, it is clear that women have more and better opportunities at the local level. Campaign costs are lower, and the demands of the job do not present a great conflict with women's responsibilities in the home (Rombaugh and Keithly, 2010). The political experience, the savvy women gain at the lower levels, has the potential to propel women to higher positions in the U.S. government. In the mid-term elections of 2010, more women were found to be involved at the local level. In the recent elections, it seems that more new women ran in primaries – and won - than ever before, particularly Republican women, with some of them also winning in the general election. Two high-profile Senate races, in Delaware and New Hampshire, yielded female Republican nominees. That makes a total of five Republican women nominated for Senate in the 2010 cycle (Kornblut, 2010). One new woman, Republican Kelly Ayotte (NH), won a Senate seat. At least eight new Republican women, including one woman of colour, will join the House of Representatives, besting the previous record of seven Republican newcomers in a single election. All three new women governors are Republicans, including two who won woman-versus-woman races. Two of the new governors are women of colour, the first women of colour to head state government (CAWP 2011). Some credit high profile women like Hillary Clinton, who was Barack Obama 's main opponent in the 2008 presidential primary and is now Obama's Secretary of State, and Sarah Palin who was John McCain's vice presidential running mate, for the push of more women into primaries and then general elections. When Palin appeared at a recent breakfast fundraiser for the Susan B. Anthony List, Dannenfelser, head of the organisation, called her the "wind in our sails" — someone who "embodies the energy" of what she characterised the new conservative women's movement (Halloran, 2010).

It is debatable whether this influx, of mostly Republican women into primaries at the state and national level, is a sign of major shift. First, when we look at long-term trends, the numbers are not as staggering. In 2002, there were actually more Republican women in office than in 2010. In the early 2000s, their numbers began to dwindle. Secondly, according to the head of Emily's List, Stephanie Schriock, "candidates that are making it through these primaries are more and more extreme, radical right-wing folks" who, even though they are female, do not appeal to independent and moderate women (Kornblut, 2010). Moreover, many feminists argue that these women do nothing to change the conditions and opportunities of women structurally or ideologically. Conservative women generally do not push for gender neutral public policy and in fact blatantly argue against women's equality and rights on many fronts. Thus, except for the few women who somehow are fortunate enough to rise up through the educational and corporate hierarchy, which is increasingly becoming the path to politics, the majority of women in the U.S. will not have a chance to enter U.S. politics, particularly at the higher levels.

In order to promote more women to rise at the top of U.S. government, there must be a shift in family and gender ideologies such as that woman are as likely as men to be seen as breadwinners and leaders because the dominant ideologies that construct women as passive, dependent, soft, nurturing, relative to men, disadvantage them in the political sphere. Women who counter these beliefs appear "too" masculine and thus deviant (e.g. Hillary Clinton), and women whose image reflects these ideologies are not taken seriously as leaders (e.g. Sarah Palin). It is ironic that, although there is a global "ideal" that paints a picture of the Western (especially white, American) women as more "progressive," than elsewhere in the world, women in the U.S. are actually more constrained by rigid gender norms and expectations in some ways. This is especially the case when women enter motherhood.

Judith Warner, author of *Perfect Madness* (2005) examines the "hypermothering" that takes place in the U.S. society. She describes her experience of giving birth to her first child in France, then moving to the U.S., where she gave birth to her second. In France, the expectation was that she would continue with her career and have a life of her own. She noticed that, in the U.S. the middle class, suburban mothers, she met, spoke about nothing but their children and spent almost all their time making sure their homes (and children) were spotless and that their children were exposed to the right activities, getting the right foods, seeing the right doctors, interacting with the right playmates in the right venues. When they weren't making appointments and running from activity to activity, they were worrying excessively about whether they were making the right choices. She observed that this left no time or energy for self-fulfillment as women. As a result, their marital relationships were less than exciting, and they were exhausted and mostly miserable. These middle-class mothers, who actually have the resources and education to enter politics were too absorbed in their childrens' lives than to focus on a demanding career as politician – or much of anything else for that matter. As Warner notes about one mother she observed that she had "taken up the politics of playdates..." (Warner, 2005, 12).

Dominant ideologies, asserting that women are better at domestic tasks and mothering, have had major effects on women in and out of the home. Women are concentrated in jobs and careers that are "feminised" – characterised in ways that correspond with definitions of womanhood. As such, they are devalued – they are paid less and not seen as important or serious, relative to male dominated occupations. Moreover, the idea that women have natural talent or ability for housework and, childcare, places an enormous burden on them, physically, mentally, and emotionally, especially for women who engage in paid labour. These ideologies, and the increasingly intense focus on the home and children rather than their own lives, helps explain why women's primary identities are wrapped up in their roles within the family. This in turn leaves them feeling desexualised, unattractive, and undesirable. Men, in contrast, not only have more leisure time than women, but continue to think of themselves first as men, whose identities are primarily connected with their jobs in other arenas, and secondly with their roles within the family. This leads to a power imbalance and helps explain why men are more likely than women to have extramarital affairs, particularly at earlier stages in the marriage. It also helps explain why women are less enthusiastic about seeking highly demanding careers like those in public office. From the time they are very young, men are socialised to take risks, make decisions, take charge. Michael Messer, in *Guyland*, looks at the "culture of entitlement" in which boys are raised in the U.S. He says "this culture of entitlement is the reward for subscribing to the Guy Code. As boys, they have felt powerless as they heroically live up to impossible conventions of masculinity...". But they know that, "someday, if I play my cards right, if I follow all the rules, the world will be mine. Having worked so hard and sacrificed so much to become a man – it'll be my turn to payback I'm entitled." (Messner, 2008, 59). We need to teach women, from an early age, that they too are entitled to power. They should be encouraged to think for themselves, take risks, and make decisions – independent of men and children. Women need to be supported in their attempts to rise to leadership positions. Most importantly, we need to break the silence around male power, at times, violence and silence around women's relative vulnerability. We need to critically examine the systems and structures that turn little boys into men and little girls into women, and how the construction of gender in different societies around the world work to provide both opportunities and constraints for all their citizens. Only then will we see a substantial change in U.S. government, and only then will women's rise to leadership positions have real meaning for women's power.

REFERENCES

Abrahams, N: "Negotiating Power, Identity, Family, and Community: Women's Community Participation." *Gender & Society*. Vol. 10, No. 6, December 1996, pp. 768-96.

Baker, Ashley: "Reexamining the Gender Implications of Campaign Finance Reform: How Higher Ceilings on Individual Donations Disproportionately Impact Female Candidates". *The Modern Americas*, fall 2006, pp. 18-23.

Benoit, Denise: *The Best Kept Secret: Women Corporate Lobbyists, Policy, and Power in the United States.* New Jersey: Rutgers University Press, 2008.

Bureau of Labour Statistics: *Women at Work. U.S. Department of Labor*, March 2011. http://www.bls.gov/spotlight/2011/women.

Burns, Nancy, Kay Lehman Schlozman, and Sidney Verba: *The Private Roots of Public Action: Gender, Equality, and Political Participation.* Cambridge, Massachusetts: Harvard University Press, 2001.

Center for American Women in Politics (CAWP): "Republican Women Follow National Winning Pattern: Newcomers Take Many House Races, But Only One New Senate Seat, Three New Governors; Many Democratic House Incumbents Fall." *Eagelton Institute of Politics*. Rutgers University, November 3, 2010.

Center for Responsive Politics: *Open Secrets*. http://www.open secrets.org.

Cherlin, Andrew: "The Deinstitutionalisation of Marriage", in Susan Ferguson (edt.) *Shifting the Center.* New York: McGraw Hill, 2011, pp. 174 .

Cherlin, Andrew: *Public and Private Families: An Introduction*. 6th Edition. New York: McGraw Hill, 2009.

Coontz, Stephanie. "Historical Perspectives on Family Diversity," in Susan Ferguson (edt.) *Shifting the Center.* New York: McGraw Hill, 2011.

University of Illinois at Urbana-Champaign. 2008. "*Women's Milestones in U.S. Government*." http://www.library.illinois.edu/doc/researchtools/guides/subject/womengov.html

Crittenden, Ann. 2001. *The Price of Motherhood: Why the Most Important Job in the World is Still the Least* Vol. NY: MacMillan.

Di Leonardo, Micaela: "The Female World of Cards and Holidays: Women, Families and the Work of Kinship." *Signs*. Vol. 12, No. 3, 1997.

Bianchi, Suzanne M., Melissa A. Milkie, Liana C. Sayer and John P. Robinson. 2000: "Is anyone doing the housework? Trends in the gender division of household labour." *Social Forces* 79, No. 1 (September): 191-228.

EMILY's List. http://emilyslist.org/

Estrich, Susan. "*The Money Primary*." Creators.com. http://www.creators.com/opinion/susan-estrich/the-money-primary.html

National Abortion Rights Action League (NARAL). http://www.naral.org.

National Institute on Money in State Politics: Show Me the Money http://www.followthemoney.org.

Halloran, Liz: "For Republican Women, 2010 Is Already A Huge Year." NPR (National Public Radio), 2010. http://www.npr.org/templates/story/story.php?storyId=127369770.

Heberle, R: Disciplining Gender: "Or, Are Women Getting Away With Murder?" *Signs*. Vol. 24, No. 4, 1999.

Hennessey, Kathleen: "For GOP Women, 2010 may not be their year." *The New York Times*, July 24, 2010.

Hochschild, Arlie: *The Second Shift*. New York: Viking, 1989.

Kornblut, Ann: "Primaries push more women into general elections, but most fresh faces now belong to Republican Party." *Washington Post*, September 15, 2010.

Mathews, T.J. and B.E. Hamilton: "*Delayed Childbearing: More Women Are Having Their First Child Later in Life*," NCHS Data Brief, No. 21. National Center for Health Statistics, Hyattsville, MD, August, 2009.

McCafferty, E. J.: *Taxing Women*. Chicago: University of Chicago Press, 1997.

McDonagh, Eileen: "It Takes a State: A Policy Feedback Model of Women's Political Representation." *Perspectives on Politics*. Vol. 8, No. 1, 2010, pp. 69 – 21.

Postrel, V.: "The U.S. Tax System is Discouraging Married Women from Working." *The New York Times,* November, 2000.

Postrel, V.: Wives' Tale: "The 'Marriage Penalty' Taxes Women for Working, Not Wedding." *Boston Globe,* April 13, 2003. http://dynamist.com/articles-speeches/nyt/marriagepenalty.html

Rombaugh Shirley and Diane C. Keithly: "Women in Politics: An Analysis of Personal Characteristics Leading to Success in Gaining Local Elective Office." *Race, Gender and Class.* Volume 17, Number 3-4, 2010, pp. 173-88.

Shear, Michael: "How Much Does It Cost to Run for President?" *The New York Times,* May 23, 2011.

Tovar, Marcela: *Women Candidates and Campaign Finance.* Revised and Edited by Women's Environment and Development Organisation, 2007.

United States Department of Agriculture. Center for Nutrition and Policy. *Cost of Raising a Child Calculator.* http://www.cnpp.usda.gov/calculator.html

Vab Assendelft, L and Stottlemeyer C: "Women in Public Office: A Case Study of Southwest-Western Virginia." *Virginia Social Science Journal,* Vol. 44, No. 1, 2009.

Women's Economic and Development Organisation (WEDO)." *Women Candidates and Campaign Finance.* December, 2007.

SECTION III

CASE STUDIES

10

Women's Participation in Decentralised Governance in Garhwal Himalayas: A Case Study of Uttarkashi District

— *Annpurna Nautiyal*

Women in Uttarakhand have always played an important role in the socio-political arena. It has been seen that their experience of working amidst severe geographical and physical hardships allows them to develop a better understanding of the issues and problems. Hence; they take a keen interest in the resolution of the socio-political problems and working for social welfare. Women due to their capacities of integration have also been associated with the various movements organised from time to time in Uttarakhand, like *Chipko Movement, Anti Liquor Movement* and *Uttarakhand State Movement* etc. However, unfortunately their high work burden, lack of awareness and knowledge, poor socio-economical status hamper their continuous activism and participation in the socio-political and developmental process. Though, there is no denying the fact that the women, by taking advantage of the clauses of reservation of seats in the Panchayati Raj Institutions, are entering the political arenain large numbers and becoming the part of the decision-making process. But the lack of awareness and knowledge about their rights and duties and social and financial independence is still not allowing them to show their full potential and caliber. More so, as these provisions have facilitated the entry of ignorant or totally illiterate women, who remian completely dependent on their husbands, sons or male relatives for performing their duties in these bodies. Therefore, in such cases, the real authority is still being enjoyed by men, because the women are just acting as rubber stamp or people's representative for name-sake. Such women are humiliated and devalued in the panchayats, on account of their ignorance and illiteracy, and they not only lack self esteem but also feel demoralised. With the result, despite potential, they remain unable to deliver the results. Women's ignorance, illiteracy, lack of awareness, superstitions, coupled with the unwanted interference by the male members of the family, make the position of the women representatives pathetic in these institutions. Sometimes women are also found to be suffering from the conservativeness and complexes of considering themselves inferior to men. This also show social contradiction as if women are illiterate, so they are mocked. But if men are illiterate, they do not face such humiliation. (Jayal 2000 and Buch 2000) Such disparity and attitude, towards women, also demoralise the women and despite potential they remain unable to deliver the results.

Moreover, it has also been found that the husbands also aspire to fulfill their own agenda through their wives due to this reason, even after winning the election the women representatives' husbands could be seen dictating terms. This scenario presents an interesting contradiction about the women of the Garhwal Himalayas as, on the one hand, they are found to be eager to work for the welfare of the family, people and society and their participation in different movements stands in testimony to this. But, on the other hand, their heavy work burden, their weak status in the society, lack of awareness and knowledge always place them at the receiving end. However, it is also true that women are naturally inclined to work on fundamental issues, like making provisions for drinking water, because it is the women who generally look after the management of water in their homes, like how to obtain water, carry it or distribute. Therefore, women are capable of handling the small and basic issues. (Borba, 2000). As women also focus their attention towards creating the basic facilities like roads, schools etc. than on high-flying projects. Therefore, it is also being felt that bringing women in larger numbers into the decision-making bodies at the local/village level would certainly improve the working of these bodies and fulfill the aim of the real village development as well as regional development. But at the same time, it is also felt that to bring overall improvement in the working of these institutions, education among the women urgently needs to be promoted, because only the educated women possess the capacity of making a difference in the situation through their working and understanding capacity.

As a matter of fact, in a democratic system based on people's active participation, involvement and interest, the activism of the people is primarily reflected through participation in the political debates, electing their representatives, showing interest for their rights and using them for their well-being and empowerment and voicing their concerns towards any violation or infringement of their rights. The activism and participation of the people is required not only for making the system responsible, but it is also ideal for good governance. The absence of the activism and participation of the people promotes lack of responsibility among the policy-makers, corruption, red tapism and socio-political problems which are harmful for the growth and health of the democratic system. In the Indian constitution, men and women have been given enough and equal rights and opportunities for their active participation in the political process, from the local level institutions to the national institutions, through various socio-political forums. As political participation and activism is directly related to the awareness of the people, particularly of the women, towards their constitutional and legal rights, therefore, every work, which involves the women in some type of work, related to the enrichment and growth of the political system, can be taken as an indicator of their activism. From this point of view, participation in the voting process, meetings, rallies, strikes and elected bodies can be seen as an indicator of their activism in the political process.

Actually, women's empowerment and activism is interrelated; because if women are empowered and aware about their rights, it becomes easier for them to actively participate in the political or social decision-making process and also in the elected bodies. This means that for promoting socio-political activism, women need to be empowered in the real sense of the term. (Femida, Feeney and Ranade: 2006) It has also been observed that women usually try to perform their roles very sincerely, as they always remain under the scanner of the society. Therefore, whenever they are given any leadership or decision-making role, they try to leave their mark behind and this quality provides a strong basis for more activism of the women in the political process. The study by Hughes, Ginnett and Curphy also supports this, as they have found that women take more time in taking any decisions as they prefer to evaluate all the information, options, possibilities and inputs received from various sources, before reaching to some conclusion. Besides, weighing all the options they also try to execute any programme or activity by consensus. Since they have a different way of doing things as well as building capacities which allow them to try new things, commit mistakes and learn by those mistakes just like mothers do with their children while teaching them new things. (Hughes, Ginnett, and Curphy, 2002) Women also believe in creating a healthy and caring atmosphere for learning so that others can learn without being intimidated by the pressures or the circumstances. On account of these qualities, women's leadership styles not only reflect their feminine values, behaviour, natural instincts, welfare concerns and characteristics but also their attempts to encourage other women by sharing power and information to be self confident, believing and appreciating their significance. This style of leadership comes more naturally to the women than to men, as men while in decision-making capacity usually tend to behave more autocratically than women. (Rosener, 1990) These qualities certainly advocate for more participation and involvement of women in leadership roles so that the best decisions for the welfare of the society and community could be taken.

However, despite various arguments in the favour of women's working styles and concerns as well as provisions, women's participation and leadership role in the political arena is still not as significant as it should have been in comparison with their population, because the implementation part of such measures always lacks commitment. It is also noteworthy that despite representing 50 per cent population and part of 50 percent vote share, even after sixty years of India's independence, the women could not get sufficient and proper representations in the decision-making process. In the 13th Lok Sabha, only 47 women could be elected, in the 14th Lok Sabha only 44 women and in 15th Lok Sabha only 59 women could be elected. The percentage of their representation in Lok Sabha has been only 5.5 percent and in the Rajya Sabha it has been 9.3 per cent. In the state assemblies also their representation has been very poor. In Bihar, it has been 4.3 percent, Kerala 4 per cent, Madhya Pradesh 3.6 per cent, Uttara Pradesh 5.4 per cent and in Rajasthan 4.1 per cent. Actually the increase in women's representation could never cross the average worldwide 10 percent bench-mark and therefore, women have remained unable to leave any imprint in the decision-making process as a group. In the rural areas, particularly the women have not been able to take advantage of the clauses of their empowerment due to their ignorance and lack of awareness. The system as well as to some extent, the women themselves are also responsible for this weakness, because, on the one hand, they do not show much interest in becoming the part of the decision-making process due to their excessive work load in domestic and agricultural sector and on the other hand, due to their training from childhood to accept the superiority of the male members and work as per their direction, also prohibits them from taking independent decisions, hence, their participation and activism in the socio-political arena is always found to be less.

In the present paper, an attempt has been made to understand and analyse the contribution, the vision of the women about the village and regional development, emerging leadership trends, problems being confronted and future prospects of women's participation and empowerment in the hill areas, on the basis of a field study conducted in a few villages of district Uttarkashi in the Garhwal Himalayas.

Administrative and Demographic Profile of Uttarkashi District

Uttarkashi is one of the largest districts of Uttarakhand, Tibet is situated to its north-east border and the district Kinnor of Himachal Pradesh is located to its west. The nature has bestowed it with immense natural wealth, useful medicinal herbs and other forest resources. Besides the famous shrines of Gangotri and Yamnotri, the ancient temples of Kashi Vishwanath and Parashuram Dattatrey also make it an important pilgrimage destination. Its Nehru Mountaineering Institute (NIM) is all time favourite with the mountaineers and hikers. Spread in a geographical area of 8,01,6 sq km, this district has been divided into six Blocks for the administrative convenience. The forest area covers 6924 sq km, rural area 7998.83 sq. km and urban area 17.17 sq. km. It has 36 Nayaya Panchyats, 427 Gram Sabhas and 264 Panchyat Houses.

Table 10.1 : Block-wise details of Nayaya Panchyat, Gram Sabha and Panchyat Houses

Year/Block	*Nayaya Panchayats*	*Gram Sabhas*	*Panchyat Houses*
2001-02	36	395	250
2002-03	36	423	264
2003-04	36	427	264
2003-04 Block-wise			
Morie	4	60	34
Purola	3	38	25
Naugaon	10	107	64
Dunda	6	81	44
Chinyalisaur	6	69	49
Bhatwari	7	72	48
Total District	36	427	264

Source: *Statistical Diary,* District Uttarkashi 2004, *Arth and Sankhya Officer,* Uttarkashi, 2004, p. 54.

According to the 2001 Census, the total population of Uttarkashi district is 29, 5013, male population is 15,2016 and female population is 14,2997. The sex ratio per 1000 male population is 941. However, the provisional estimates of the census 2011 shows an increase in the population of Uttarkashi. The total population has now become 32, 96,86 with an increased sex ratio of 959.

Table 10.2: Block-wise Forest, Rural and Urban areas, Number of Household and Families and Total Population of Uttarakashi District

Year/Block	Area sq. (km)	No. of Resid-ential Houses	No. of Families	Total Population		
				Total	Male	Female
1981	8016	37441	38174	190948	101533	89415
1991	8016	44282	45900	239709	124978	114731
2001	8016	92646	55558	295013	152016	142997
		Block-Wise 2001				
Morie	88.83	NA	5538	33374	17251	16123
Purola	56	NA	4998	27187	13842	13345
Naugaon	421	NA	10097	57685	29422	28263
Dunda	127	NA	10679	55848	27997	27851
Chinyalisaur	133	NA	8211	43962	21431	22531
Bhatwari	249	NA	10495	51995	27538	24457
Total Block	1074.83	NA	50018	270051	137481	132570
Forest Area	6924	NA	483	2044	1256	788
Rural Area	7998.83	85981	50501	272095	138737	133358
Urban Area	17.17	6665	5057	22918	13279	9639
Total Block	8016	92646	55558	295013	152016	142997

Source: *Statistical Diary*, District Uttarkashi 2004, *Arth and Sankhya Officer*, Uttarkashi, 2004, p. 13.

The mainstay of 80 per cent population is agriculture. The provisional estimates of the census 2011 indicate towards an increase in the literacy rate also. According to these estimates the total literacy rate of Uttarkashi district has now become 75.98 per cent, male literacy has become 89.26 per cent and female literacy 62.23 per cent respectively. The female literacy rate shows an impressive rise of almost 15 per cent but these are still estimates and could only be verified only, once the final census report is released. (Census-2011) However, in comparisons to other districts (like Dehradun 79.61 per cent, Pauri 73.26 per cent, Nainital 78.21 per cent, Rudrprayag 70.94 per cent, Pithoragarh 72.97

per cent, Chamoli 73.20 per cent) the female literacy in Uttarkashi is still below 65 per cent which cannot be said to be satisfactory. As per the 2001 census, the total literacy rate of Uttarkashi district is 65.71 per cent, male literacy is 83.60 per cent and female literacy rate is 46.69 per cent respectively. The literacy profile of the district has been presented in the following table which shows that the female literacy rate is below 40 per cent in Morie and Naugaon blocks of Uttarakashi. (Morie 33.65 and Naugaon 39.49 per cent) As women's empowerment and awareness is also related to literacy and education, therefore, the low literacy rate is not only a sign of underdevelopment but also women's poor status in the society at large.

Table 10.3 : Block-wise Literacy Profile

Year/Block	*Literate Persons*			*Literacy Percentage*		
	Male	*Female*	*Total*	*Male*	*Female*	*Total*
1981	47030	8195	55225	46.32	9.17	28.92
1991	70134	21865	91999	68.74	23.57	47.23
2001	105663	55498	161161	83.60	46.69	65.71
2001 Block-wise						
Morie	9570	4374	13944	67.66	33.65	51.37
Purola	9345	4922	14267	81.40	44.75	63.47
Naugaon	19003	9174	28177	79.13	39.49	59.64
Dunda	20264	10944	31208	87.50	47.11	67.27
Chinyalisaur	14721	7785	22506	84.66	41.52	62.27
Bhatwari	20902	11432	32334	89.56	55.58	73.64
Total District	105663	55498	161161	83.60	46.69	65.71

Source: *Statistical Diary*, District Uttarkashi 2004, *Arth and Sankhya Officer*, Uttarkashi, 2004, p. 18.

Analysis of the field survey conducted in the three blocks of Uttarkashi District

Since the female literacy rate as per the census 2001 in Morie, Daunda and Chinyalisaur blocks ranges from 33.65 per cent to 47.11 per cent, therefore, these three blocks were selected for field survey as well as to evaluating and understanding the level of socio-economic and political awareness and activism of the women, particularly under the system of decentralised governance. From each block 04 villages and 25 respondents between the age group of 18 and above, representing all groups population were randomly selected. Although all the selected blocks were far-flung but Mori was located at such a farthest corner of

Uttarkashi that some of the villages of this block can still be found to be deprived of the road transport network and the common distance of such villages from the road head happens to be between 10 to 15 km. The villages Gangar, Usola and Pawani of Morie block, selected for survey, were located at a distance of approximately 15 km from the road head and the general mode for transportation of ration and other necessary items in these villages is still through the mules and horses. These

Location Map of the Surveyed Blocks in Uttarakashi District

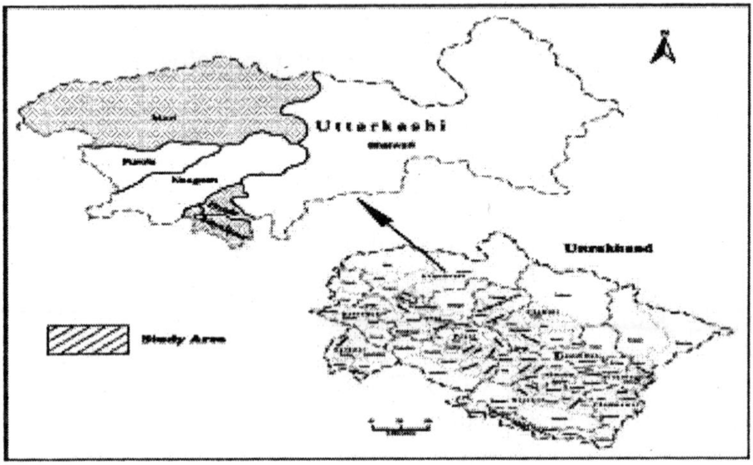

villages are also not connected with any communication and electricity network and the schools located in these villages work for name sake only, as regular teachers are not available and it was also informed by the inhabitants that the schools normally operate for two to three months only. As a result most of the children were found playing at their homes and the school building totally locked with no traces of any activity.

Interestingly, it also came to light that the Gram Pradhan, who is not only considered the representative of the people in the first tier of the local self government institutions and also responsible for carrying out the developmental schemes, was himself not residing in the village but in Uttarkashi town for looking after the education of his children which makes it clear as why development has not taken place in these areas. The inhabitants also informed that the government officials rarely visited their areas, therefore, their problems and life style has remained unchanged even after the creation of the Uttarakhand state. These villages present a glaring example of the governmental neglect and apathy. For most of the villagers who have yet to see a train, getting electricity is also a luxury. The main crops of these areas are Ram Dana, Potato and Kidney Beans However, the lack of facilities for transportation and markets near their areas forces them to sell their produce which is of very good quality and totally organic to the contractors at throw away prices. The situation of the other villages in Chinyalisaur and Dunda blocks was also not well. Though the villages in these blocks were connected to the road head but the inhabitants also informed that the construction of Tehri Dam has adversely affected their life. The people were found to be frustrated because of the insufficient and inappropriate compensation package provided to them by the construction agency which in their view point was hardly enough to bring changes in their life style. Moreover, due to the submergence of the connecting bridge over the river Bhagirathi, the people were forced to trudge a long distance to visit their family members residing at the other side of the river or for schooling of their children, as schools were also located at the other side of the river which has increased their problems and miseries. In view of the apathetic attitude of the state government machinery towards their problems, the respondents also expressed their disappointment and dissatisfaction. It was also found that in the Morie block, due to the forest rules, the roads could not be constructed on the basis of the logic that such construction would lead to a large scale felling of trees which would be disastrous from the environmental point of view. But the environmental concerns have forced the inhabitants to remain largely cut off from the mainstream of development and also the other facilities. The surveyed villages in Uttarkashi district generally bore a deserted and sad look and the respondents also looked irritated and unhappy. The plight of the people who have been living in serious hardships, due to geographical, factors as well as apathy and neglect of the government machinery reflected in their responses and attitudes also as the people also complained about the vainness of various surveys being conducted by different agencies to highlight their troubles, status and developmental profile but with no attempts for the resolution of their problems and pain.

An analysis of the data collected from the surveyed villages has been presented in the following tables which clearly show the differences of perception, awareness and development. From the point of development and availability of various sources of awareness, it was found that Morie block was so much cut off from the normal facilities that only a few people had access to newspapers or TV, because of the lack of electricity and modes of communication and transportation. In comparison to Morie, the respondents in the Dunda and Chinyalisaur blocks were found to be much more aware about the various issues, because of the easy availability of the sources of information. Actually, the lack of the transport and communication facilities has created this divide in these areas which can be understood from the data presented in the following table.

Table 10.4: Availability of the Sources of Information in the three blocks

S.N	Name of the Block Views of Respondents	Morie		Dunda		Chinyalisaur	
		Yes (%)	No (%)	Yes (%)	No (%)	Yes (%)	No (%)
1.	Read Newspapers	11	89	57	43	65	35
2.	View TV News, programs	22	78	62	38	73	27
	Total	33	167	119	181	138	62

All figures in percentages (Sample Size 300).

As news papers, internet and Television are the main sources of information and awareness in the present age, therefore, the availability of these can also affect the level of awareness and judgment of the people. As shown in the above table that in Morie block only 11 per cent respondents informed that they read newspapers and 22 per cent viewed TV news. However, in Dunda 57 per cent people read news papers and 62 per cent viewed TV, in Chinyalisaur 65 per cent read the newspapers and 73 per cent people watched T.V. Since Mori is still one of the most backward and remote part of Uttarakashi, therefore, in the absence of the sources of awareness, communication and connections, the people of this area generally lacked knowledge and interest about various issues of national or regional importance, whereas, in Dunda and Chinyalisaur blocks people were found to be well informed. The easy accessibility of sources of information and also presence of a small village *market*, where usually villagers assemble, shop for goods, share their views and also gossip, created a difference in the awareness and attitude of the respondents of the three blocks, because for the villagers of Morie, the nearest small market was also located at a distance of 15 km. This situation, on the one hand, shows the isolation of the area and on the other, the pitiable state of development. This has made the issue of regional development very important for most of the respondents and it reflected in their criteria of casting votes also.

Table 10.5 : Respondents Criterion of Casting Vote

S.N.	Criterion of Casting Vote	Morie	Dunda	Chinyalisaur
1.	Personality of the candidate	12	22	64
2.	Political party	11	42	20
3.	Regional Development	72	36	16
4.	Any other reason	5	-	
	Total	100	100	100

Though, as shown in the above table that the respondents of the each block had different opinion about the criterion of casting votes, because, in Morie block, only 12 per cent people accepted that they cast their votes on the basis of the personality of the candidates whereas 72 per cent people accepted that they cast their vote on the issue of regional development and expect that the candidates would work towards the basic developmental issues of their areas. In the villages of Dunda block 42 per cent respondents admitted that they follow the party line and only 36 per cent informed that they considered the issue of regional development as an important issue. However, in the villages of Chinyalisaur, the picture was rather different because, most of the villages were located at the road head. Therefore their condition was better from the point of view of access and facilities. Therefore, for only 16 per cent people, the issue of regional development was important. For 64 per cent respondents, the personality of a candidate was an important criterion to cast their votes and 20 per cent followed the party line. The agenda of development was a top most priority for the respondents of the Morie block and generally people were neither associated with political parties nor did they show any type of political awareness. Since this area also lacks good educational institutions, therefore, due to lack of education, the people also lacked awareness and this is also one of the reasons of the backwardness of this area. However, in Chinyalisaur block the people were found to be more active and politically aware in comparison to Dunda and Morie blocks. So far as the active participation in political activities is concerned, people accepted that the degree of their participation differs according to the body/type of election. Fifty-seven per cent people in Morie, 45 per cent in Dunda and 68 per cent in Chinyalisaur accepted that they participated actively in the elections of the local bodies; however, their activism was found to be different for the Assembly and Lok Sabha elections, as most of the people informed that they did not participate actively in these elections.

Table 10.7 : People's Activism in different Elections

S.N.	Activism in Elections	Morie	Dunda	Chinyalisaur
1.	Gram Pradhan/ Local Bodies	57	45	68
2.	Assembly Elections	17	20	15
3.	Lok Sabha Elections	6	15	2
4.	No Opinion	20	20	15
	Total	100	100	100

People were found to be more enthusiastic towards the elections of the Gram-Pradhans, because they related the activities of the Gram Panchayat with the local area development. They also opined that as the Village Pradhan was supposed to work for the village development and be available to the people as and when required, therefore, it was always easier for the villagers to get hold of the Pradhan to discuss their problems. The respondents informed that they found it difficult to approach other representatives and members of assembly and parliament because of their non accessibility and unavailability during the time of need. Therefore; they did not take active interest in the Assembly or Lok Sabha elections. The people also accepted that with the 50 per cent reservation in the local bodies for the women, their participation in the political activities has increased. Most of the respondents also shared that as women, by and large tend to be honest, less corrupt, devoted to the cause and sincere, therefore, the chances of corruption in the day-to-day working of the Gram Sabha also gets to be reduced and need based activities are undertaken. As shown in the following table that 71 per cent people in Morie, 41 per cent in Dunda and 77 per cent in Chinyalisaur accepted that women's participation in the local bodies is likely to reduce corruption but, in Dunda block 59 per cent respondents opined that corruption could not be reduced if uneducated women would make entry in the local bodies, as these would largely depend on the male members of their family for planning developmental activities and carrying out their work. Such situation would not only make them just a rubber stamp to be used by their male relatives, but no difference in the working would be witnessed by the participation of such representatives in the local bodies. As literacy rate of the women is less than 45 per cent in all the three blocks, therefore, most of the women respondents had a low educational level which also gives weight to the apprehensions of the people expressed about the pitfall of the entry of the less educated and illiterate women in the Panchayati Raj Institutions.

Table 10.8 : Impact of Reservation and Women's Participation in Local Bodies

S.N.	View of Respondents	Morie		Dunda		Chinyalisaur	
		Yes %	No %	Yes %	No %	Yes %	No %
1.	Women's participation to reduce corruption	71	29	41	59	77	23
2.	Reservation would help their entry in politics	91	9	88	22	81	19
3.	Participation increased in local bodies	73	27	66	34	74	26
4.	Better understanding of the needs of the area	22	78	32	68	33	77

As the above table shows that 59 per cent respondents in Dunda block felt that due to the women's dependence on their male relatives, they would not be able to use their own judgment. However, most of the respondents felt that reservation for women would help their entry into politics. Ninety-one per cent respondents of Morie, 88 per cent in Dunda and 81 per cent in Chinyalisaur believed that reservation would help women's entry in politics, as it has also increased women's presence in the local bodies. As Morie block is very backward and in the absence of exposure, the people were not only found to be very orthodox and conservative, but they also did not have a good opinion about the women and their capabilities. Therefore, 78 per cent people opined that women, due to their weak knowledge and intellect, were unable to understand anything. In their opinion, women do not have any idea of the developmental needs of the area and their perception about the needs was limited to the household things only.

(*Yah Raj Kaj Aurotin ka bas kee baat nahi hai, unko ghar kay kaam ka alwa aaur aata hee kaya hai. Unsay is tarah kee koyee umeed karana bakar hai. Achhaey gahr kee aurotain to yah kaam kartee bhee nahi hain*)

In Dunda and Chinyalisaur blocks also, 68 per cent and 77 per cent respondents expressed the same opinion about the women's understanding about the developmental needs of the area, which clearly shows that men still do not appreciate women's entry and work in the political institutions, because of their mindset and other reservations. In informal meetings, the women also complained that males of their families never allow them to act independently, rather they always thrust their ideas or force them to respect or follow their whims and fancies.

(*Mard hamko apney sa hamesha kam samjatay hain unko lagta hai ke ham aurotin to bavkoph hoti hain aur ghar ka kaam ka alwa kuch na to samj sakti hain aur na sooch sakti hain. Iseeliya koee bhee kaam unsay puchha bina to nihi ho sakta hai aur unhee kee baat manane parti hai.*)

Though, ironically, in Morie block, 78 per cent respondents, in Chinyalisaur 77 per cent and in Dunda block 68 per cent people did not have much idea about the rights provided to them under the Panchyati Raj system. However they strongly felt that for effective participation in these institutions the women need to show their worth, and contest election on their own and not as a filler for their husbands. They also opined that the women need to be more vocal and develop the capacity to express their views more often in the meetings of the Gram Panchayat as well as attend them regularly. It was also told that, generally, the women fail to turn up for the meetings of the Gram-Sabha because they lack time due to their over indulgence in various

Table 10.9: Status of working and satisfaction with the representatives and the governmental schemes

S.N.	*View of Respondents*	*Morie*		*Dunda*		*Chinyalisaur*	
		Yes %	*No %*	*Yes %*	*No %*	*Yes %*	*No %*
1.	Work independently to fulfill the responsibilities of the post in the local self governments	23	77	36	64	58	42
2.	Satisfied with the work of their representatives	26	74	52	48	33	67
3.	Satisfied with government's regional development plans	51	49	67	33	43	57

household and farming related works which they have to perform every day. As shown in the following table that only 23 per cent respondents in Morie and 36 per cent in Dunda accepted that they performed their duties themselves in the bodies of the local self government; however in Chinyalisaur this number was comparatively high, as 58 per cent respondents accepted that they performed their duties without the support of others. Twenty-six per cent respondents in Morie, 52 per cent in Dunda and 33 Per cent in Chinyalisaur accepted that they prefer working through their representatives. Twenty-six per cent respondents of Mori, 52 per cent of Dunda and 33 per cent respondents of Chinyalisaur accepted that their representatives were doing good work for their area and also for the solution of their problems.

As shown above that, in Morie block, 74 per cent respondents informed that they were not satisfied with the working of the local bodies as their area was totally underdeveloped and lack all the basic facilities. In Dunda 33 per cent respondents were found to be disillusioned with the development and in Chinyalisaur 57 per cent shared the same opinion. Though more than 50 per cent respondents were found to be satisfied with the governmental schemes, launched for the regional development, but the people told that while implementing such schemes their opinion is never sought which affects the value and impact of these plans. Forty-nine per cent respondents of Mori block, 33 per cent of Dunda and 57 per cent respondents of the Chinyalisaur were not found to be satisfied with the present plans being undertaken at the local level in the name of development, whether being done under Gram-Sabha, Gram-Panchayat, Kshetra-Panchayat, and the Zila-Panchayat; because they have failed to work according to the requirements of the area and many projects of development could not be completed in time. As the villages of the Mori block could not be connected with the road, transport and communication network, therefore, majority of the people were not happy with these plans and schemes. However, the people of Mori block were found to be happy with the Mahtma Gandhi Gramin Rojgar Yojana (MNREGA) of the government of India. Most of the people of Dunda block also appreciated and viewed it favourably. Though generally, people were not found to be very much inclined towards participating in politics or political activities, but 60 per cent respondents in Morie, 65 per cent in Dunda and 72 per cent in Chinyalisaur shared that if any of the family members holds political post in the local self bodies, it gives inspiration to others and encourage the participation of the family members. (See Table No. 10)

Table 10.10 : Participation in socio-political Activities and Contesting Elections

Sl. No.	*View of Respondents*	*Morie*		*Dunda*		*Chinyalisaur*	
		Yes %	*No %*	*Yes %*	*No %*	*Yes %*	*No %*
1.	Family members, holding Political post, encourages political participation	60	40	65	35	72	28
2.	Receive help from the family in political participation	12	88	19	81	35	65
3.	Participation in Socio-Political Activities	67	33	43	57	66	34
4.	Capable of Contesting Election	49	51	25	75	61	39
	Consider themselves capable of holding political posts	57	43	66	34	70	30

Only 12 per cent respondents in Morie, 19 per cent in Dunda and 35 per cent in Chinyalisaur accepted that they receive support from their family members in registering their political participation. The majority of the respondents in Morie and Dunda block informed that they do not get help from the family members in the conduct of political activities. This opinion was expressed largely by the women who informed that their participation in the political sphere was not appreciated by their family members because of their conservative mindset and also due to their belief that women's place is only inside the household or performing the farm activities. Studies by Gurung has also highlighted this fact that as women are still seen just like helpers of men, therefore they are not expected to be active and loud in outside activities, (Gurung and Gurung, 2006) and as their entry into politics is not likely to reduce their workload, therefore performing the double responsibility of family work and Panchayat work becomes difficult for them. As far as the participation in socio-political activities is concerned, more than 50 per cent respondents admitted that they participate in the social functions and activities and take part in the meetings of the village Panchayat and also canvassing in the favour of their candidate in the Gram panchayat elections. However, in Morie block 51 per cent respondents informed that they never participated in these activities. Despite showing reluctance in participation in socio-political activities, 57 per cent respondents in Morie, 66 per cent in Dunda and 70 per cent in Chinyalisaur accepted that they considered themselves capable of holding the political posts in the local bodies and given the chance, they would work with full capacity to realise the aim of village development by implementing different welfare and developmental schemes launched by the government. The confidence of the people clearly reflected the benefits of the Panchayti Raj institutions and the exposure, experience and training being provided by these institutions to the grass-root people. Since Chinyalisaur is the most developed block in comparison to other two blocks, therefore, the number of the respondents considering themselves capable of holding the political offices was found to be the largest. Only 30 per cent respondents in Chinyalisaur accepted that they did not consider themselves capable of holding political positions, whereas in Morie block, 43 per cent respondents accepted that they were not capable of holding such positions. In Chinyalisaur block, people were generally found to be politically aware and alert, because, on the one hand, it has large number of people with political affiliations and on the other, the

Table 10.11: Contribution for Development by Representatives

S.N.	*Public representatives who actively work for village Development*	*Morie*	*Dunda*	*Chinya-lisaur*
1.	Gram Pradhan (Village Head of Panchyat)	73	91	86
2.	Kshetra Panchayat member (Area)	11	5	4
3.	Zilla Panchayat member (District)	5	-	5
4.	Member of Legislative Assembly (MLA)	4	2	3
5.	Member of Parliament (MP)	7	2	2

percentage of the people, who considered themselves capable for holding the political responsibilities, was also more than the other blocks. Hence, from the political point of view, the people of Chinyalisaur block were found to be most active and aware in comparison with the other two blocks.

As the above table shows that all the respondents of the three blocks fully agreed that the Gram Pradhan actively works for the village development of a particular area. In Mori block 73 per cent respondents, 91 per cent in the Dunda block and 86 per cent in the Chinyalisaur block supported it. Though in the villages of Morie block the respondents also complained about the absence of the Gram Pradhan but they were still found favouring the Gram Pradhan. The second preference in this regard was given to the Kshetra-Panchayat member by the respondents of the Mori block, and the third preference to the member of the Parliament. However, in Dunda and Chinyalisaur blocks, only 2-3 per cent respondents believed that member of Legislative Assembly and Member of Parliament work for the village development. The poor opinion about the contribution of MLA and MP reflected people's loss of confidence with the performance of these representatives, as people also informed that they generally get to see the MLA or MP during the elections only and once, elections are over, no one bothers to visit these areas for fulfilling the promises made in the party's election manifesto. They also shared that Gram Pradhan, being the head of the village body, remains available to the people and more so holds a better understanding of their needs and therefore should be expected to perform according to their expectations or satisfy them. But other categories of representatives, particularly MLA and MP, remain mostly

Table 10.12 : Impact of Uttarakhand's Creation

S.N.	*Impact of Creation of Uttrakahnd on Village development*	*Morie*	*Dunda*	*Chinyalisaur*
1.	Better Condition with improvement	19	40	38
2.	Condition Deteriorated	13	16	18
3.	Distance and remoteness unchanged	38	16	30
4.	No better availability of facilities	30	28	14

unavailable to the people and therefore show little interest and understanding towards their needs. However, people's general opinion was that, due to the indifferent attitude and the knowledge of the area specific needs, the condition of the villages has not improved much, even after the 11 years of the creation of Uttarakhand state.

In Morie 19 per cent respondents, 40 per cent respondents in Dunda and 38 per cent in Chinyalisaur accepted that the condition has become better with some improvements in regard to the amenities and availability of facilities and only 13 per cent respondents in Morie, 16 per cent in Dunda and 18 per cent in Chinyalisaur accepted that condition has become worse with the creation of Uttarakhand. However, the respondents of Morie clearly opined that the distance and remoteness of their areas has remained the same, even after the creation of Uttarakhand state, because they were still deprived of the basic facilities like electricity, schools, roads and health facilities. Thirty-eight per cent respondents in Morie were found to be perturbed with the distance and remoteness of the area and 30 per cent were found to be disturbed due to the unavailability of the basic amenities. In Dunda and Chinyalisaur also, 16 per cent, 28 per cent, 30 per cent and 14 per cent respondents respectively were found complaining about the condition of their area which in their opinion was same even after the creation of Uttarakahnd state because the representatives never find any time to visit their areas.

(*Uttarakhand banney say bhee to hamiri muskilay kam nahi huai hain, kyoki pratinidhi to yahin tak aataey hee nahin hain to unko kya pata kee ham kis haal main hain*)

This indicates towards the people's frustration with the condition of the development even after the creation of Uttarakhand. Since the government, machinery is also not very sensitive towards the needs of these villages, therefore, people's irritation was apparent when they informed that the officials seldom visit these areas to have firsthand information of the grass-root realities. Actually, the neglect was seen in all the areas from roads to schools which were running without teachers and infrastructural facilities. This has promoted a culture of agitation and movement in the hill areas, because the people feel that without agitation, the officials never pay any heed to the needs, whether it is related to water supply or electricity, health facilities or anything else and the best mode of showing their resentment was through blocking the main highway which happens to be the only connecting road of that area. Due to this reason, in the recent years, the incidences of blocking the road by observing sit ins or placing some objects has increased drastically, which creates inconvenience to the common people, small children, tourists or travelers without any connection or fault of theirs.

Conclusion

In view of this, it can be said that people generally feel that there has been not much change in their life styles with the creation of the Uttarakhand state. The people of these areas are also not happy with the construction of the Tehri Dam, because the government has failed to provide them with a proper compensation as well as connection with their families and relatives, by not constructing the bridges or providing frequent boat services in the submerged areas. On the one hand, due to rapid revolution in the field of transport and communication, one talks about the idea of the global village, whereas, on the other hand, even today there are areas, that are devoid of the modern means of communication and transportation which has not allowed them to connect with the outside world and share the prosperity and progress. Therefore, the people of these areas are lagging behind in all respects. The respondents also opined that if the government is unable to improve their condition, they should be rehabilitated to some other areas with better facilities, as the underdevelopment has also blocked all the employment opportunities for them. In the absence of alternative sources of employment, they had no means except making use of animal husbandry (sheep farming) and selling the agricultural products like potatoes and Rajma (Kidney beans), as the only means of livelihood and sustaining their families. But it was also informed that these are also not very profitable in the absence of market facilities near their villages and the lack of refinement in the handmade woolen products, as per the needs of the market, also fetches a very little amount of money for their products which are sold through the contractors who purchase their goods in a very low price but make profit by selling these products at a very high cost in the cities. The people felt that the government should provide them market facilities and also good seeds so that they could get good yield from their produce. The people also earnestly felt that for better development, their areas need to be connected with the road network. On the other hand it was also seen that though women have entered the local bodies, on account of reservation but due to the secondary status and poor opinion about the women's capabilities and performance, most of the women representatives informed that they always faced difficulties in discharging their duties. Some of them even informed that the male members not only try to create hindrance but sometimes also defame them because of their false ego and being unable to see a woman holding such position. Actually, it is still a challenge for the rural women to prove their potential in a conservative and male dominated society, where most of the time they have always to undergo a social micro scrutiny. The watchful eyes of the male members sometimes unnerve the women and they tend to be confused about the issues. However it was also found that women have a better idea of the developmental needs of the village, like schools, facilities for children, drinking water, community halls, footpaths and they also shared a better rapport with the fellow women. It also came to light that with the woman Gram Pradhan, the other women are able to develop a kind of informal relationship and as when their comfort level increases, they do not hesitate in opening up and sharing and discussing the problems. It was also found that once the women are able to establish themselves and their good work is recognised by the people they are generally elected unopposed, because there were some women representatives who informed that they have been serving for the last one decades. This provides a base for not only promoting good workers among women, but also information about their duties so that they are able to fulfill their given task without any difficulty.

Observations and Suggestions

The following observations and suggestions about the developmental needs of the people can be made on the basis of this study of the three blocks of Uttarakashi:

- People need to be consulted by the agents of local self government about their specific developmental needs.
- Network of roads and other basic facilities like electricity, water, toilets, and health facilities need to be urgently developed in the area for a better and improved life style as well as connection among the people.
- The needs of the people displaced by the construction of Tehri Dam also to be seen and dealt sympathe-tically.
- The focus of all the developmental activities should be development at the grass-root level or as desired by the people.
- Government machinery should be used to provide assistance to the Gram Pradhans to fulfill their duties by frequently imparting training and organising awareness camps for generating awareness about their role.
- For improving and bringing qualitative changes in the working of the women representatives. their participation in such training camps should be made mandatory.
- The mindset of the society about women's role and capabilities also needs to be changed, so that women are not considered incapable of handling their responsibilities.

- The government officials should make field visits regularly to assess the ground realities and make them available to the representatives of the Panchayati Raj Institutions. The paper work needs to be taken to the field for better and practical results.
- Since the Gram panchayat is the basic unit for village development, therefore, for the overall development of the villages of the hill areas, the focus of planning and centre of activity should be the Village Panchyat and people's participation in its meeting needs to be encouraged or be made compulsory.
- Uniform facilities and area specific development should be the goal of all plans and schemes taken for village development; then only the dream of Gram Swaraj and self sufficient villages would be fulfilled.
- The civic sense also needs to be imbibed in mins the people so that the surroundings could be kept clean, the waste and litter management must also be looked after by the Gram Panchayat.
- Exposure and training for managing disaster must also form part of the duties of the Gram Panchayat.

Acknowledgement

The field work, data collection and analysis done by Dr. Rakesh Negi, Project Officer, Women's Studies Centre and a few other students with the financial assistance from the UGC- SAP –DRS Programme and Women Studies Centre is thankfully acknowledged.

REFERENCES

Jayal, Niraja Gopal: *Gender and Decentralisation.* "Unpublished manuscript, Centre for the Study of Law and Governance, Jawaharal Nehru University", New Delhi, India and Buch , Nirmala, (2000) *From Oppression to Assertion: A Study of Panchayats and Women in M.P, Rajasthan and U.P.* New Delhi: Centre for Women's Development Studies, 2000.

Borba, Maria-Lucia G.: "Capacity Building for Women in Water Supply and Sanitation," in Cecilia Tortajada Edt. *Women and Water Management: The Latin American Experience.* OUP New Delhi, pp. 27-28, 2000.

Handy Femida, Meenaz Kassam, Suzanne Feeney, Bhagyashree Ranade: *Grass-roots NGOs by Women for Women. The Driving Force of Development in India.* SAGE Publications, New Delhi, p. 37, 2006.

Hughes, R.L., R.C. Ginnett, and G.J. Curphy: *Leadership: Enhancing the Lessons of Experience.* New York Mc Graw Hills et al. p. 38, 2002.

Rosener, J.B.: Ways Women Lead: "The Command and Control Leadership Styles Associated With Men Is Not the Only Way to Succeed". *Harvard Business Review.* November/ December, pp. 119-25, 1990.

Census of India-2011, Provisional Population Totals and Data Products www.censusindia.gov.in

Gurung Chanda and Nawraj Gurung: "The Social and Gendered nature of Ginger production and Commercialisation". In Ronnie Vernooy edt. *Social and Gender Analysis in Natural Resource Management.* Sage Publication, New Delhi, pp. 62-63, 2006.

11

Empowering Hill Women for Sustainable Livelihoods and Natural Resource Management: A Case Study of Opportunities and Issues of Governance in Garhwal Himalayas

— ***R.K. Maikhuri*** and ***Shalini Dhyani***

Seventy percent of the world's poor are women; many of them rely on forests and agriculture for their livelihood. Though both women and men play different roles in biodiversity management, but both have knowledge about, and skills in, use and protection of biodiversity resources. With the absence of men from the hills, on account of migration, the women serve as the backbone of the hill societies, due to their work in domestic and agriculture sectors. They represent more than 50 percent of the population living in the hills and actively participate in the social, cultural and economic activities. They are the major contributors of labour in farming, livestock, domestic and forest resource collections/ utilisation systems etc. They play a significant role in the natural resource management, on which the livelihood and the very survival of hill families/communities depend. They have also an enormous source of traditional knowledge related to daily life and use of bioresources around them. Unfortunately, women's contribution in conserving and managing forest resources is seldom acknowledged and even their capacity to contribute in this field is also not recognised. One of the reasons for this avoidance is the lack of gender-friendly perspectives in biodiversity research and documentation. Hill women have other challenges also to face, they belong to societies that are marginalised, traditional, inhabited in remote and far flung areas and cut off from the mainstream societies. Hardship of living amidst remote and harsh environment, difficult steep slopes, tough topography and long distances to cover, make their tasks more arduous. The increasing tendency of men folk to migrate for employment is also responsible for women's abnormally heavy workload. Unfortunately, despite contributing immensely for the society and family, there is a general lack of appreciation of women's role and skills in managing the responsibilities of their own families. They are often left out of the various capacities building programmes and training in rural development and decision-making processes. The gender bias also allows the society to ignore women's perspectives, needs, knowledge and contribution, whereas for a balanced growth and development, both women's and men's perspectives need to be integrated in biodiversity studies to gain a complete account of biodiversity characteristics, people-plant-wildlife relationships, causes of biodiversity loss, and the efforts required for conservation and management. Such integration would help achievement of the three objectives of the Convention on Biological Diversity (CBD) on conservation and sustainable use of biodiversity and the fair and equitable sharing of benefits from genetic resources. The adverse impact of Climate Change (CC) on water and other forest products, such as, fodder, medicinal plants, dyes etc. has forced the societies to select new species of crop and fodder. CC is also leading to declining fertility of soil, erratic rainfall and temperature leading to food insecurity and more labour intensive work. Climate Change has also added another dimension to biodiversity management, because it has direct and indirect impact on both biodiversity and the people who depend on the services it provides.

Natural resource management represents priority issues for the entire Indian Himalayan Region (IHR). Globally, women own less than 2 percent of all land and their unpaid work in care economy produces an output of $11 trillion (global GDP c $23 trillion (UNEP, 1995). It has been highlighted in some reports that women's income generally remians US$ 10.5 trillion and men on the other hand, receive $23.4 which clearly indicates that woment receive 30-40 percent less payment than the men for the same work. The women though form 46.5 percent work force in US but less than 1 percent are in natural resources management (USDoL, 2008). The absence of women from international dialogue on (REDD) Reduced Emission from Deforestation and Degradation and REDD+ and under representation of women even if they are trained professionals, at all levels of policy and decision-making in natural resources and environmental management indicates towards a total lack of understanding about women's concern and their point of view. The comprehensive studies are not available on gender issues, dealing with the environmental and livelihood situations, in Garhwal. There is also a paucity of information on governance issues and participation of women in decision-making activities in forest management of their village. Though, the issue has been addressed consistently but there are fewer efforts to analyse the women's situation, climatic changes and governance in the context of natural resources management in the Garhwal Himalayas. The present paper attempts to bridge this gap. It provides a detailed overview of the associated problems and suggests some cost-effective solutions to relieve pressures of the hill women and forests of the Garhwal Himalayas. The information provided in this paper is based on more than six years of research and development activities in Upper Kedar Valley which would be helpful in improving the condition of existing forest and conservation policy dialogues with respect to women in the Garhwal Himalayas.

Study Area and Climate

The state of Uttarakhand encompases an area of 53,485 sq. km, which accounts for nearly 15.5 per cent of the total geographical area of the Western Himalayas and 1.63 per cent of the total land area of India (Anonymous, 1991). It has two distinct traditional politico-cultural regions known as the Garhwal and the Kumaon. The state of Uttarakhand, which lies to the east of the river Yamuna, actually acts as an intermediate zone between the Western and the Central Himalayas in almost all respects including the diversity of species. The study area of the Kedarnath Wildlife Sanctuary (Fig.1), located in the Chamoli-Rudraprayag district in the Garhwal Himalayas the is one of the bio-diversity rich and protected areas of Uttarakhand.

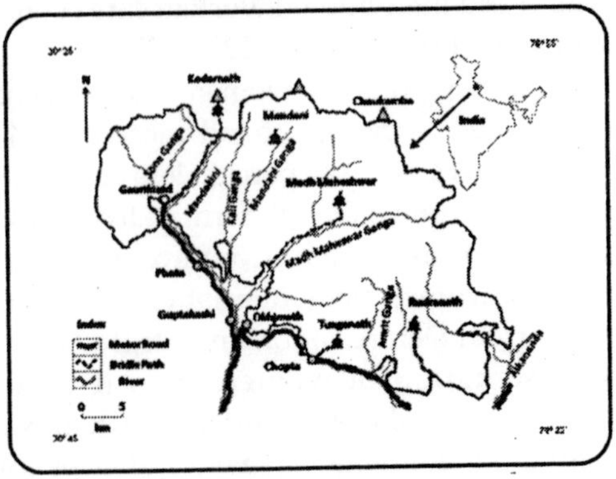

Fig. 11.1 : Location map of Kedarnath Wildlife Sanctuary, Uttarakhand, the Cenral Himalayas.

The floristic and faunistic richness of KWLS (Kedarnath Wildlife Sanctuary) can be attributed to its location that is at the junction of Indian sub-continent and Indo-China biogeographic regions (Prabhakar et al, 2001). This area covers a wide altitudinal range from 1600-2800 m amsl with a varying mean annual temperature range of -2 to 30°C and mean annual precipitation of 1752 mm during the study period (Dhyani et al, 2011). Relative humidity was high throughout the season recorded in Shersi village. There are 182 villages inside the core zone of the KWLS (as the entire sanctuary is treated as core zone) whereas, 5 km extending area from the core boundaries is treated as buffer zone having many more villages (Prabhakar et al, 2001).

The study area during summer is inhabited by a large number of local transhumants, and visitied by tourists and pilgrims as the famous Hindu shrine of Kedarnath and other Panch Kedars are located in this area. The main pressure on the forests of the area involves local graziers, herders and transhumants; more so the heavy influx of national, international tourists and extraction of fuelwood, fodder and leaf-litter by local villagers. For the present study, the five villages viz. Maikhanda Shersi, Rampur, Sitapur, Triyuginarayan and Tosi in upper Kedar valley (1400-2800 m amsl) were selected. In these areas, the agriculture and animal husbandry along with tourism related jobs are the main source of income. Extension of croplands under Potato and Kidney bean have increased manifold which has promoted the practice of abandoning traditional and indigenous crops and these cropping practices are adding more pressure on forests to remove fodder and leaf litter for preparing Farmyard Manure (Dhyani et al, 2011).

Approaches and Methodology

The approach of the study has been designed to improve livelihood options for empowering women of the study area by using local bioresources through cost effective technological interventions (Maikhuri et al, 2011). Baseline survey of natural resources, Participatory Rural Appraisal (PRA), Capacity building programme and documenting the indigenous knowledge base was initiated at village level. Data on seasonal dependence of local inhabitants on forests and related traditional beliefs were documented following focussed group discussions and interviews with women folk (Dhyani et al, 2011). Indigenous knowledge and locally used indigenous medicinal and aromatic plant species and off season vegetables were identified for cultivation by using simple and modern scientific, rural development techniques for protected cultivation and training. As the aim was to improve socio-economic conditions of the women by reducing their work load, therefore, a fodder bank model was developed by the active participation of local women folk. Attempt was also made to generate awareness about the fact that the goal of sustainable development is possible only through the empowerment of the grass-root people of the area. The study has been initiated in Upper Kedar valley in Ukhimath block of Rudrapryag districts of Grahwal. Keeping the uniformity of sampling in mind, about 60 households were selected for questioning in all the target villages. Lottery sampling technique was used to minimize any potential bias and to capture the heterogeneity of the local population. Semi-structured questionnaires were used to collect the data. Before collecting the actual data, the survey questionnaires were tested and edited in order to increase their efficiency. The linkages and dependence of the community with the forests was assessed by undertaking formal, informal group discussions and personal interviews with more than 50 local women inhabitants involved in collection of leaf litter by accompanying them in the collection areas. Data verification was carried out by actual field checks. As the rural women of the study area have been targeted as direct beneficiaries, therefore, the sample largely comprises of women from marginal and small farm households.

Results and Discussion

The Himalayas provide ecosystem services for the well-being of all the mountain communities and people living in other parts of South Asia. The livelihoods lack resilience and are highly vulnerable to shocks and stresses. Thereofore, climate changes in the Himalayas would reduce their ability to provide life and livelihood security. Rapid socio-economic transformations are taking place in Indian Himalaya Region (IHR). Women though are able to cope up with these changes and somehow try to manage their diverse roles, but these coping strategies are mostly limited to household levels. According to 2001 census of India, the population of Uttarakahand was 84.89 lakhs, which includes 43.26 lakhs males and 41.63 lakhs females, the male-female ratio was 964, with a literacy rate of 72 percent and population density of 159 people per square kilometre. As per the provisional population totals of 2011 census of India, the population of Uttarakhand has become 1, 01, 16, 752. It shows a rise in both male and female population. The male population has now become 51, 54, 178, and female population 49,625,74, with a sex ratio of 963 and population density 189. The demography of Uttarakhand also indicates that about 74 percent of the total population of Uttarakhand resides in its rural areas. As per the 2001 census, 12.56 lakh people belong to the Scheduled Castes. This comes to around 83 percent of the total scheduled caste population in the state. The total scheduled tribes in the state add up to 2.56 lakhs and out of this 2.40 lakhs are rural. The study area lies in upper Kedar valley of the Western Himalayas and majority of the settlements of the region practices agro pastoralism. A general profile of the study area was prepared on the basis of door-to-door survey (Table 1). Like other high altitude communities, animal husbandry is practised by the residents of studied villages, which is an inevitable part of their social system. Therefore, each family maintained 5-8 cattle of indigenous breed i.e. a cow, a pair of bullocks, a buffalo and a horse or mule that are reared on traditional lines. Livestock units varied from the lowest of 180.14 in Sitapur to 363.14 in Maikhanda village (Table 1). Agriculture is the main occupation of the population and is practised on steep terraced slopes under rainfed conditions. The average landholding per household is approximately 0.01 ha. The area is well-known pilgrimage route as the famous Hindu shrine Kedarnath is situated here. Farm area and cropping intensity has changed over the last two decades and shows a shift from traditional crops *i.e. Eleusine coracana* and *Amaranthus frumentaceus* to cash crop as *Solanum tuberosum*. Cultivation of other traditional crops such as *Echinocloa frumentocea, Glycine max, Setaria italica, Panicum miliaceum and Pennisetum typhoides* have been abandoned. The area under *Solanum tuberosum* and *Phaceolus* species has increased in almost all the villages adding more pressure on forests as floor biomass is used for farm yard manure and local *ringal* bamboo and branches of some shrubs and trees (*Deutzia staminea* and *Bahunia vahlii*) used for supporting the legume crop plants. Earlier 15-20 crops that comprised of cereals, millets, vegetables, pulses, oil yielding, condiments, spices and medicinal plants were grown by the farmers, however, now only a few are grown on large scale.

Table 11.1: A general profile of the studied villages of Upper Kedar Valley in Garhwal

Parameters	*Villages of the study area*				
	Shersi	*Rampur*	*Sitapur*	*Triyugi-narayan*	*Tosi*
1	2	3	4	5	6
Altitude (m amsl)	1800	1900	2000	2500	2750
Households (Number)	48	170	37	195	23
Population (Number)	241	936	203	1125	145

1	2	3	4	5	6
Female (Number)	127	464	102	559	70
Scheduled Caste females (Number)	36	0	0	0	0
Total Agriculture Land (ha.)	33.35	60.64	-	66.50	9.33
Reserve forest (ha.)	16.86	135.46	25.26	29.66	2.64
Community Forest (ha.)	150.01	7.94	-	128.57	0
Livestock (Number)	302	302	288	926	749
Livestock Units	214.57	249.14	180.14	638.71	336.86

Resource Collection from Forests

Resource collection is a major and everyday activity of a hill woman that adds to her drudgery. Women folk of the study area visit forests twice (in morning and evening) for harvesting fodder, fuelwood, leaf litter or wild edibles from forests and sometimes from a very far off location. (Table 2). It was observed that, women of Garhwal region are now walking longer distances for fodder, because regular lopping (both

Table 11.2: Indigenous resource use pattern in the villages of the study area

Resource Type	*Extraction Process*	*Species*	*Frequency*	*Consumption*
Fuelwood	Felling Lopping Collecting	*Q.leucotrichophora, Prunus cerasoides, Lyonia ovalifolia, Pyrus pashia, Alnus nepalensis*	Once in 2-3 days	Entire year
Fodder	Lopping, Chopping	*Q.leucotrichophora Myrica esculenta, Debregeasia salicifolia*	Twice a day	February-May and August-September
NTFP and Wild edibles	Lopping , Chopping, Uprooting	*Myrica esculenta, Rhododendron, Diplazium esculentum, Paeonia emoddi*	2-3Times a week	March-June
Leaf Litter	Collecting	Leaves of *Alnus Aesculus and Acer caesium*	Twice a day	November-April

partial and complete) has not only resulted into degradation of forest vegetation near their village settlements but has also affected their health and education.

Change in cropping pattern (Maikhuri et al, 2000a; Nautiyal et al, 2007) from traditional millets and cereals to cash crops like potato, kidney bean and hybrid wheat varieties (with small height and low crop residue) has also considerably reduced the availability of agricultural by-products of crop residue as fodder leading to receding forest boundaries has been observed in other parts of the Himalaya (Moench and Bandhopadhyay, 1986). Developing fodder bank model among a few village clusters is an inspiring idea using fast growing, high biomass yielding, nutritious and production enhancing tree, shrub and grass species. These fodder banks help in generating awareness regarding preservation and storage of surplus fodder, availability of nutritious fodder during the period of fodder scarcity, steps to enhance nutritive value of crop residue and other cellulosic waste for animal feeding and to minimise the waste of conventional and nonconventional fodder. There is a vital need to train people to introduce fast growing, high biomass yielding grasses on their cropland bunds, kitchen gardens and degraded community wastelands that can be harvested throughout the year.

Bioresource Based Organic Farming

A number of initiatives have been undertaken by various R & D Institutions in Uttarakhand state to address conservation and developmental needs of the ever growing population in the region. Establishment of Rural Technology Demonstration and Training Center (RTDTC) could be helpful in generating and providing viable options for conservation and efficient management of available natural resources while developing appropriate technologies for sustainable rural development in the central Himalayas. Agriculture in this region is still practised on traditional lines due to unique socio-economic and ecological factors, coupled with mountainous topography that require technologies according to the needs and conditions of the area for making suitable and successful intervention. Technological intervention and change is considered as an important instrument in the continuous process of socio-economic development. However, poor access to suitable technologies due to factors already mentioned is one of the main causes of poverty, drudgery, and natural resources degradation in the central Himalayas. Despite increasing levels of economic investment and multiplication of developmental projects in this region, the worsening economic and environmental conditions speak for the need of a critical re-examination of prevailing developmental planning approaches in this mountainous region. With this background, the Garhwal Unit of the G.B. Pant Institute of the Himalayan Environment and Development (GBPIHED) at Srinagar Garhwal established a Rural Technology Demonstration and Training Centre (RTDTC) at Triyuginarayan village in upper Kedar valley of district Rudraprayag. The main objectives of this centre is to train and build capacities of local farmers and other user groups to adopt some of the simple, low cost, hill specific rural technologies in participatory mode. It was done with the hope that the improved capacities of local farmers would be able to promote widespread adoption of rural technologies in Uttarakhand and expand the existing limited livelihood earning opportunities in remote and isolated areas of this Himalayan state.

Economic Stability through Cost Effective Technologies

In this centre fifteen (15) appropriate and hill specific rural technologies, such as, rehabilitation of degraded land through slopping watershed environmental engineering technology (SWEET), low-cost rain water harvesting tank technology, bio prospecting and value addition of wild edibles and traditional agro biodiversity, farm produce particularly vegetables storage technique (zero energy cool chamber), protected cultivation (use of polyhouse, shade nethouse and poly-pit), vermicomposting, biocomposting, vermiwash, azolla culture, bamboo propagation, drip irrigation, biobrequetting, apiculture and mushroom cultivation, have been successfully designed/ demonstrated based on science and technology inputs. The major objectives are: (*a*) exploration, documentation and preparation of an inventory of indigenous and modern technologies which are hill specific and simple to use, (*b*) demonstrations of improved /alternative and already available hill specific technologies in the rural technology demonstration and training center at selected field sites, (*c*) capacity building of women and marginal groups through training/live demonstrations/ field exercise of target groups, and training of trainers (TOT) on a regular basis, (*d*) guidance and support for field implementation of technology packages and subsequent monitoring, and (*e*) to develop a framework for achieving self-sufficiency within the system in the short and long run.

Livelihood Versus Natural Resource Conservation

Banning the collection of resources may affect the marginal hill societies disproportionately, and increase the workload of women. Such restriction on bioresources on which they have traditional rights over centuries can also lead to rapid depletion of resources as the sense of ownership is lost. *Mahila Mangal Dals* has established effective control over management of the village forest as collection of fuelwood, fodder and water is almost exclusively women's work in the hills. Decisions about when to open the forest for grass, leaf and firewood collection, the rules for collection, the fines for violation, etc. are taken by the *Mahila Mangal Dal* and communicated to the *Van Panchayat Sarpanch* (president). The women's control over forest use decisions enables them not only to make a choice about the forest to be used but also to ensure that forest product's collection is not in conflict with periods of heavy agricultural work, soon after harvesting the monsoon *mandwa* crop in October. During the October season, they generaly visit the nearest forest and the most far-off forest is visited in December when all agricultural work is finished and women feel that they can devote most of their time to stocking up firewood and grass before the snow fall. Cutting of bushes and pruning tree branches is generally done from April to May. This practice of harvesting with recommended calendar is mostly related to fodder and forest floor litter which if removed unsustainably can cause low rate of tree species regeneration as well as leaching of nutrients from the forest floor. As the stall feeding of livestocks also reduces the grazing pressures in these areas, therefore, in order to control the adverse effect on the carrying capacity of the forests only one or two patches of forest in a year/ season is opened for resource extraction and the remaining patches are reserved for the next three to four years so that the forest get proper time for their regeneration. Fodder resource extraction is mostly done by partial lopping or just by pruning method instead of complete lopping (Misra, 2010).

Conserving and Managing Resources

The main pressure on the forests of the area is witnessed during summers due to the heavy influx of local graziers, herders, local transhumants, tourists and local collection. As this study was conducted to generate an understanding and awareness about the role and impact of the resource removal from forests, involvement of women folk, forest accidents involving women and drudgery of rural women interlinked with resource collection activity, therefore an attempt was made to focus on the observations, interactions, discussions and dialogue with the local people. From the field observations it has been estimated that due to faulty system of feeding of dry fodder to the livestock about 40 percent of the dry fodder goes waste with urine, dung and trampling with animal hooves. During the rainy season, the availability of fodder is in excess but there is fodder crisis during winters and summers, because farmers are ill-equipped for management of grass for the use in lean months. As this study was also underataken with an aim to make an assessment of the fodder related needs and possible options and solutions through the developing fodder bank model. For this purpose Maikhanda village in Upper Kedar valley was identified as one suitable and potential site, because it is mostly inhabited by BPL and scheduled caste population. A total area of more than 5 hectare of village wasteland has been acquired with the permission of villagers for the model fodder bank development site. Besides indigenous grass and indigenous tree species, other grass species like Hybrid Napier, Joint star, Makuni, Cox food are also being used for developing this model site. A nursery site is also developed near the fodder bank site where trials of vegetative propagation of some lesser known but preferred and nutritious tree fodder species are under progress. To reduce the impacts of fodder harvesting in villages with ample area under forests, a self regulated, rotational approach of 3-5 years was discussed and suggested during capacity building workshop. For better utilisation of dry fodder, women are also being motivated and trained to use the feed after chopping them in small pieces and soaking in water for the lean season.

Governance Issues in Natural Resource Management

The role of women in Eco Development Committees is generally pathetic, because the men in the villages dislike promoting and involving women in activities outside the household. Majority of the women in these areas are not well educated, therefore, their participation and view point is never considered important by the men folk. While the incorporation of gender concerns into governance framework increases the efficiency and sustainability of the system, therefore, to achieve best results the, it is desirable that international and national planning processes include gender responsive indicators and targets as part of performance-based funding. In the implementation of various national projects and activities, special attention need to be given to gender implications of benefit sharing and payment structure frameworks. Projects also need to comply with the international agreements related to women's equal access to land ownership and resource rights. Equal and timely access to information and capacity-building opportunities also need to be made available to women as well as the decision-makers to ensure the formulation of gender responsive schemes. The effective participation of women, their capacity and skill development requires innovative approaches, institutional development, awareness and education and socio-economic motivation. In addition to this, rural women need to be made fully aware about the other rural development programmes supported by central/state governments and being executed by state/central line agencies/department in the following sectors: (*a*) agriculture, irrigation and water management, (*b*) social forestry and forestry, (*c*) small scale village and cottage industries, (*d*) rural housing, (*e*) drinking water, (*f*) rural road network, (*g*) rural electrification and non-conventional energy sources, (*h*) poverty alleviation, (*i*) education, (*k*) cultural activities, health family welfare and sanitation, (*l*) women and child development, social welfare, (*m*) social welfare of weaker sections/SC/ST/youth, (*n*) public distribution system, and Panchayati Raj, etc.

Major Constraints (National and International Scenario)

Women's lack of access to and ownership of productive resources is the major cause of the vulnerability of women in the Garhwal Himalayas. In India, at the national level the sixth five year plan provided the joint title to spouses in distribution of lands and home sites whereas, the eighth five year plan strengthened it by asking state governments to allow 40 percent of the surplus land to women alone and the rest jointly. The 73rd Constitutional Amendments Acts of 1992, can be seen as the landmark achievement in the history of women's empowerment and their involvement in the governance and decison-making in the three tiers of local self government institutions. This has not only ensured the entry of women in these bodies by making 33 percent reservation or 1/3rd of total seats for women in all elected offices in local bodies in rural and urban areas but the rural women have also benefitted by these immensely, because from devising the plans for their village development to the implementation of the plans the women are involved in each stage of the developmental process. Actually, this should be the spririt of all the developmental activities and plans because unless the plans have people's support, their success becomes doubtful.

At the international level, almost 25 years ago the, United Nations for women's empowerment and development issues as well as to voicing concerns about the gender issues declared International Year of Women in 1975 and UN Decade of women- 1976-1985. In the 1990s women's organisations struggled to put gender on the global policy agenda at key UN conferences namely Rio declaration and UN Millennium Summit 2000. These platforms have not only endorsed women's role and contribution in conservation and natural resource management, but they have also stressed the need to incorporating women's view point while making policies in these sectors. The article 20 of the Rio

Declaration says, "Women have a vital role in environmental management and development, and their full participation is, therefore, essential to achieve sustainable development." The World Forestry Congress has reaffirmed its commitment for conser-vation projects.

Conclusion

Gender mainstreaming, with its promise of gender transformation, equality and empowerment has become a central pillar of development discourse, policy and practice. Yet the implementation of these promises has been largely disappointing. While the gap between policy and practice is well known, proposed 'solutions' also bring little new to the table. Technical fixes don't work, and will not work to address complex gendered issues and inequities. Transforming gender requires staying on the edge of what we know, questioning our own certainties and through that, creating openness to risk that allows 'another way of knowing and of living in the world' and expanding 'our capacity to imagine the human'. There is a need to provide detailed information about rural development programmes/activities to women (being executed by the state/central governments and their line departments) and make them empowered through education and awareness programmes. Education needs to be encouraged as a means of empowering women from the grass root level. Educational and awareness programmes for women need to incorporate capacity building and skill developmental activities in the field of rural development and livelihood, formal decision-making processes, leadership and strategic planning skills as well as confidence building, role in decision-making in local level governance etc. Policies that support mainstream gender issues, acknowledge women's mangerial capacities in family responsibilities but also their resources and environment need to be formulated. Thus, hill women need to be involved in various programme activities that improve their capacities in addressing the issues relevant to rural development. Besides, this they also need to be involved in policy making at local, regional and national levels and given equal opportunities to participate in decision making and selection of appropriate programme/activities for rural development.

Acknowledgement

We thank all our informants, who shared valuable information and knowledge with us. We are grateful to the Director, G.B. Pant Institute of the Himalayan Environment and Development and Development, Kosi-Katarmal, Almora for facilities and TSBF/GEF/UNEP for financial support.

REFERENCES

UNEP: *Global Biodiversity Assessment*. Cambridge, Cambridge University Press, 1995.

USDoL: *Unemployment Insurance Financial Data, Employment and Training Handbook* 394. Washington, DC: Employment and Training Administration (ETA), U.S. Department of Labor (USDOL), 2008.

Anonymous: Census Data of Garhwal region of Uttar Pradesh. 1991.

Prabhakar B, Sharma SS, Singh RL: *Management plan of Kedarnath Muskdeer Sanctuary (from 2000-2001 to 2009-2010) part I and II*, Wildlife Preservation Organization. Uttar Pradesh: Forest Department, 2001.

Dhyani Shalini, Maikhuri, R.K. and Dhyani, D: "Energy budget of fodder harvesting pattern along the altitudinal gradient in the Garhwal Himalaya, India." *Biomass and Bioenergy*, 35. pp. 1823-1832. 2011.

Maikhuri RK, Nautiyal S, Rao KS, Chandrasekhar K, Gavali R, Saxena KG.: "Analysis and resolution of protected area-people conflicts in Nanda Devi Biosphere Reserve." India. *Environmental Conservation*, 27. pp. 43-53. 2000a.

Maikhuri, R.K., Rawat, L.S., Negi, V.S., Purohit, V.K., Rao, K.S. and Saxena, K.G.: "Managing natural resources through simple and appropriate technological interventions for sustainable mountain development". *Current Science*, 100(7). pp. 992-97, 2011.

Nautiyal S, Kaechele H. : "Adverse impacts of pasture abandonment in Himalayan protected areas: testing the efficiency of a Natural Resource Management Plan (NRMP)." *Environ Impact Assess Rev*; 27. pp. 109-25, 2007.

Moench M, Bandhopadhyay J. : People forest interaction? neglected parameter in Himalayan forest management. *Mountain Research and Development*; 6:3-16, 1986.

Misra Shalini: *Impact of natural and man-made disturbances on vegetation structure and diversity in Guptakashi Range of Kedarnath Forest Division, Uttarakhand* [Ph.D. thesis]. Dehradun [India]: Forest Research Institute University. 2010.

12

Role and Significance of Women Representatives in Panchayats in Garhwal Himalayas: A Case Study

— ***Prashant Kandari***

Women, of the hill areas of Uttarakhand, though, contribute a great deal in the socio-economic sector, they are still not considered equal partners in the developmental process, despite several resurrecting policy interventions by the government. The reservation of seats for women in the Panchayats is one such policy action, which have worked to change the picture slightly. However, despite the 33 percent reservation of seats, the women are still found to be working as proxy to their male relatives, husbands or guardians. The use of '*pradhan pati*' has become quite common in this context. Keeping in mind the contribution of women in the hill regions, it becomes highly important to assess the impact of women's participation in governance. The present study, carried out in micro level in Pauri district of Uttarakhand, attempts to examine the problems which the women face in the governance in the hill areas, their role in the decision-making process, contribution towards development process and efforts for their empowerment.

Rural areas of the Garhwal Himalayas, due to tough geographical and environmental conditions coupled with the very poor infrastructural facilities, present immense challenges to the people for leading a comfortable and problem free life. The lack-luster approach of the Government towards these areas helps in making the situation murkier. About 87 percent of population of Pauri Garhwal district region is residing in rural areas. This shows the largely rural nature of this district. Agriculture is the basic source of occupation for the people of the rural areas and service and entrepreneurship is the main mode of earning for the population residing in the urban areas. Majority of villages in Pauri district have still the kuccha road, with immense water and irrigation problems, poor health facilities, differentiation on the basis of caste, creed and gender, domestic violence and alcoholism. Poverty and unemployment are the other problems which add to women's problems in these areas. Ironically, women though live a life of negligence, but they also act as the major bread earners for their families. The women not only conduct their household activities, collect water, fodder, fuel and nuture the domestic animals, but also the outdoor economic activities like agriculture is also mainly carried out by women of these areas. As majority of males in these rural areas migrate to the urban areas for employment, therefore the males are rarely found engaged in the agricultural or other rural activities which forces, on the one hand, the women to take up all the work burden in these areas and on the other, the remittance sent by the migrant relatives helps to convert the economy into money order economy. On account of these problems, the women remain poor and suppressed in the rural areas.

In view of the dominant role of women in the rural economies but their poor status and lack of real empowerment, the government in 1992 enacted 73rd constitutional amendment act to empowering and involving the rural women in the local governance and developmental process by making provisions of reserving 33 percent seats for the women in all the three tiers of the Panchayat Raj Institutions. With the result, women's participation in local governments has increased quite radically. Some studies on women's parliamentary participation indicate that though women members participate more actively in 'women's issues' – health, welfare, atrocities against women, crimes like dowry and violations of human rights, but this participation is confined to the more articulate women. In issues such as the, defense, finance, politics, etc. their participation is relatively limited. (www.unescap.org/huset/"reports india" Although the states have also implemented the quota system in village water and sanitation committees under the Panchayati Raj system and allocated a small fund also for it, but women still remain marginal in the decision-making process. A range of factors, from economic status to caste and importantly patriarchy, play a role in determining women's participation in the public sphere. (www.indiawater portal.org). For successful participation of the women there is a need to enhance the capacity of women to fight elections and reduce or remove the preventive barriers. (http://www.csrindia.org) Women representatives face problems at every stage of their participation—from the Gram Sabha to Zila Parishad. 'In an Open Forum, organised by the Rural Litigation And Entitlement Kendra for 300 elected women representatives of PRIs of Uttar Pradesh, it was opined that women representatives were generally branded as 'incompetent' and forced to quit through the passing of no-confidence motions, and widespread use of corrupt practices, among the male members and local bureaucrats also discourage them from performing their functions.' (Gill, 2006) Women representatives also suffer from the weakness of lack of literacy and education, high work burden, male dominance, lack of communication skills and poor socio-economic background etc. These faetors also affect their capacity of delivering the results. (Ravi and P. Sunder Raj 2006),

Study Area and Methodology

To assess the role of rural women in Panchayats of Pauri Garhwal district, the rural areas of Pauri were selected for the study. As of 2001 Indian census, the Pauri Garhwal district has a population of 6,96,851, with a high sex ratio of 1104. The total literacy rate of Pauri district is 77.9 percent and the females' literacy rate is 65.6 percent. Its 87 percent population is residing in the rural areas and the main occupation of the rural population is agriculture. Army / para-military forces and teaching are also major sources of employment for the young people. Due to lack of required infrastructure and the geography of the area, there are no major industries in the district; however, some industrial units have been established around Kotdwara. For the study, 24 villages and 24 women Panchayat representatives were selected on the basis of judgment sampling method. Further, a sample of 55 women and 60 men, which were not the part of local governance system, were also interviewed for knowing the common people's perception about the women represntative's role and development scene. To deduct the information related to the study structured questionnaire were utilised. Observation, interaction and dialogues with the respondents were also used for collecting suitable information.

Observation and Discussion

Since Panchayati Raj system, introduced through the 73rd Constitutional Amendment Act, has emerged as the most definitive step towards re-energuising democracy in the history of independent India, by making 33 percent reservation of seats in the Panchayats for the women, compulsory. Therefore, it becomes necessary to assess the role and contribution of the empowered women. Keeping in mind, the importance of women in rural areas of Uttarakhand, the study was conducted with an aim to mainly assess the role of rural women in local governance, perception of the local community towards women's significance in the governance, problems faced by women in the local governance system and the factors influencing women's participation in governance as well as to verify the validity of the term 'Pati Pradhan' which is more often attached with the woman politicians. The aim was also to examine the various factors affecting the performance of the women in the governance process as well as to deduct the various policy actions which can lead to more effective representation and performance of women in the local governance system.

Profile of Women Engaged in Governance in Sampled Villages

Sixty-seven percent female respondents belonged to the age group of 25 to 35 years and 22 percent were above 35 years. This shows that majority of the female respondents belonged to the child bearing group and which could hamper their participation in governance activities. More so, 86 percent female respondents were married and this is also a major factor in determining the working hours of the female PRI members. Sixty-five percent of the females had joint families and majority of them came from the male dominated households and 86 percent of these households had agriculture as the main means of occupation. As far as the participation of these elected women representatives in the village Panchayats was concerned, it was found that though women have become part of these bodies on account of the reservation but increasing representation was not an indicator of their empowerment and active participation. As shown in the following table that women's participation has not automatically led to a more gendered analysis of the issues confronting local governments because women are largely brought in the governance by the family members. More soas most of the elected women representatives often act as proxies for their male relatives

Table 12.1 : Motivation Factors for Joining the Local Governance System

Motivation factors	*Percentage of Women*
Self-decision	23
Suggested by family	42
Suggested by the rural community	6
Connection with political groups	-
Connection with women groups	17
Others	12

Source: Field Survey (2009).

and guided by their advice, therefore, the concerns about women's need and interests generally remain unattended. The motivating factors for participation in the local self government, compiled in the following table, clearly suggest that majority of women are mainly pushed by the male members who are either related to politics or are interested to be a part of the local governance in direct or in indirect manner.

As 42 percent women entered these bodies, because of their male relatives, therefore, it was also found that such women elected to village councils are either not performing well or not performing at all. The cultural norms, historical bias, and unfamiliarity with local politics etc. still hold back the women from successfully serving in village councils. (http://web.worldbank.org) It was also found that the politically active male relatives mostly support their female relative's entry into politics. In the sampled population, 41 percent women respondents accepted that their male relatives were engaged in politics and they supported their entry also in the Panchayts. (Table -2)

Table 12.2: Male family members earlier/ presently engaged in politics

Category of Male Family Members	*Percentage of Female Representatives*
Engaged in politics	41
Not engaged in politics	30
Engaged in social activities	17
Engaged in social local groups	12

Source: Field Survey (2009)

The above table depicts that only 30 percent female representatives did not have any male members engaged in politics or social programmes. This clearly indicates towards the possibilities of male member's interference in the working of their family female representatives in the governance.

Rate of Women's Participation in Governance Activities

Women's participation rate in the local governance activities is also decided by their working hours which are contributed by them in performing various activities in and outside household. These activities include domestic activities

Table 12.3: Distribution of Working Hours of Women Involved in Local Governance

Family work activities	*Women involved in such activities (in Percentage)*	*Time contributed and percentage of women in such activities (in hrs)*
Indoor Household activities	100	1 to 2 hrs. 0 2 to 4 hrs. 0 4 to 6 hrs. 70% 6 to 8 hrs. 15% More than 8 hrs. 15%
Outdoor household activities	85	1 to 2 hrs. 80% 2 to 4 hrs. 20% 4 to 6 hrs. 0% 6 to 8 hrs. 0% More than 8 hrs. 0%
Family income generation activities		
Agriculture and other allied activities	75	1 to 2 hrs. 10% 2 to 4 hrs. 0% 4 to 6 hrs. 10% 6 to 8 hrs. 65% More than 8 hrs. 15%
Others	10	1 to 2 hrs. 0% 2 to 4 hrs. 30% 4 to 6 hrs. 70% 6 to 8 hrs. 0% More than 8 hrs. 0%
Services	0	

Source: Field Survey (2009).

like looking after children, fetching water, cooking, rearing cattle and farm activities. The income is mostly generated by the farm activities carried out mainly by these women. The table given below shows the distribution of working hours of women engaged in local governance system.

The following aspects came into light about the working hours of women representatives:

- Majority of all the women, actively involved in the governance, share the household and farm activities.
- Maximum percentages of women contribute around 6 to 8 hours in domestic activities.

- Majority of women contributes around 1 to 2 hours for outdoor household activities.

Ninety-five percent women are engaged in agricultural activities and 65 percent women, who are engaged in local governance, are involved in agricultural activities and contributing 6 to 8 hours in it.

This clearly suggests that women even if they are engaged in local governance are overburdened by the domestic household and income generating farm activities. The collection of water leads to extra outdoor household activities fo the women, which increases their work pressures. These activities leave very little time in their hands for the governance and rural development activities. And if they some-how find time for performing their roles in Panchayts, the half-hearted attempts just do not allow them to achieve the goals or deliver the results. The table given below shows the overall work hours these women have to contribute for the work activities other than the governance and development activities.

Majority of the women either from female headed or male headed households have to work for more than twelve hours in household and income generating activities. This reflects the amount of time that is left with these women to undertake the local governance and development activities in these hill rural areas. The lack of time often leads to both divergence and negligence or involvement of male member, mainly husbands in the governance activities on belhalf of the women (husband acting as proxy for the female member).

Table 11.4: Distribution of Overall Working Hours of Women Engaged in Local Governance

Working hours for the household and income generating activities	*Percentage of women involved in household and income generating activities*	
	In Male-headed household (MHH)	*In Female-headed household(FHH)*
0 to 1 hrs	-	-
1 to 2 hrs	-	-
2 to 4 hrs	10	-
4 to 6 hrs	10	-
6 to 8 hrs	-	-
10 to 12 hrs	30	30
More than 12 hrs	50	70

Source: Field Survey (2009)

Community Perception towards Women's Significance in Governance

For knowing the perception of the local rural community about women represntative's significance and importance in local governance system, 60 males and 55 females were interviewed from the sampled villages. As shown in the following table-5, that 74 percent respondents accepted that women have an important role in family and 63 percent accepted that they have a vital position in the society also. The majority of respondents did not have a favourable opinion about women's leadership qualities and the role in governance as only 29 percent respondents acknowledged that the women have a significant role in governance and only 32 percent said that they have a potential for leading developmental activities but on the other hand, 72 percent respondents emphasized that men are the better leaders than women in the governance sector and they have a better potential and perception about development. Though 39 percent respondents accepted that women act as proxy to the male members, but majority of respondents (61 percent) did not agree with it. But majority of the females felt that women act as a proxy to their husbands and follow their directions only.

Table 11.5: Community Perceptions towards Women's Significance in Governance

Perception of the Respondents	*No. of Males (in %)*		*No. of Females (in %)*		*Total Respondents (in %)*	
	Yes	*No*	*Yes*	*No*	*Yes*	*No*
1	2	3	4	5	6	7
Women's role important in family	62	38	85	15	74	26
Women's role important in society	68	32	58	42	63	37
Women's role important in local governance	27	73	30	70	29	71
Women have potential for leading rural development activities	22	78	41	59	32	68

1	2	3	4	5	6	7
Men are better leaders than women in governance activities	17	83	58	42	75	25
Male members act as proxies for Females members	35	65	42	68	39	61

Source: Field Survey (2009)

The above table, depicting the perception of rural community, reveals the following aspects:

- Majority of females and males from the local community consider that women have an important role in the family and society.
- For majority of the people, women's role in the local governance system is not so important.
- They also felt that women do not have a potential for leading rural development activities.
- Majority of males opined that males are better leaders than women in governance.

Community's opinion about women's role and significance in the family and the society while shows its faith but its view about women's role and leadership cabilities in the governance sector depicts the lack of confidence among the rural community towards women for caparrying their responsibilities in the governance process. This also shows the lack of gender sensitisation among the people.

Factors Influencing Women's Participation in Governance and Development Activities

The participation rate of the women engaged in the local governance system in the rural areas of Pauri Garhwal is poor and restricts their effective role in the system. The following factors influence/ reduce women's participation in the governance and development process in the rural areas.

Illiteracy

In Pauri district female literacy level is very low in comparison to male literacy. As per the 2001 census, 90 percent males were literate, while only 66 percent of females were literate in the state. Illiteracy has been the major reason not only for the poor socio-economic conditions of the women in the rural areas, but also for their exclusion from community development, low awareness about their rights, trouble in getting jobs, going to the bank or helping their children with their studies etc. The follwoing table shows the literacy status of females engaged in governance in the Pauri Garhwal district.

Table 12.6: Percentage of Literacy among Females engaged in Governance

Educational status	*Percentage of females*	*Percentage of dominant male members in the family*
Illiterates	7 (29%)	7 (22%)
Literates	17 (71%)	25 (78%)
(a) Read and write	10 (59%)	6 (24%)
(b) High School	4 (23%)	3 (12%)
(c) Intermediate	2 (12%)	8 (32%)
(d) Graduation	1 (6%)	5 (20%)
(e) Post Graduation	-	3 (12%)
Total Females	24	32

Source: Field Survey (2009).

As per the data shown in the above table, the majority of women representatives in local governance are literates but the above data also reveals that only 59 percent of these literates are capable of reading and writing. This clearly projects the strength of women representatives on the basis of education. The poor education results in the inadequate confidence level of women and also acts as a formidable stumbling block to realise their full leadership potential.

(B) PATRIARCHY AND CORRUPTION

Women are oppressed on a personal basis by the individual patriarchs who share their lives. The segregationist strategy of patriarchy excludes women from the public arena by using various structures to subordinate them. In the study, it was found that the patriarchal values, political intimidation from the opposition parties or men from the same party, vested groups, and the political and administrative system were the major obstacles in the effective participation of the elected woman members. Hostility, ridicule and insensitivity from the government functionaries were the other factors. Around 39 percent respondents accepted that males work as the proxies for the women representatives in the local governance and this clearly reveals that despite the participation of the women in governance, the dominant role was being played by their male relatives. Additionally, many women are coerced by their husbands or family members to run for election and such women simply lack interest or will to be part of the institutions. It was revealed from the study that when these women have to meet officials or elected representatives in the town, they preferred to take their family members (mainly male members) along, which makes them appear dependent on others to get their work done. As the males are better and more educated than the females, therefore, it also affects their confidence.

Table 12.7: Problems Encountered by the Female Representatives in the Governance Process

Problems encountered by the females in governance system	*Percentage of females*
Mis-guidance by male officials	46%
Mis-treatment by males	36%
Men's reluctance to share public space with women	42%
Lack of Cooperation from male Colleagues	46%
Priority given to males	40%

Source: Field Survey (2009)

The above table clearly shows that female representatives in local governance have to face alot of problems in governance process, not only from their colleagues but also from the male officials. Forty-six percent of the female representatives revealed that they are misguided by the male officials, which results in their lack of effective performance in the development activities. Majority of females opined that importance is not given to them during the official meeting and mostly either they are ignored or mistreated by the male colleagues. Their suggestions are not given due importance in any meetings, while their lack of knowledge and experience becomes the main factor for the male dominance over them. Corruption in the offices is the other factor which inhibits the working of the females in the local governance system. The huge presence of commission system in the official working process also hinders the working of the women.

(C) OTHER FACTORS

Lack of Appreciation of Women's Role in Governance

The acceptance, by a large number of women respondents that men are better leaders than women, makes it clear that unless the local community, particularly the women extend support to the women representatives and respect the women at leadership positions, the effective representation of the women in the local self governance canot be assured.

Poverty

Poverty is the other constraining factor that results in poor and inactive participation of the women in the local governance. Twenty-eight percent of the women from the local rural community accepted that poverty is the major obstacle for the women representatives in the local governance in the rural areas, as it restricts their active participation in the governance.

Poor Family Support

As majority of women are contributing almost half a day for the household and income generating activities, which leaves them with very less time for governance related activities. The poor family support also prohibits their active participation in the governance.

Lack of Confidence

The lack of confidence and hesitation among the women, mainly in public speaking, in sharing their ideas and in asking questions, also inhibits their role in the governance.

Besides these, the respondents also confirmed that lack of transport facilities/assistance in the rural areas also hamperes their activeness. Forty-six percent women respondents accepted that due to lack of adequate transport facilities they often fail to regularly visit the district offices for various purposes. A large number of respondents accused the officials and the males that instead of serving them with adequate information, they misguide them to an extent that their work gets largely affected. Lack of economic independence also affects their freedom of action and decision.

Positive Aspect of Women's Participation in Local Governance

However, despite the constraints, it was found that women at the Panchayat level also take an active part in social programmes, such as, mass literacy drives, pulse polio administration and midday meal schemes, and they even visit buildings for electricity meter reading. The issues, in which women representatives generally take interest, involve drinking water supply, primary health, child care, public distribution system and environmental protection. They show patience to hear the problems of the public and capacity to work in adverse circumstances. It has been observed in various studies that women representatives are honest and accurate in presenting issues to the decision-making bodies and authorities and they bring new ideas in local governance. They believe in a sustainable development and protection of the natural resources management. Women representatives working at the grass-root level also believe that communal harmony is an important element of development and they strive to achieve this objective and they also do not indulge in corrupt practices. (Sree Kumar , 2006) Women are considered an extremely pivotal point in the process of change in the rural areas and their participation, a most effective instrument in bringing about a change in their way of life in terms of economic well-being and adoption of new technology. (Rajeshwari, 1996) Women leaders in the Panchayati Raj are transforming local governance by sensitising the State to the issues of poverty, inequality and gender injustice. Through the PRI, they are tackling issues that had previously gone virtually unacknowledged, including water, alcohol abuse, education, health and domestic violence. The enormous expansion of women's representation in decentralised government structures has highlighted the advantages of proximity, and the ability to mobilise struggle at a local level, where it is most meaningful. Thus women are helping to radicalise local government. Large women participation in governance has led to increase in the women's awareness about their basic rights. Women participation has the potential of reducing the commission tendency in the Indian official working system.

Policy Prescriptions and Suggestions for More Productive Role of the Women in Governance

The following suggestions could be helpful in improving women's role in the governance.

On Women's Level

It is women who can inspire confidence and offer stimulus for social change, especially, among other the women in the rural areas. Hence, effective leadership among women must come from the women themselves. The women should accept the importance of women in the leadership positions and promote the women in such activities.

Community awareness programmes should be undertaken by the local social groups for this purpose. Women leaders should conduct regular meetings with the local women to discuss their problems and to evolve suggestions and new ideas from them. The women leaders should take the help of Mahila Mangal Dals (rural women councils) for conducting such meetings, while recognising their importance.

On the Government Level

The active participation of the women can be achieved through training, awareness and information. Hence, the government should recognise the importance of imparting training to the newly appointed women in the governance. Mahila Mandals could be activated for this purpose where women could learn skills. The government (Ministry of Women and Child Development) should take the responsibility to make the rural women aware about their rights and responsibilities. Government should further ensure that the women are not marginalised in the revenue and expenditure committee structures. For that Links have to be strengthened between the village and the bureaucracy at the lower level. Further, the lack of confidence arising out of poor communication skills and fear of public speaking should be dealt in the training sessions. Training is one of the most important venues for a newly elected women representative to become comfortable with their new position. Trainings give women a chance to ask questions, acquire new information, make networking connections, and learn how to speak in public and assert themselves. Leadership training should be given to these women for strengthening the identity and feminist consciousness of women representatives.

Capacity building training should be given to the women to make them believe their worth and to be independent. Women MLAs and MPS from the constituencies should visit the villages and interact with these women at all forums. This will not only serve as a confidence building measure for the rural women, but also serve as a medium to push their demands to the higher level for effective and quick action. Further, campaigns and training programmes to prepare the women both as electors and elected should be carried out with the help of NGO's and other local social activist groups. The government should further facilitate their meetings across the districts, offering women representatives forum to discuss issues and ideas among themselves.

On the Level of Other Actors (NGO's, Bureaucrats, etc.)

Finally, as society is made up of many entities, the role of other actors like non-government, bureaucrats, and social activist groups should not be ignored. Gender sensitisation is not only needed for men in the villages, but also for the bureaucrats who interact with women representatives. Bureaucrats, while interacting with females, should not treat women indifferently and help them by giving them adequate and timely information. Non-governmental organisation should also play a role by spreading awareness, training the women to build their confidence and leadership abilities through various capacity building programmes.

Women leaders in the Panchayati Raj are transforming the local governance by sensitising the state to issues of water scarcity, alcohol abuse, poor education, health, domestic violence, poverty, inequality, gender injustice etc. The need of the hour is to encourage and strengthen these women more towards leadership which would go a long way to not only their real empowerment but will also help in delimiting the corruption in the development of the rural areas in an effective way.

REFERENCES

www.unescap.org/huset/**HYPERLINK "http://www.unescap.org/huset/women/reports/india"**

www.indiawaterportal.org

http://www.csrindia.org

http://web.worldbank.org

Gill Rajesh:"Empowering Women Through Panchayats". In *Man and Development*, Vol. XXVIII, No. 4, Chandigarh: CRRID, 2006.

Ravi Venkata R.R. and P. Sunder Raj: "Decentralisation and Development in India". In *Man and Development*, Vol. XXVIII, No. 4, Chandigarh: CRRID, 2006.

Sree Kumar S.S.: "Representation of Women in Legislature: A Sociological Perspective in the Indian Context". In *Indian Journal of Political Science*, Vol. LXVII, No. 3, Meerut: Indian Political Science Association.2006.

Rajeshwari A.: *PRIs and Women, in G. Palanithurai (ed.) Empowering People—Issues and Solutions,* New Delhi: Kanishka, 1996.

Giriappa S. : *Role of Women in Rural Development*, Daya Publishing House, Delhi, 1988.

Mahipal: "Empowering Women through Panchayati Raj Institution". *Kurukshetra*, Journal of Ministry of Rural Areas and Employment, Government of India, New Delhi. 1994.

Purushothaman, Sangeetha.: *The Empowerment of Women in India: Grassroots Women's Networks and the State.* Sage Publications, New Delhi. 1998.

13

Decentralised Governance, Empowerment of Women and Village Development—The Road Ahead

— ***R.R. Nautiyal*** and ***R. Datta***

The whole idea of decentralised governance is based upon some key factors like people's participation, accountability, transparency and fiscal transfers (Braun and Grote 2002; Tanzi 2001; Crook and Manor 1998; Litvack et. al. 1998). These are interlinked and their effects on development cannot be measured in simple equations. A number of studies find that female participation in legislative processes can help overcome gender bias, as female legislatures may be more likely to support policies in favour of family issues and women's rights (Paxton and Hughes 2007, Reingold 1992). Another way, through which participation in decision-making can affect outcomes, is by allowing greater participation so that results of political processes will reflect the median of all eligible voters rather than only those who had traditionally participated in the political process. Such participation can also improve outcomes by increasing the pool of talent which the system can draw upon (Franceschet et al, 2009).

The critique of decentralisation is valid in those regions of the world, where poverty and a dysfunctional democracy are rampant for various reasons. A large part of literature talks about issues of quality of citizens' participation and broader questions of democratic control. The critical democratic theorists have noted that the predominant mode of social organisations is not a vertical relationship of authority between selfish individuals and the supra state, but a series of horizontal associations embodying groups of individuals, who are capable of regulating and expressing themselves as members of a community, rather than as self-promoting individuals (Roy Chowdhury, 1996).

Decentralised governance has been effective in some parts of the world, where people are active, vigilant, and participative. In such societies, civil society groups assume far greater roles in educating people and, ultimately, people themselves seek greater accountability (fairness) from the elected members and officials in meeting their immediate needs. On similar lines, the theory of social capital has been receiving increasing attention and it has begun to generate a remarkable consensus, regarding the role and importance of communities and local organisations in making decentralised governance effective (Marjit 1999; Slater and Watson 1993). Matching with the global trend, developing countries often initiate decentralised governance to promote development and India is not an exception to this trend. India has been experimenting with the decentralised governance process for quite some time. The block as a center of Community Development (CD) came into existence throughout the country in 1952. However, as per recommendation of Balwant Rai Mehta Committee 1959, CD was replaced by the Panchayati Raj Institutions (PRIs) to ensure people's involvement in development programmes.

The broad framework for decentralised governance was laid down in India under the provision of the 73rd Constitution Amendment Act with the objective of achieving faster social and economic development. This has ushered in a greater degree of uniformity in the structure (three-tier), composition (reservation for SC, ST and women), powers and functions (financial and planning) of these institutions. The three-tier structures of the PRIs are Zilla Panchayat at the district level, Taluk Panchayat at the intermediate levels and Gram Panchayat at the village level. The 73rd Amendment Act has given an impetus to panchayats for promoting development in terms of infrastructure, education, and health and poverty alleviation in rural India.

However, the experiences of panchayats in different states in India reveal that this Act is yet to be implemented successfully in all the states (Bardhan et al 2005;Verma 2002; Upadhyay 2002; Pal 2002; Palanithurai 1994). Studies suggest that reservations which intend to empower the women remain ineffective as the women are poorly educated and easily manipulated by traditional elites that dominate politics and are unlikely to give up power. This means that the elected female may just be a front for a powerful husband or family members who pulls the strings behind the scenes (Rajaram and Gupta, 2008). The power devolved to the panchayats with women pradhans over plans and implementation of various development programmes appears not to have been utilised fully. In this paper an attempt has been made to examine the experience of such panchayats through a case study conducted in the Kirtinagar block of Tehri district of Uttarakhand with particular reference to the Mahatma Gandhi National Rural Employment Guarantee Act (MGNREGA), the largest single rights-based social protection initiatives in the world. We have tried to find out whether decentralised governance has helped in promoting efficiency in such poverty alleviation and employment generation programmes. Has it helped in looking after the interest of women? Has decentralisation helped in increasing professionalism among the village women? How far such programmes under the decentralised regime have affected the lives of rural women through village development or how far the village women really contribute to village development? We have attempted to answer such questions through the case study.

This paper has been divided into seven broad sections. Subsequent to the introduction in section I, section II discusses the problem and the rationale of the study. Section III describes the methodology and limitations while section IV gives an idea about the study area and the women population. Section V discusses the main findings of the study followed by discussion and conclusion in section VI and suggestions in section VII.

The Problem and the Rationale

The issue of participation in the PRIS is primarily associated with the grassroot people, including poor and weaker sections (caste-wise, gender-wise or area-wise), not only because they are the most disadvantaged within the society, but also because the rural areas in contrast to urban areas have been relatively ignored by various development strategies. This philosophy of a 'people based' development 'from below' assumes that participation is not only an end in itself but also an elementary condition and a tool of decentralised governance and successful development. Sharma (2000) observes that the failure of past development strategy is fundamentally linked to absence of decentralised governance and people's participation. Actually, people's participation has become the heart of good governance for a number of reasons. First, it is a means of obtaining information about local conditions, needs and attitudes without which development could fail. Secondly, people's participation in planning and implementation not only portray people's commitment but also identify with it and see it as their own project. The contribution and assistance of the people in the construction and maintenance of the project is not only a guarantee of success but it also exhibits people's power. It is the only mechanism by which the people can express, protect and promote their interests. It is assumed that they are always looking out for opportunities for participation to protect their individual and collective interests.

Article 40 of the Indian Constitution says that, *the State shall take steps to organise village panchayats and endow them with such powers and authority as may be necessary to enable them to function as units of self-government.* Individual opinions and their voices can affect the game of policy-makers, if they are allocated to participate in the political and decision-making process. A recent study (Feininger, et al, 2010) observes that female reservation has a very positive effect on their overall willingness to make contribution to public goods. With the enactment of 73rd Amendment Act in 1992, a new system of decentralised governance was brought into being. This institutional arrangement promised an alternative to the hitherto followed bureaucratic mechanism of local self governance which in place of strengthening the PRIs in true spirit, depended on the initiation of other various programmes without making the PRIs effective in the real sense. Several parallel programmes were running and being directly funded by union/state governments and monitored by state government officials. These actions undermined the role of PRIs and their effective presence in the development. Therefore, a dilemma of decentralised governance with the nature of political process, local organisations and their temperament towards development emerged and continued. This paper in particular analyses this dilemma with particular reference to the rural women in the decentralised governance process in the villages of Uttarakhand. Since Uttarakhand is a state with very high male outward migration with the result an increased work load of the women forces them to lead a very hard life. Therefore, it becomes necessary to understand how decentralisation has helped empowerment of the rural women and to what extent it is helping in village development through a case study of MGNREGA.

Methodology

To understand the experiences of the panchayats in the study area as well as the experiences of the women within the panchayats, two schedules were prepared- one for the women pradhans and the other for the women of the villages working under the MGNREGA. For this purpose four Gram Panchayats having women Pradhans were selected through purposive sampling. Within each Gram Panchayat, all the revenue villages were chosen in the sample. From each village, on the basis of random sampling women and also job card holders under MGNREGA were chosen from all group population. The villages where population was less than 25 female, an attempt was made to cover almost all the samples. The total sample of women workers under MNREGA in the study was 120. In most of the villages, workers were interviewed at the worksite except in two villages where interviews were conducted at the households.

Tehri district was chosen for the study for three reasons: (1) it is one of the districts in Uttarakhand where MNREGA was implemented in the first phase [Chamoli and Champawat being the other two districts]. (2) MNREGA data of Uttarakhand reveals that expenditure on MNREGA is the highest in the district (www.nrega.nic.in) (3) unemployment is comparatively high in the district. In order to concise the study, the Kirtinagar block of Tehri district was chosen and the Gram Panchayats chosen included Maletha, Jialgarh, Naithana and Ranihat consisting of villages Maletha, Semwalgoan and Ringolgoan in Maletha Gram Panchayat, Choparya, Jialgarh and Chham in Jialgarh Gram Panchayat, Naithana in Naithana Gram Panchayat and Ranihat in Ranihat Gram Panchayat. Thus a total number of 08 villages were taken for this study. The secondary data was collected from the Block Development Officer's (BDO) office of Kirtinagar block as well as from the website of MGNREGA (www. nrega.nic.in). The main objectives of the study were:

(i) To understand how far decentralisation has helped in women empowerment in the study area.

(ii) To evaluate the bottlenecks of implementation of the programme by the women Pradhans.

(iii) To assess the advantages as well as the disadvantages of the scheme by the women beneficiaries.

(iv) To investigate the contribution of women's participation in village development through the decentralised practice.

Profile of the Study Area and Position of Women:

Kirtinagar block has an area of 54635 hectres with a total population of 44860, according to the 2001 census. Women population in the block is 23762 against the male population of 21098. There are total 9371 households in the block. Out of total 82 Gram Sabhas, 44 Gram sabhas have Women Pradhan and out of 82,41 Gram Sabhas had reserved seats for women.

However the data shows that at least in 3 Gram Sabhas women were elected as Pradhans on non reserved seats which is a positive sign for women empowerment.

Table 13.1: Administrative Profile of the Kirtinagar Block

Area	54635 Hectre
Total Population	44860(2001 census)
Total no. of households	9371
Total Male Population	21098
Total Women Population	23762
No of woman *Pradhans* in the block	44
No of woman *Pradhans (where the seat was not reserved for a female candidate)*	3
Nyaya Panchayats	08
No. of Gram Sabhas	82
No. of villages(*Rajaswa Gram*)	154

Source: Block Development Office, Kirtinagar

Table 13.2: A profile of the sample Gram Sabhas

Panchayat		Maletha			Zialgarh		Naithana	Ranihat
No. of Revenue villages		3			3		1	1
Names of the villages	Rangoli goan	Semwal goan	Male-tha	Chham	Jial-garh	Chop-arya	Nait-hana	Rani-hat
Total Households	5	7	2006	3	56	26	231	73
Total Population	14	21	1191	13	272	119	1158	311
Female population	9 (64.2)	13 (61.9)	612 (51.38)	5 (38.46)	147 (54.0)	60 (50.42)	570 (49.22)	163 (52.41)
Female Literacy rate (percent)	50.0	50.0	45.4	50.0	46.4	34.9	44.94	43.25
Total job cards issued		219			91		295	81
Job cards issued in the name of a woman		125			50		168	50
Total man-days generated (2009-10)		678			2109		666	370
Mandays generated by women		370 (54.57)			1023 (48.5)		442 (66.36)	240 (64.86)

Figures in parenthesis represent the percentages.

Source: Compiled from the data obtained from Kirtinagar block office and www.nrega.nic.in

Table 2 gives the profile of the sampled Gram Sabhas and villages. Gram Sabha Maletha has three revenue villages with a population of 14 in Ringoligoan, 21 in Semwalgoan and 1191 in Maletha. In Ringoligoan female population is 64.2 percent and women literacy rate is 50 percent. In Semwalgoan total population is 21 with 62 percent women population and literacy of women is 50 percent. Maletha has a total population of 1191 with female population of 51.38 percent and female literacy rate of 45.4 percent. Under the Jialgarh Gram Sabha, there are three revenue villages, namely, Jialgarh, Choparya and Chham. In Jialgarh female population is 54 percent and female literacy is 46.4 percent. Chham has a female population of 38.46 percent with female literacy of 50 percent. Choparya has a female population of 50.42 percent with female literacy 34.9 percent. The other two Gram Sabhas, Ranihat and Naithana have 01 revenue villages each. The female population of Naithana is 49.2 percent with female literacy of 44.9 percent while Ranihat has a female population of 52.4 percent and literacy rate of 43.25 percent.

The figures of number of job cards issued in the name of a female against total job cards issued in each Gram Sabha show that more than 50 percent job cards have been issued in the name of females in all the sample villages [57.07 percent in Maletha, 54.94 percent in Jialgarh, 56.94 percent in Naithana and 61.72 percent in Ranihat]. Moreover, the

Table 13.3: A profile of the Pradhans in the sample Gram Sabhas

	Maletha	*Jialgarh*	*Naithana*	*Ranihat*
Pradhan's name	Sita Devi	Km. Lata	Rekha Devi	Km. Seema
Age	35	25	38	26
Educational qualification	8th	MA,B.Ed	High School	MA
Works carried out in the GS so far	Flood retention walls, Land development, a Panchayat room is in progress	Flood retention walls, Land development, Irrigation canals, Village common bathrooms, A SHG named 'Durgadevi' was formed	Flood retention walls, Land development	Flood retention walls, land development, plantation programmes.

Source: Primary data collected from the Pradhans.

figures of the mandays generated by women against total mandays generated show that in Maletha 54.57 percent mandays have been generated by women, in Jialgarh 48.5 percent, in Naithana 66.36 and in Ranihat 64.8 percent. The percentage of mandays generated by women shows that in all the Gram Sabhas, it is more than 50 percent except Jialgarh. This is an encouraging figure for the contribution of women in village developmental and economic activity.

Table 13.3 gives a brief profile of the Pradhans showing their age, educational qualification and the works carried out in their Gram Sabha for village development during their tenure so far. One point is clear from the table that along with less educated, middle aged women; the young educated female Pradhans are also joining the educated and young women in the process which is encouraging for women empowerment. During the interview, it was found that the young educated women Pradhans and/or Upa Pradhans possessed all the information regarding the villages under their aegis in their fingertips. However, the middle aged, less educated pradhans were being promoted by their family members (husbands in most cases) and were mostly working on behalf of them.

Working of the Programme and the Main Findings of the Study

Before the issues are discussed, it is important to under-stand how the programme works under the decentralised system.

Village panchayats are not the only nodal implementing bodies for the MGNREGA, but they also plan, design and execute the works to be taken up, under this scheme. It makes the act participatory and empowers people at the grassroot level. A perspective plan is prepared for each district indicating the works to be undertaken under the programme. The listing is done in the 'muster rolls' . A "muster roll" is essentially a labour attendance register, pertaining to a particular worksite and a particular period (e.g. two weeks). It is also used as a receipt, to claim funds from the Programme Officer for the payment of wages. Typically, the completion of a particular work would involve several muster rolls. Thus, if a worksite has 50 labourers and lasts six weeks, 9 muster rolls would be involved. The village-level information on the missing infrastructure, its costs and the employment generated is compiled in the block level plan; the block-wise information is compiled in the district plan. Based on these plans, a district perspective plan is formulated, which presents on yearly basis, the works and employment to be generated at the district level.

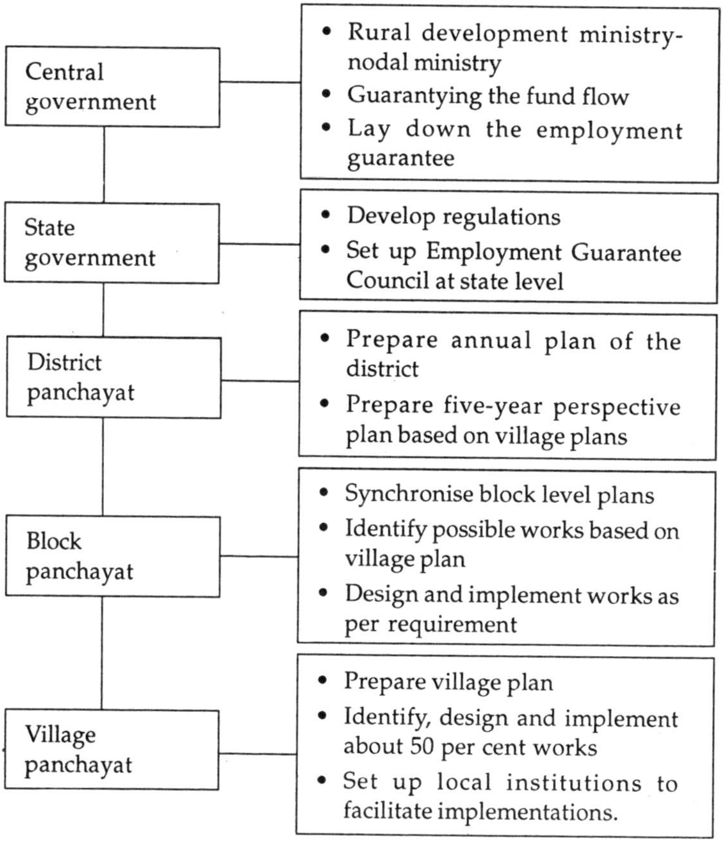

Source: Compiled by the researchers.

Fig. 13.1: Flowchart showing how the decentralised process works in implementing such schemes as MGNREGA.

NREGA was not designed to be led by government officials, because lessons learnt from the outcomes of the previous schemes called for the necessity of designing and implementing developmental programmes in the villages on the basis of their needs and labour. Under this scheme the village has to make a development plan and the projects have to be cleared by the Gram Sabha and implemented by the Panchayat. It is a better way of decentralisation and empowerment of the people.

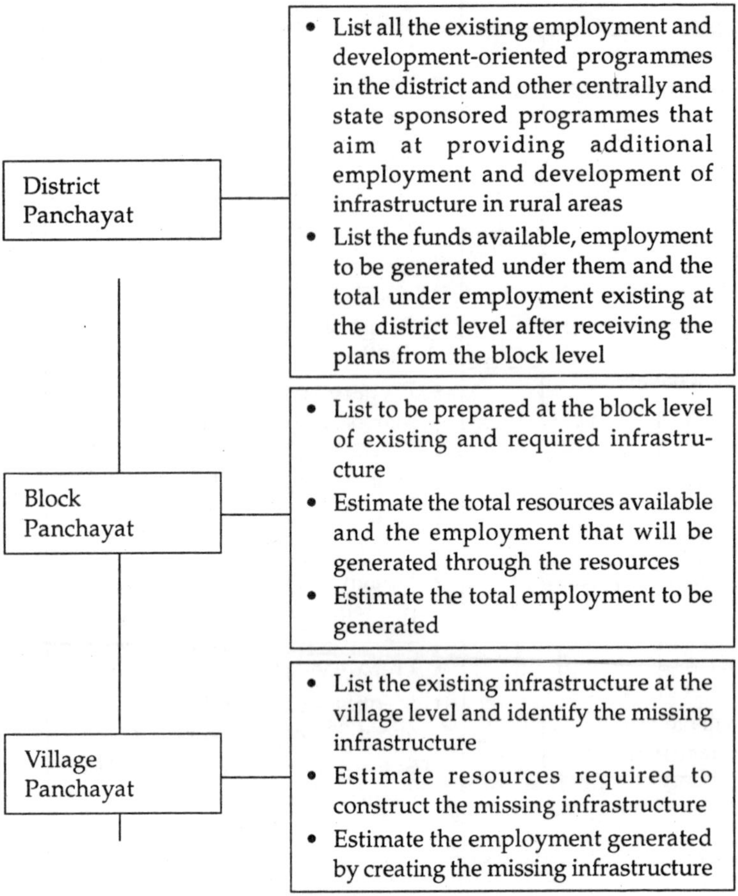

Source: Compiled by the researchers.

Fig. 13.2: Flowchart showing how the perspective plan is prepared.

The main findings from the primary data collected through the structured interview schedules are summed up below.

The Pradhans and the Upa Pradhans informed that decentralisation as well as women reservation has helped them to become part of the village development process. Awareness has increased and women who never used to have a say in the administrative process of the village, now feel free and empowered to share their opinions. MNREGA, besides providing a source of their income, have also allowed them to become a part of the decision-making process of the family. Their opinion is valued in the family expenditure and education of their children. The women also accepted that they would like to work for promoting education for the female child and stopping discrimination against them. With growing awareness, the female members are also coming forward to protest against the injustice against them or any other women in the village. However, they opined that they also feel more secure if the Pradhan is a female. But, on the other hand, almost all the Pradhans and/ Upa Pradhans revealed that they face problems in management and monitoring within their GS and they are often threatened about their tenure in the position, if they are strict to other women of the village. This also creates problem within the family as well as among the households of the village. With particular reference to MGNREGA, it came to the light that since the scheme was for every individual who was an unpaid labour, quite often the women from well-to-do families also apply for the job but show their unwillingness to work on the worksite. This creates problem of measurement in the worksite and more over many women have a misconception that the Pradhan has the power to give jobs for more than 100 days under the MGNREGA scheme, which also acts as a hindrance and increases acrimony. Another problem faced at the worksite is regarding the working hours. As it is not possible for the Pradhan to monitor the work continuously, therefore, in the absence of continuous monitoring, the women workers in the worksite often could be found sitting and gossiping. All women Pradhans were of the opinion that strong monitoring by Government officials, from the block as well as district level, is also required for improving the situation.

From the analysis of the second schedule prepared to assess the profile of the beneficiaries, it was found that the age of women workers varied from 18-75 years. The highest numbers of workers belonged to the age group 25-35 followed by above 60 age group. The women of both the age groups faced difficulties as the first category had less mobility, due to small children and family responsibilities. And the second group, because of age barriers, could not work elsewhere and also were less mobile. Eighty-seven per cent of the sample belonged to the general category in terms of caste, and their average family income varied from Rs.800 per month to Rs 25,000 per month, Eighty-two per cent of the labours in the sample accepted that they got 100 days of job in a year since NREGA was implemented. The other 18 per cent, who did not get job for 100 days, informed that since the worksite was not at the vicinity of their house, therefore, they did not get the job. The wage rate offered to them was Rs. 100 for unskilled workers and Rs. 160 for semi skilled workers. But unfortunately no women worker was treated as a semi skilled worker in these villages. Hundred per cent of the workers under MNREGA in the sample opined that they feel free to communicate their problems through a woman Pradhan/Upa Pradhan, rather than the male Pradhan or Upapradhan . They even suggested that if the Pradhan is male, then the Upa Pradhans seat should at least go to a female candidate.

Since male outward migration is a main problem in the villages, therefore, 87 per cent of the sample felt that if some employment could be generated through village development schemes (like cottage industries) the migration could be controlled to some extent. Seven per cent people felt that male migration has not affected their life too much, as the workload of a woman in a family will not reduce even if the male member is present at home. The other 6 per cent did not have a very strong opinion about the issue of migration and their hard life. Since in most cases semi-skilled labour (*Mistri*) is a 'male domain', therefore in the absence of such worker in the village, a male semi-skilled labour (mason) is hired from outside the village at a higher 'wage rate' which they have to adjust as it cannot be mentioned in the accounts. Eighty-three per cent of the labours informed that they work for maximum 5 hours while the others told that it varies between 6-7 hours. Seventy-seven per cent beneficiaries of the MGNREGA, however, admitted that if the maximum number of days of work could be increased, it would help in improving their standard of living. However, 23 per cent people opined that if the MGNREGA issues separate job cards to every adult woman in the village, it could boost women empowerment. Women also observed that many of the male members work in the scheme just to have money to buy 'liquor' for themselves. However, 86 per cent women admitted that the income from MGNREGA has helped them in improving their living conditions and they also try to make some savings out of it; because they do not spend money on liquor or make other wasteful expenses like their male family members. The women, however, had no complaints against regular wage payments.

As far as their contribution in village development is concerned, 27 per cent women felt that it has largely contributed to the development, 56 per cent felt that it has helped to some extent while 17 per cent felt that it has not really contributed towards village development, because the priorities of the villages have been different. The respondents also informed that a new project initiated recently under MGNREGA is to grow the 'NAPIER' [the grass that re-grows within almost 7 days] grass was good as it will help in solving the problem of fodder for the cattle and make women's life somewhat easy by reducing their drudgery of collecting fodder from forest. Only 5 per cent workers felt that there has been some value addition in their skills as they could learn some major techniques of construction while working on the sites. The other 95 per cent felt that there has not been any difference. The grievance redressal mechanism against the allocation of work was not found to be very strong in the villages, due to lack of proper awareness, education and mobility. Actually, the study suggests that due to such types of inherent problems, the decentralised governance has reduced professionalism and promoted personalism. It also highlights that majority of the women felt that MNREGA has made a positive effect in their life, perception and attitude. However, the women preferred a woman Pradhan for ensuring betterment in their socio-political conditions.

Discusson and Conclusion

Our study shows that there is a huge potential of unskilled women labour force in Uttarakhand villages. If the labour force can be channelised in a proper manner through proper skill development, it can be a good source for the development of the region. However, the priorities for development have to be region specific. The list of priorities of the MNREGA ranks rural connectivity as the eighth priority, but from the survey, it was observed that rural connectivity was a prime demand of the villagers in the hilly district. Therefore, the provision in MNREGA to carry out the plans, as per the order of priorities, seems to be unjustified. For achieving the desired goal for village development, the order in the priority list becomes a barrier as there are economic, social, geographical as well as climatic variations across the regions. The prime requirement of a district like Haridwar and that of Champawat or Chamoli may not match in view of their different geo-physical set up. Therefore, a decentralised approach with more of 'bottom up' planning and participatory approach is the need of the hour to make such schemes successful as the people of the area are the best judge to assess and identify their priorities and plans that can sustain in the long run. Women of Uttarakhand villages have a major role to play in such planning process as they are the real residents of the villages, because in most of the villages male outward migration is very high. Therefore, their views need to be given importance to understand the pros and cons of any project for village development.

It was observed from the study that personal relations had overpowered professionalism in many casesas the personal relationship mattered more than the professional status to the village Pradhan / Upa Pradhan. A major problem for development in MGNREGA scheme was the lack of continuous monitoring at all levels for fruitful results. It was also observed that the work carried under MNREGA like construction of the flood retention walls were without cementing. Therefore, the walls were weak in nature to sustain the 'acute natural disasters'. Along with planning at the village level, it was felt that more freedom is needed at the district level and block level to generate actual priorities for region specific village development with proper technical expertise. The Pradhan and the Upa Pradhan should represent the demand of the villages in such cases. A lack of belongingness, towards the government sponsored schemes, was also witnessed which indicated towards the perception that the government was bound to allocate funds under the scheme whether work is done or not. This attitude of the beneficiaries allows raising a very pertinent question at this juncture; whether the scheme will be a burden for the national exchequer in the near future? However, one good information that came out of the study was whatever decision is taken in the gram sabha meeting or at the GP level was implemented (though not in the stipulated time frame in most cases). It indicates towards some achievement of the decentralised planning and also village development.

Suggestions

The level of awareness and the right kind of perceptions about the decentralised governance and participation of the people are essential for achieving better development. Therefore, the study revealed that there was a good relationship between awareness, perception and participation. Without this, the village development or decentralisation could not be achieved. In this study the level of awareness and perception of females was found to be encouraging. But it also came to light that some information were not given to them intentionally, to minimise the complexities of official work. More awareness among the rural women needs to be developed so that they may be really conscious and responsive to their rights and duties. For this, the study showed that literacy level of women can help in boosting up such awareness. Gram Panchayat and Gram Sabha meetings were the prime mechanisms of obtaining inputs for planning and implementation. Therefore, meetings at regular intervals and unbiased decisions regarding village development is of prime importance for a successful planning process.

Accountability and transparency are also viewed as the most important pillars of the decentralised governance as these ensure the successful delivery of the services at the grassroot level. The officials of the GP and the employees are answerable to the elected members. This is a necessary condition for democratic institution and their smooth functioning like planning, monitoring and evaluating public services. In view of this, more powers to the Pradhans with proper accountability and transparency are required. Thus awareness needs to be generated among the people about decentralized governance by frequent training programmes. The Pradhans must also be trained for effective and efficient management by the concerned government authorities.

Many safeguards for transparency and accountability are built into the MNREGA Act, and also in the MNREGA Guidelines. For instance, the MNREGA Guidelines require 'muster rolls' to be available at the worksites, displayed at the Panchayat Bhawan, and submitted to the Gram Sabhas, but unfortunately these are not made so transparent in most of the Gram Sabhas. If this could be really done, it could go a long way in preventing corruption in wage payments. However, public vigilance is required to ensure that these and other transparency provisions are implemented. And since women of the villages are the majority in the workforce of MNREGA in Uttarakhand, their awareness, attitude and understanding counts a lot for the successful implementation of any project. However, despite the loopholes and shortcomings, our study suggests that decentralised governance is helpful in women empowerment as well as village development; because, it helps in attaining efficiency in the face of different local preferences for local public goods (women who had to walk miles to bring water, now have some sources of water in the vicinity of their house; women, who had to collect fodder from forest, have options through growing grasses like NAPIER in the village. It also promotes good governance, people's participation and women empowerment as women can now also voice their concerns. Our data on mandays generated reveal that though male population is higher in all villages but mandays generated by women is more. This shows the contribution of women in village development as well as their empowerment. It has also helped the growth of social organisations within the village, such as, groups and network which promotes coordination and cooperation among people, local officials and office bearers.

Thus, this study throws light on the fact that decentralised governance is effective in providing better community services as well in promoting social and economic development. It has helped in empowering village women but the awareness and attitude of the masses about government scheme affects the end results. The feeling that *'sarkar ka paisa hai, tum thori na apne jeb se de rahe hon'*, needs to be changed for better results. A sense of belongingness needs to be created for the village, the block as well as higher level of administration. It is, therefore, the need of the hour that the state should initiate pro-active steps to create such an environment for promotion of social capital by extending not only financial support but moral support also. The different organisations like NGOs, SHGs should also be made partners with panchayats for better governance and women empowerment and participation at local levels.

REFERENCES

Bardhan, P and Mookherjee, D: "Pro-poor Targeting and Accountability of Local Governments in West Bengal," *Journal of Development Economics.* http://people.bu.edu/dilipm/wkpap/wbtarg1105.pdf. 2004

Bardhan, P and Mookherjee, D and Parra Torrado, M: "Impact of Panchayat Pradhan Reservation on Targeting in West Bengal." *Working Paper,* Boston University. http://people.bu.edu/dilipm/wkpap/wbtreserv.pdf. 2005.

Braun, Foachim Von and Ulrike Grote:, "Does Decentralisation Serve the Poor." In Ahmed Ehtisham and Vito Tanzi (eds.), *Managing Fiscal Decentralisation,* London: Routledge. 2002.

Chandrashekhar, S. : "Willingness to contribute to public projects - evidence from India." *Working Paper. Mumbai: Indira Ghandi Institute of Development Research.* 2008.

Cohen, John and Norman T. Uphoff.: "Participation's Place in Rural Development: Seeking Clarity Through Specificity." *World Development.* 8 (3): pp. 213-35, 1980.

Crook Richard C and James Manor: *Democracy and Decentralisation in South Asia and West Africa.* London: Cambridge University Press 1998.

Feininger K, Jin S, Nagarajan H.K: "*Can Political Reservation Improve Female Empowerment? Evidence from Local Panchayat Elections in Rural India.*" available at www.rural gov-ncaer.org. 2010

Franceschet, S., M. L. Krook, and J. M. Piscopo: "The Impact of Gender Quotas: A Research Agenda." *MPSA Conference Paper*. Chicago: Midwest Political Science Association National Conference. 2009.

Lieten, G K. : *Development Devolution and Democracy. Village Discourse in West Bengal.* New Delhi: Sage Publications. 1996.

Litvack, Jennie, Junaid Ahmed, & Richard Bird: *Rethinking Decentralisation in Developing Countries.* Washington, DC: The World Bank. 1998.

Marjit, Sugata: "Decentralised Financing, Governance and Public - Private Cooperation." *Economic and Political Weekly,* XXXIV (20): pp. 1197-1201, 1999.

Mathew, George: "Panchayati Raj Institutions and Human Rights in India." *Economic and Political Weekly.* XXXVIII (2) : pp. 155-62. 2003.

Oakly Peter and David Marsden: *Approaches to participation in rural development.* Geneva: International Labour Office,1984.

Pal, Mahi : "Empowerment at Grassroots. *Economic and Political Weekly.*" XXXVII (38): pp. 3923-24. 2002.

Pal, Mahi: "Women in Panchayat Experiences of a Training camp." *Economic and PolitIcal Weekly*, XXXIII (4): pp. 150-52. 1998.

Palanithurai, G: *Capacity BuildIng for Local Leaders*, New Delhi: Concept Publishing Company, 2001.

Paxton, P. and M. M. Hughes: *Women, Politics, and Power: A Global Perspective.* Los Angeles: Pine Forge Press. 2007.

Rajaraman, I. and M. Gupta: "*Further Evidence on the Policy Impact of Randomised Political Reservation.*" New Delhi: National Institute of Public Finance and Policy. 2008.

Roy Chowdhury, Supriya: *Rethinking Co-Operation: Towards A Non-Essentialist*, 1996.

Conception, National. *Seminar On Rediscovering Co-Operation.* Institute of Rural Management Anand (November): pp. 1-10.

Reingold, B: "Concepts of Representation among Female and Male State Legislators." *Legislative Studies Quarterly* 17 (4): pp. 509-37. 1992.

Sen, A.: *Lead Article, Panchayati Raj Update.* Institute of Social Sciences, 60 (December): pp. 1-2, 1998.

Sharma, Keshav: "Popular Participation for Good Governance and Development at the local level: The case of Botswana." *Regional Development Dialogue*, 21 (1): pp. 176-91, 2000.

Slater, R.P. and J.R. Watson: "Decentralised Planning and the Anti-Poverty Programmes. Some Possible New Direction. In Hooja, Rakesh and B. Yerram Raju (eds.) *Decentrallsed Planning in Multilevel Framework.* New Delhi: Rawat Publications. 1993.

Tanzi, Vito: "Pitfalls on the Road to Fiscal Decentralisation." *Working Paper*, No. 19. Washington D.C: Carnegie Endowment for International Peace, 2001.

Upadhyay, Vides: "Panchayats and Paper Laws." *Economic and Political Weekly*, XXXVII (29): pp. 2988-9, 2002.

Verma, B. M.: *Social Justice and Panchayat Raj.* New Delhi: Mittal Publications, 2002.

14

Role of Mahila Samakhya in Empowerment of Women: A Case Study of Uttarakhand

— *Jaya Pande*

Women empowerment refers to the ability of the women to transform economic and social development and to participate in the decisions that effect their life (Nayar, 2008). Sustainable and long term change, in the subordination of women and their total development, has always been an issue, since renaissance in India. Initial reformers like Raja Ram Mohan Rai, Ranade, and Ishwar Chandra Vidya Sagar immensely contributed for bringing changes in the status and improving the conditions of Indian women. However, since independence, various constitutional arrangements have been made to establish an equitable society and ensuring women's participation, development and real empowerment. Government's welfare schemes also aim to achieve the aim set by the constitution and work according to its spirit to provide equty, justice and development to all the genders. The approach of the welfare schemes has also been shifting from gender and development to gender in development as per the focus and need of the developmental programmes.

Mahila Samakhya (MS) is also one of the projects where Government has changed its focus from Gender and Development to Gender in Development. The thought leading to this change was the argument that women should not only be the recipient of welfare scheme but they should also be active agents in their own transformation in the spirit of the term "empowerment". The project evolved through a large scale discussion and debate involving Government officials' and women's groups. These discussions laid out the fact that socio-economic constraints reinforce a negative self image among the women and their work receives little recognition and respect. The entire range of social, cultural and economic factors restricts women's access to knowledge, information, education, mobility and justice. The complex socio-personal restraints cannot be tackled without active participation of women in bringing about a basic change in the mindset of individuals and society. The paper tries to evaluate Mahila Samakhya's responsibility in empowering women in Uttarakhand. It also attempts to assess its role (i) in providing information, knowledge and skill for political, economic and social upliftment of women, (ii) in developing rational and logical attitude in women, (iii) in building a positive attitude of women in society, (iv) in changing the patriarchal mindset and values. The primary data for this study has been collected through field survey, questionnaires and personal interview etc.

The MS programme was the result of National Policy on Education initiated in 1986 (NPE 1986). It was deliberately put under education department in the Human Resource Development, because it was recognised that the participation of girls and women in the educational process is possibly the most critical pre-condition for the empowerment of women. Education was supposed to be the main tool for achieving equitable society and generating awareness about the women's rights and to uphold their dignity. Without education, the women cannot play their roles and without changing the mentality of women, a positive education inducing atmosphere cannot be created for them. In view of this, the MS takes education in a broader and practical perspective, not only to enhance women's knowledge but also to develop their capabilities, generating awareness among them and using their education in handling their day-to-day life. At present the MS programme has been launched in 11 states, Uttarakhand is one of them. It covers six districts, i.e. Pauri, Nainital, Udham Singh Nagar, Tehri, Uttarkashi, and Champawat in Uttarakhand and 2377 villages of 21 blocks of these six districts.

Table 14.1 : Areas Covered and Programmes under Mahila Samkhya in Uttarakhand

S.N.	*Programme*	*Pauri*	*Tehri*	*Nainital*	*U. Kashi*	*U.S. Nagar*	*Cham-pawat*	*Total*
1.	Covered Villages	560	320	447	350	350	350	2377
2.	Dev. Blocks	5	3	4	3	3	3	21
3.	Women Sangha	560	320	447	350	330	350	2357

S.N.	Programme	Pauri	Tehri	Nainital	U. Kashi	U.S. Nagar	Cham-pawat	Total
4.	Sangha Members	10336	7610	12260	525	8365	6838	50659
5.	Kishori Sangha	49	45	54	122	25	139	434
6.	Kshr. Sangh Members	196	868	885	1890	498	1906	6743
7.	Cluster Sangha	43	-	47	48	-	-	138
8.	Mahansangha	4	-	4	-	-	-	8
9.	Villages in Roll Back Process	195	-	250	180	-	-	625
10.	Libraries	26	-	3	-	-	-	29
11.	Women Shelter (Thikana)	6	-	11	-	-	-	17
12.	Saving Funds	166	130	184	266	92	72	910
13.	Saved Capital (Rs.)	208513	4574023	86683	1850810	737735	274062	5603543
14.	Apani Adalat	4	-	2	-	-	1	7
15.	Health Centers	22	-	-	-	-	-	22
16.	Mahila Shikshan Kendra	1	1	1	1	1	1	6

(**Source:** Annual Report 2008-2009 Mahila Samakhya, Dehradun).

Table 14.2: District Implementation Units of Mahila Samakhya

S.N.	Post	Pauri	Tehri	Naini-tal	Uttar Kashi	Udham Singh Nagar	Campa-wat	Total
1.	Sahayogini	20	32	09	17	33	35	146
2.	C.R.P.	05	-	08	08	-	-	21
3.	J.R.P.	07	05	05	05	06	06	34
4.	Messenger	02	02	02	02	02	02	12
5.	D.E. Operator	01	01	01	01	01	01	06
6.	Off. Assistant	01	01	01	01	01	01	06
7.	Accountant	01	01	01	01	01	01	06
8.	R.P.	01	03	03	04	02	03	16
9.	D.C.P.	01	-	01	01	01	-	04

(**Source:** Annual Report 2008-2009 Mahila Samakhya, Dehradun).

The Mahila Samakhya programme was initiated with the following objectives:

- Enhancing self-esteem and self confidence of women.
- Building a positive image of women by recognising their contribution to the society, polity and the economy.
- Developing women's ability to think critically.
- Fostering decision-making through collective process.
- Ensuring equal participation in developmental processes.
- Providing information, knowledge and skill for economic independence.
- Enhancing access to legal literacy and information relating to their right and entitlements in society with a view to enhance their participation and equal footing in all areas. (*www.india. educationdiary.in. edupolicy)*

Institutional arrangement for achieving these goals, have five characteristics. First, it is totally run by women from top to bottom. Therefore, the responsibility lies with the women to carry out and plan activities under this programme.

Second, its structure is flexible and vibrant as it is neither Government nor non-Government organisation, but adopts the best elements from the both. It has checks and balance system of the Government structure and flexibility and openness of non-governmental structure. There has been considerable streamlining of budgets, plans and procedures and its strategies are continually being reviewed and changed to ensure sustainability of processes. Selection of programme, functionaries, trainers and resource support is made on the basis of commitment; aptitude and quality. The programme of the MS are not laid down just to achieve the set targets or specific agenda only, but it takes cue from the problems and issues of the women working in the ground level for better and fruitful results. Due to this factor, it has been seen that in Nainital district, the women have taken issues of water, forest and land and in Udham Singh Nagar, literacy has been taken up by the MS as its target.

Third, Mahila Samakhya is a time bound programme and after completing its time period, its women empowerment programme is rolled back and shifted to another area. MS believes that after the roll back from an area, the Mahasangha constituted would play an important role in sustaining the activities of women empowerment and awareness in the roll back areas. The continuity of activities and the awareness created in the field is necessary for establishing the usefulness of the MS in carrying out the programmes.

Fourth, Mahila Samakhya is an ideologically grounded programme (Sharma, 2010) initiated with the objective to bringing change in the psychological mindset of the patriarchal society. By meetings, discussions, trainings and workshops, attempts are made to generate awareness among the women, about the social status of women and factor behind the poor condition of the women. Women's issues, social circumstances and social structure are understood and analysed with feministic perspective. The women are helped in developing skills, capacities, attitudes and analysing power by participating in these discussions. Through continuous upgrading of information skill and collective strategies, the capabilities for critical analysis among women is developed. A strong effort is made to build a different culture and model of powers by continuously searching for alternative values so that inequitable power relationship of patriarchal society could be changed (Batliwala, 1996, p. 1251).

Fifth, it adopts a holistic approach for bringing real empowerment, among the women, through a variety of activities which are helful in achieving the aim of all-round development of the women. The various activities, which it conducts for women empowerment, include gender sanitisation activities, health programmes, Panchayat related awareness programmes, literacy programmes, economic empowerment and natural resources management programmes. These programmes are carried out through trainings, workshops, rallies and publication of booklets and pamphlets.

MS's basic strategy is to organise rural women into collectives through building of Mahila Sangha by the programme's activists (Sahyoginies), each working in about 10 villages. The Sangha, instead of externally and forcefully created entities that would collapse as soon as the MS rolls back its programme in that area, were expected to evolve gradually over a period of one year as a unique forum needed and owned by its members. There are three levels of Sangha: village level – comprised by village women; cluster level – comprised of two or three villages of the Sangha and Mahasangha to be developed at the block level. The focus of the Mahasangha's activities is to strive for women's emancipation and work as a pressure group in the region for women's issues.

The Mahila Samakhya and its different Sangha's activities are multi-dimensional. For positive intervention in Panchayats, its members are motivated to participate in the meetings of the Gram Sabha and divulge their views on women issues. Members are also motivated and informed about the importance of casting votes and selecting a competent candidate. Workshops and training programmes are organised for elected representatives. For economic empowerment of the women Mahila Samakhya organises various training for entrepreneurship and also sets up saving funds at village level which are created by the small savings of its members. The Sangh members conduct all the activities of saving fund themselves and its members are entitled to take loan from the small savings. It also organises training programmes for capacity building and generating income by undertaking economic activities like producing bakery products, fruit preservation, candle making, flower making etc.

For creating an education-oriented environment, MS has Mahila Siksha Kendra for girls of the age group of 14 to 18 years, who due to their age remain unable to get admission in 5th to 8th classes and for the adolescent girls who wish to appearing in examination privately, a district level bridge course is also operated. Besides literacy camps for the adult women, the MS also runs alternative health system, known as Sanjeevani Health Centre at village level, through local resources. For accessible and free justice, Apani Adalat is also conducted by forming an executive committee, consisting of vigilant and aware women. The Apani Adalat provides an opportunity to both the conflicting parties to present their argument about the case. The case is decided by identifying the root cause and discussing the problem with the victim. If a dispute cannot be resolved, women are guided in various workshops to put their cases effectively in the Courts.

However, any scheme or plan becomes meaningful, only when the implementing authorities and the target group are in co-ordination. There is no doubt that government has launched various schemes for the women, but the lack of information and shortcomings in the implementation part blocks their success rate. In view of this, the Sangha and Maha Sangha are motivated for networking with the government and non-governmental agencies at village and cluster level meetings. Lately, the MS workers, Sangha and Maha Sangha have started networking with CRCS and BRCS of Education Department and National Open Board for conducting exams for literacy camps and bridge course.

For receiving information about MNREGA scheme and to bring transparency in releasing job cards, the Block Development Offices are approached by the MS and integrated Child Development Scheme Officials and Anganbadies are networked for child care. (Annual Report

2008-09, Mahila Samakhya, Dehradun, p. 59) As information plays a vital role in empowerment by helping a person to work in right direction, benefit from it and put his or her arguments with facts. Hence, in its process of empowerment and to fulfill the objective of providing information, MS organises various workshops and trainings in different direction. The follwoing table provides an example of the workshops/ trainings being conducted by the MS in various sectors.

Table 14.3 : Workshop and Training Organised by the Mahila Samakhya at Various Levels

Particulars	*Sangha level*	*Cluster level*	*Block level*	*District level*
Gender Sensitisation	1816	126	10	26
Panchayat Empowerment	2588	428	14	10
Health Training	1317	125	33	11
Economic Empowerment Training	2593	655	30	10
Legal Literacy	1332	79	20	05
Domestic Violence	1924	44	44	08
Right to Information	301	52	30	-

Source: Annual Report 2008-2009 Mahila Samakhya, Dehradun.

The impact of these trainings and workshops has been seen in the following sectors:

Capacity building: It was found that on account of the workshops and trainings provided by the MS, the women who were illiterate and had been limited to their home, were acquring leadership roles. They have not only established themselves as role models but also become more vocal, articulate and aware about their rights. They were more competent to handle their own lives and also have a clear understanding of the objectives and goals of the Mahila Samakhya Programme. Discussion in the MS programmes has increased their rationality and participation and experience in the meetings have improved their decision-making power and confidence. Devaki Devi in Nathuakhan Block said, "Mahila Samakhya has changed our lives. Before attending Samakhya, we even hesitated to stand infront of men. But now we openly speak to our elders and discuss the problem before Panchayat, participate in the local Andolans, and also fight the Panchayat elections." The following table, from four blocks of Nainital district, shows the number of different categories of women workers helped by

Mahila Samakhya to participate in various developmental schemes:

Active existing Pradhan related with Sangha	—	21
Ward Members	—	42
B.D.C. Members	—	5
Active Asha workers from Sangha	—	42
Active Anganwadi workers from Sanghs	—	26

Source: DIU Nainital.

Gender Sensitisation: As it was not easy to change the persisting patriarchal mindset, even in woman herself, therefore, through continuous discussions and interations Mahila Samakhya has been able to develop a rational and logical attitude among the women. In a survey, conducted in Dhari block in Nainital district showed that the women now have a logical and changed attitude towards different issues, like on asking whether son is the sole carrier of the clan. Ninety percent of the respondents opined that son is not the sole carrier of clan. Rest of the 10 percent included those respondents who had recently joined the Mahila Samakhya. A participant, of the gender workshop at Champawat, organised by the MS very beautifully illustrated the role of M S : "After participating in the workshop, I came to realise that how much misfounded are our views on the girls. They are as capable as we are; only that they are not given the opportunities. We knowingly or unknowingly, discriminate with them." (Annual Report 2008-09, Mahila Samakhya Dehradun, p. 5) The following table shows the impact of MS on the critical and analysing power of the women.

Educational Upliftment: A unique feature about the Mahila Samakhya programme in Uttarakhand seems to be the interest shown by the women to become literate. The fact that women have been attending literacy camps in large numbers and attending the bridge classes to take class 3, 5 and 8 exams shows that MS has been able to create the necessary conditions for the education of women. Moreover, the women have also realised the importance of literacy skills to make progress in their life and to access information for strengthening their *Sangathan and Sangharsh*. The success of the literacy campaign can be evaluated by the fact that 2637 women enrolled themselves for examination at various levels. (Annual Report 2008-09, Mahila Samakhya Dehradun, p. 26) Educational certificates have helped active Sangha women to get employment as Asha worker (NRHM), Bhojan Mata (cook) for mid-day-meal scheme and also as Anganwadi workers. When asked, why they are appearing for examination in such a mature

Table 4: Logical and Analysing power of the Women Involved With Mahila Samakhya

Question	*Various Answers*		
1. Is son the sole carrier of clan?	1. If anyone has no son, can his clan will stop.	2. If there is a female, then only can a clan survive, men alone cannot make a clan.	3. Daughter can also carry her parent's clan ahead.
2. Is widow marriage the right thing?	1. If a men can marry after his wife's death, why a woman cannot.	2. If widow is not permitted to marry, she will satisfy her biological needs anywhere. Then why she be prohibited to marry?	3. It does not matter, she should be permitted or not, but the disabilities should be banned. It is nonsensical to prohibit widow from wearing red clothes, ornaments.
3. Should the daughter be married after she becomes economically self -dependent?	1. Marriage is not necessary, but daughter should be economically self-dependent.		

Source: Author's Interaction with the Respondents.

age, a literacy camp participant at Nainital replied, "This is being done to spread the message to those guardians who have removed their daughters from schools for domestic chores. They should realise that even these mature women know the importance of education while those guardians do not know. At least this will embarrass them enough to send their daughters to school." It is evident that the Sangha women have understood the importance of literacy to liberate. The high level involvement of the women in socio-political struggles in the past has provided the necessary fillip for Mahila Samakhya's success in Uttarakhand.

Breaking Caste Barriers: MS has also been successful in consolidating women's gender perspective. Their workshops have also helped women to formulate some common agenda regardless of caste and class and also sensitising upper caste women to stay and eat together with Dalit women during the training programmes. The district co-coordinator of Nainital district informed the author, "We have not restricted them. We have not forced them to live with. We ignored their complaint. In the beginning, there was some problem. But gradually barriers were loosened automatically."

Intervention in Panchayat: Sangha women, who have become Gram Panchayat members, have not only been found to be consistently more articulate, aware, assertive and effective as Gram Panchayat members, but appear to be challenging and bringing some change in the conduct and culture of Gram Panchayat as a whole. This can be judged from the following examples indicating change in the perceptions due to women's knowledge and awareness acquired through MS meetings, trainings and workshops.

Their knowledge broke the male domination: The Gram Panchayat members of Ganghareti village presented a good example of their confidence, awareness and knowledge and through it they successfully challenged the male domination in Gram Panchayat. To run down the women typical questions were asked by the male members like "Why have you come in the meeting? What is your job here?" But the women equipped with the knowledge acquired at Panchayat workshops, replied wih confidence that they were in the meeting as members of Gram Sabha and informed them about all the rules and regulations of Panchayat Raj. The male members were stunned when the women asked the Gram Pradhan about the allocation of budget for Panchayat, its various heads and expenditure. Though, initially the Pradhan refused to divulge the information, but when the Sangha members pressed their right as Gram Sabha members to inquire about it, as shown in MS booklet on Panchayat, Panchayat Secretary advised Pradhan to acceed to their demands. (Annual Report, 2006-07, p. 55)

Their Unity changed the attitude: The awareness created by Tehri unit of Mahila Samakhya, in its newly expanded field of activities is visible in women. The women of Punar village were upset with the Gram Pradhan, resident of another village, for not fulfilling his election promise to construct a water-nallah in the village, even after repeated reminders. The Sangh women invited Gram Pradhan at their meeting and sensing the unity of the women in village, he came for the Sangha meeting. When women asked him about his promise and lack of other development work at their village, the Gram Pradhan admitted his negligence and assured that construction of Nallah would be the first thing on his agenda in the next financial year. The women also complained about the lack of information about the agenda of Gram Sabha meeting. The Gram Pradhan was amazed at the level of awareness and knowledge of women about Gram Sabha. As a result of this, not only the attitude of the Gram Pradhan changed towards the women, but the flow of information about the meetings of Gram Sabha also became regular.

In the survey conducted by MS, it was revealed that those women Panchayat representatives, who joined the workshop and trainings on Panchayat, organised by Mahila Samakhya, were regular in attending Panchayat meetings, putting their point of view with confidence and opposing the illegal activities. They were instrumental in getting development work done for their Gram Sabha from Block Development Office and they were also sensitive to women issues. It was also the result of Panchayat activities of the Mahila Samakhya that Sangha women contested election in large number in Panchayats and the Sangha members also pledged their support to honest candidates having sensitive approach to the women issues.

These are no mean achievement as the Sanghas are creating a viable mechanism for changing the dominant model of power and patriarchal mindset of the society. However, despite the positive changes, there are some problems which sometimes hinder the work of the Mahila Samakhaya as Geeta Gairola, Project Director, Mahila Samakhya, Uttarakhand, shared with the author that, "Sometimes Sangha women elected to Panchayat deceive us in such cases we do not have any option except to boycott and terminate from the membership." But she also accepted that at least a positive beginning has been made, the men have started to give women due respect and the women are bringing change in the socio-political arena which is the main aim of the MS.

REFERENCES

Nayar Sudha : *Women's Empowerment in South Asia*, Navyug Publishers & Distributors, New Delhi, 2008, p. 1.

Mahila Samakhya Programme, Monday, July, 21, 2008, *www.india educationdiary,in>edupolicy,*

Sharma, Kumud : *Framing the Discourse on Decentralised Governance and women's empowerment*, Inaugral Address, National Seminar, 18-20 February, 2010, Deptt. of Political Science, HNB Garhwal University, Srinagar.

Batliwala, Srilatha. "Transforming Political Culture: Mahila Samakhya Experience". *Economic and Political Weekly*, May 25, 1996, p. 1251.

"Move Ahead with Strength". *Annual Report 2008-09, Mahila Samakhya*, Dehradun, p. 59.

"Opening Horizon". *Annual Report, 2006-07, Mahila Samakhya*, Dehradun p. 55.

15

Political Participation of Woman Legislators: An Experience of Rajasthan State Assembly

— *Inakshi Chaturvedi*

The concept, of political participation, encompasses all voluntary actions, intended to influence the making of public policies, the administration of public affairs and the choice of political leaders at all levels of government. Political participation is concerned, not only with the organisation of the state and government and the exercise of power by them, but also seeks the reorganisation of the lives of the members of its society. Political participation means involvements of the people in the political process. In a parliamentary democarcy, the people register their participation in the political process, through their elected representatives. Political participation includes voting, campaigning, party membership, involvement in Local, State and Central legislative bodies etc. Though participation in voting process is the first step towards assimilating in the political system, but the act of voting itself does not yield the desired end of equality in a democarcy, because for bringing equality in the society it is also necessary, that all the people participate in the political process irresespective of their gender, particularly women's participation is more than required for ensuring equality. However, for bringing the women in the mainstream of development and ensuring their involvement in the political process, the women's political participation should not end at only partaking in the activities of electing their representatives once in five years, but should also include efforts on the part of the women and society at large to raising consciousness and changing the unequal system into an equal system, by participating actively in the political and governance process. In Anne Phillips' opinion : "Women's interests can be taken care of only when women articulate these interests within the legislatures and other such law-making bodies (Phillips, 1995, p.83), because unless such activism is shown and laws are made, women's concern cannot be protected."

Since, Legislature is a representative body and people's participation in the political process in this body takes palce through the representatives, therefore, in view of the importance of the political participation of the women in the legislative bodies, the present paper makes an attempt to analyse and evaluate the participation of the women in the Legislative Assembly of the State of Rajasthan, particularly, the performance of women legislators in 11th and 12th State assemblies of Rajasthan. This study becomes imprtant in view of the fact that the women though constitute 50 percent of the total population, but their overall representation in the Union Parliament or State Assembalies is not as per their numbers; and without proper and equal representation and political participation of woman, a democracy can not be called successful. The dearth of woman legislators, both at the Centre and the State level in post independent India, reflects towards the apathy for the women issues or the need to involving them for a more productive planning towards bringing gender equality and promoting women empowerment in the real sense of the term. What could be more ironical than the fact, that despite having the right to vote and electing their represntatives, women themselves are still under-represented in parliament, state legislative assemblies and governments. And Rajasthan State Assembly is no exception to it, as shown in the following table.

Table 15.1: Women Contestants and Elected Women Legislators in Rajasthan State Assembly (1952-2008)

Year	*No. of Women Contestants*	*No. of Elected Women Members*
1952	04	02
1957	21	09
1962	15	08
1967	19	07
1972	17	13
1977	31	08
1980	31	10
1985	45	17
1990	93	11

Year	*No. of Women Contestants*	*No. of Elected L Women Members*
1993	97	10
1998	69	15
2003	118	13
2008	154	29
Total	714	152

As shown in the above table that in the elections, held during the last five decades from 1952 – 2008 from 1st to 13th assemblies of the Rajasthan State, a total number of 714 women contested the elections but only 152 members was elected. But it is also heartening to note that despite the representation of women never reaching the desired proportion, the women legislators have palyed an active role, shown their efficiency in delivering the results or participating in the proceedings. This has gradually led to refuting the prevailing dogmas about women's knowledge, understanding, efficiency, capacity, quality of participation and interests in the political process. Although women are still under-represented in the State Assembly of Rajasthan, but the role actually performed in the house is qualitatively commendable. An analysis of diverse activities in the assembly, the role played, the efficiency shown, awareness and interest exhibited has been qualitatively far better than the strength of their representation. This also implies that if given proper representation, woman can change the context with their determination and efficiency.

The following factors have their influence on the performance of the women in elections and as legislators.

Affiliation with the Political Parties

Affiliation with political parties is one of the important factors for women's chances of getting elected in elections and also to work successfully as legislators, but sometimes people do not accept the changes in the affiliation of the women. The case of Smt. Narendra Kanwar a legislator, can be cited to support this argument. Narendra Kanwar got elected in the 10th legislative assembly as an independent candidate, but as she joined the BJP and contested election in its ticket, she had to face defeat in the 11th assembly. The electorate could not accept her as a BJP candidate or the voters did not approve of the change of party by the women candidates. In view of this, it can be said that political background or affiliation with the political parties is an important factor, but not the sole factor, responsible for the political career of the women. This can also be understood from the fact that in the 11th assembly, Smt. Sumitra Singh (Mahila Netritava Evam Mahila Sahabhagita, 2010. p.253) was the most animated member without political connections. In the 12th and 13th Assembly Smt. Surya Kanta Vyas was the most animated member without political affiliation.

Women's number in the assembly also depends on the party which gets the majority and forms the government in the state. In the 11th legislative assembly, Congress party was in majority, therefore, 14 out of 55 women candidates were elected from the Congress party and in the 12th legislative assembly 10 out of 13 women elected from the BJP and in the 13th assembly 14 out of 29 women were elected from the Congress party. The graph of the percentage of women representatives stand as 7 percent in the 11th assembly and 5 percent in the 12th assembly and 10.9 percent in the 13th assembly. As in the 11th and 12th legislative assemblies, the party in power had commanded a majority (Mahila Netritava Evam Mahila Sahabhagita, 2010, pp. 256-57), therefore, it did not require the support of independents but in the 13th legislative assembly Smt. Golma Devi (www.rajassembly.nic.in) an independent member extended her support to the government and in return she was rewarded with the state ministership.

Offices Held by Women Members

Offices held by the women candidates as legislators also influence their performance and their efficiency, capability and popularity is also judged by the work done by them in such offices. In the 11th legislative assembly, Smt. Kamla Beniwal not only became the minister for irrigation but she also held the office of the Deputy Chief Minister. She became a role model for the other women in the state. The holding of Chief Ministership by Smt. Vasundhara Raje was one more feather in the cap of women's participation in politics. She became the chief minister in the 12th assembly and Smt. Sumitra Singh was elected as speaker of the assembly. Another woman legislator, Smt. Usha Poonia, became the Minister for Tourism. In the 13th legislative assembly, two women members were made ministers. Smt. Beena Kak was made Cabinet Minister for Women and Child Development, Tourism, Art and Culture, Archaeology, Printing and Stationery and Smt. Golma Devi was elevated as State Minister for Khadi and Rural Industries, Home and Civil Defense. This is a pointer to the empowerment of women. (Mahila Netritava Evam Mahila Sahabhagita, 2010, pp. 258-59)

Socio-Economic and Political Background

Though socio-economic and political background also matters in the success of the women in politics, but a look into the socio-economic and political background of women legislators show that, most of the women members in both the assemblies came from the ordinary common class. The state of Rajasthan with its feudal past, has only a negligible representation of the princely class. This indicates that women legislators' success in politics is attributable not to the background of their descent but to their own merit. The family background or the political affinity may have been a factor, but on the basis of a look at their background and their success, it can be said that they have scored more, because of their education, efficiency, capacity and ability. (11th Legislative Assembly: Who's Who, Rajasthan Vidhan Sabha, Secretariat).

Educational Background

A glance at the educational qualification of the women legislators clarifies that women legislators in the 11th legislative assembly had very high educational skills. Dr. Kamla Beniwal held a doctorate degree, Smt. Zakia was post-graduate in Botany and Smt. Yasmin Abrar was M.Phil. In the 12th assembly also the women members were highly educated. Smt. Anita Bhadel held a doctorate degree (Ph.D. Degree). All these educated women legislators performed their functions very efficiently, which clearly indicates that education plays an important role in women's empowerment as well as their performance in the various offices held by them.

Age Factor in the Performance

In the 11th assembly, there were 10 women legislators in the age group of 36-50. (11th Legislative Assembly: Who's Who, Rajasthan Vidhan Sabha Secretariat). In the 12th assembly, there was only 01 member in the age group of 36-50. In the 11th legislative assembly, Ms. Meenakshi Chandrawat (12th Legislative Assembly, Who's Who, Rajasthan Vidhan Sabha Secretariat) was the youngest woman legislator. In the 12th assembly, most of the women members were in the age group of 46-50. There were no women legislators in the assembly in the age group of seventies and eighties. However, in the 11th assembly Smt. Kamla (71), Smt. Sumitra Singh (68) and Smt. Surya Kanta Vyas (68) made an impression in the 12th assembly by participating in every activity, though the youngsters also did their best by their innovative inspiration and energy. Smt. Sumitra Singh, another women legislator, has the credit of being elected 09 times in the assembly elections and Smt. Kamla has a record of winning 07 elections. In the 11th assembly 07 women members had the experience of participating in the past elections while in the 12th assembly only 03 members had the advantage of participating in the past elections. (12th Legislative Assembly, Who's Who, Rajasthan Vidhan Sabha Secretariat, Jaipur) This shows that age-wise maturity some times works for the advantage of the women legislators as the gradual experience gained by them in different positions helps them to improve their knowledge, develop a better understanding of the issues and also increases their efficiency.

Marital Status

Although marital status is not a very important factor for deciding the success or performance of the women legislators, however, all the women members of the 11^{th,} 12th and 13th assemblies, except three, were married. The state of being married or unmarried had, of course, no impact on their political activities, as most of the legislators accepted during interaction with the author that they did not face any conflict in their domestic and political life. Most of them accepted that their entry in politics became possible because of the inspiration and cooperation of their husbands, father-in-law and other family members. Only a few women legislators accepted that their domestic responsibilities sometimes acted as an impediment, because of their busy schedules or time devoted in political activities. The women legislators also acknowledged that working, for general public interest, keeps them all the time charged.

Family Background

Family background and experience in social work also hepls the performance of the women legislators. A glance at the family background of the women legislators of the 11th and 12th assembly revealed that though in the 11th assembly 07 out of 15 members had an agricultural background and in the12th assembly only 06 members had agricultural background.(www.rajassembly.nic.in); but most of the members, in interaction with the author, accepted that they had either experience of contesting elections or they had been social workers. One of the lady members of the 11th assembly had turned from education to politics.

Women Legislators' Participation in the Proceedings of the Legislative Assembly and its Impact on their Performance

For making an evaluation of the women legislators' performance and their role in the assembly, it becomes imperative to analyse the efficacy of their participation in assembly debates, discussions and other such activities of the assembly. The following tables provide an idea of the impact of women legislators' in such activities.

As participation in the debates on the Governor's address also forms an important function of the legislators, because it allows to making an appraisal of their views about the government's policies. Therefore, it is considered important for all the legislators to participate in such debates and express their opinion for and against the Governor's address.

Table 15.2: Assessment of Women Legislators' Participation on Governor's Address

Description	*11th assembly*	*12th assembly*
Total address of the Governor	05	05
Total frequency of members participated	115	175
Frequency of women members participated in debate	09 times (05 women)	05 times (05 women)
Time consumed by women members	3 hrs. 57 min.	4 hours.

Source: 11th Legislative Assembly (Who's Who) Rajasthan Vidhan Sabha Secretariat, Jaipur and12th Legislative Assembly (Who's Who) Rajasthan Vidhan Sabha Secretariat, Jaipur.

The above table clarifies, that woman legislators of both the assemblies participated on the Governor's address actively and contributed useful and important suggestions. During the 05 addresses of the Governor in the 11th legislative assembly, 05 women legislators remained active on 09 occasions and in the 12th assembly the women members were active only on 05 occasions, consuming 03 hours 57 min. in the former and 04 hours in the latter. As 13 out of 15 members belonged to the ruling party, therefore, only a limited number of women legislators in the 11th assembly participated and took interest in the debate (11th Legislative Assembly (Who's Who) Rajasthan Vidhan Sabha Secretariat, Jaipur). Usually the members of the opposition take more interest in critising the Government, therefore; the participation from the ruling party members remained limited. Besides this, there was a noticeable factor about Smt. Sumitra Singh, an independent member that, despite her being an independent member, she participated actively and gave valuable suggestions touching national and regional problems, rather than local ones in each of the addresses by the Governor, whereas the members related to the ruling party had concentrated on problems, confined to their own constituency. The same trend continued in the 12th assembly, as most of the members from the ruling party restrained themselves from participating in the debate. Smt. Pratibha Singh, Smt. Krishanender Kaur and Smt. Mamta Sharma, who were from other parties, participated actively in the debate so much so that Smt. Mamta Sharma exhibited her interest in providing constructive suggestions with regard to established procedure.

Although the interest taken by the women legislators was quantitatively not significant, in view of their smaller number yet their participation was qualitatively more pronounced. It was natural for the members of the ruling party to defend the governmental policies and for the members of the opposition parties to either oppose or suggest modifications in those policies. However, it was also noticed that sometimes the members of ruling party levelled criticism and the opposition members supported those policies, though this was done very rarely, as it accounted to departure from their party line, therefore, it was related mostly to voicing concern about the deprived classes, security, education and women empowerment issues. It was also found that though the members showed their general interest in all the subjects, but they took particular interest on the issues of education, women empowerment, child development, empowerment of Panchayati Raj and problems related with peasants. Whereas, on the one hand, they expressed their appreciation and criticism like other members, but on the other, from qualitative point

Table 15.3: Women Legislators' Participation and Impact in Formulation of Law in 11th and 12th Assemblies

Description	*11th Assembly*	*12th Assembly*
Total proposed bills	126	
Bill proposed by women ministers	06	03
Total bills passed	89	
Bills of women ministers passed	02	03
Women members participated on the bills presented by women ministers	02	03

Description	*11th Assembly*	*12th Assembly*
Frequency of women members in the discussion of the bills.	08 times (Smt. Sumitra Singh 05 times)	04 times
Name of women members participated in discussion of the bills	Smt. Sumitra Singh, Smt. Poonam Goyal Smt. Madhu Dadhich Smt. Mamta Sharma	Smt. Laxmi Barupal Smt. Anita Bhadel Smt. Raj Kumari Sharma

Source: 11th Legislative Assembly (Who's Who) Rajasthan Vidhan Sabha Secretariat, Jaipur and12th Legislative Assembly (Who's Who) Rajasthan Vidhan Sabha Secretariat, Jaipur.

of view, they affirmed their identity in the house by making significant factual and empirical information while giving important suggestions:

As shown in the above table, a total number of 06 bills were proposed by the women ministers in the 11th assembly, and 02 women legislators actively participated in the debates on these bills. A total number of 04 women members participated in the discussions on the various bills presented in the assembly. In the 12th assembly 03 bills were introduced by women ministers and 03 women legislators expressed their views thereon. Besides, the women legislators had made positive suggestions with regard to the issue of education. In the 11th Assembly, out of 15 members, 04 remained active in the discussion of the bills and out of them Smt. Sumitra Singh was most active. In the 12th assembly, 03 members remained active in the discussion on the bills.

Among these members, Smt. Anita Bhadel, Smt. Laxmi Barupal and Smt. Raj Kumari Sharma were most active participants in the discussion on the bills. These members, though belonged to the ruling party, but they made their own impression while taking part in the discussion on bills, even sometimes departing from the common trend of supporting the party line. Smt. Anita Bhadel and Smt. Laxmi Barupal participated in the discussion on the Panchayati Raj (2nd amendment) bill 2008 and Suresh Gyan Vihar University, Jaipur 2008. (www.rajassembly.nic.in)

The women legislators participated 03 times in the discussion on the bills. Equal interest was shown by the women members of the 11th and 12th assemblies, with regard to the bills concerning education and tourism. The common feature, in both the assemblies, was that the lady members showed their interest and offered important suggestions on the common subjects, like Panchayati Raj, Women Empowerment and Cooperatives. Although the numerical strength of the women members was proportionately less in legislative functions, yet the suggestions offered by them or the issues raised by them were useful. The women legislators' presentation of the bills in the assembly, participation and intervention in these discussions, not only exhibited their self confidence, but their replies to the questions also showed their logical style and factual information on the bills presented by them. Their sensitivity, to public issues, legislative business and active participation in the discussions, was also reflected by their interventions and replies.

Table 15.4: Participation on Financial Matters in 11th and 12th Assemblies

S.N.	*Description*	*11th assembly*	*12th assembly*
1.	Total members participated on general discussion on budget	129 times	140 times
2.	Total women members participated	16 times (10 women)	18 times (06 women)
3.	Total time consumed by women members	04 hr. 40 min.	04 hr. 35 min.
4.	Total number of demands discussed	50	70
5.	Number of demands on which women members were active	35	53
6.	Number of women members active in discussions	10	11

The table-4 corroborates the fact that the women members' discussion, on the budget and grant-in-aid, was engineered with sufficient interest and activeness. In the 11th assembly 10 women members participated in the discussion on 16 occasions and consumed four and half hours. Most of the women members, except those who were ministers, participated in the discussion of the budget. In the 12th assembly Smt. Anita Bhadel took the lead in carrying her discussion on the budget for about 16 minutes. The members most actively participated in the discussion on the expenditure incurred on public utility and showed their interest and made appropriate suggestions, in relation to the budgetary aspects, involving education, Gram Swarajya, agriculture, deprived sections of the society and the issues related to their own constituency. The members of the ruling party appreciated the budget, whereas the independent member like Smt. Sumitra Singh demonstrated the deficiencies of the budget. But the members reviewed the merits and demerits honestly, in the interest of the people without following the general trend of the ruling party and the opposition party. They attracted the attention of the house on the problems of their constituency and by their budgetary speeches they made important suggestions for the solution of the problems.

Likewise, in the matter of grants-in-aid, the members took a keen interest in both the assemblies. In the 11th assembly out of 50 demands, the women members participated in the discussion of 35 demands. In the 12th assembly out of 70 demands, the women members participated in the discussion of 53 demands. In the 11th assembly the extent of the participation of the woman members in the discussion of demands was meagre, because they belonged to the ruling party; but the participation in the 12th assembly was comprehensive and unaffected by their party affinity.

In the 11th assembly Smt. Sumitra Singh was most active, since she participated 12 times in the discussion of demands. In the 12th assembly Smt. Surya Kanta Vyas was most active and she participated 10 times in the discussion of the demands. The women members showed their activeness on demands relating to public works department, road and bridges. This analysis verifies that the women members had been equally and keenly interested in the matters like education, art and culture, medicines and health and the achievements in both the assemblies of these members can be counted on highlighting the deficiencies of the government, appreciation for the constructive provisions, raising useful demands and issues and making valuable suggestions. The women members expressed their token resentment or raised the demands of their own constituencies through the cut motions.

It was also observed that all the members were very active and sensitive towards the problems of their constituency. But they also took active interest and exhibited sensitivity to public issues also. Cutting across the party lines, woman members were united on the issues of women reservation, women's education and other interest of women. While the women members had shown their interest and awareness in financial matters through their statements, they also created an impression of their efficiency by their effective replies. They expressed their notional resentment against the policies of the government through the cut motions on various demands and they simultaneously put/ forth the demands of their constituency.

In the question hour of both the assemblies, the women members had taken considerable interest, in respect of all the departments, although the number of questions was large regarding their own constituency; but the women members also proved their activeness in highlighting the weakness of the government and restraining it through supplementary questions. On the other hand, the women members in both the assemblies offered adequate solutions to the questions on the basis of their experience and efficiency. The activeness on the part of the woman ministers was more prominent in the 11th assembly rather than in the 12th assembly, which had only one woman minister. The women members brought to focus the errors and omissions on the part of the executive. The women ministers also succeeded in disposing of the questions with confidence. Whereas the woman members baffled the ministers through their eloquence in the swarm of their questions, the woman ministers, at the same time, also succeeded in encountering questions and disposing them off by placing the relevant data efficiently. Several questions, of urgent public importance, were raised by women legislators through the slips, some times without prior information and some times by demanding a discussion on the adjournment motions in the zero hour but they fared well in the face of such challenging situations also. On the whole, the women members proved themselves as intelligent, efficient and dignified.

These incidents illustrate that all the woman members had drawn the attention of the government to the local problems of their constituency in the question hour and they conducted themselves fairly well by discharging their responsibilities. In the 11th assembly no petitions was ever presented in the house; but in the 12th assembly 10 petitions were presented in the house, not a single, government and non-government, resolution was proposed by woman members in the 11th assembly; but two resolutions were presented by women ministers in the 12th assembly. Moreover, the woman legislators raised various urgent problems of public importance, ranging from national to local levels under rule 295. Thus the woman legislators took advantage of rule 295 for drawing attention of the house towards the various local problems of their respective constituencies. The role of woman legislators in legislative functioning proves their capacity and insight and contradicts the standing patriarchal notions about women's knowledge and performance. Besides this, the woman members conducted themselves well as the members of the various committees. They exhibited a keen interest in the woman and child welfare committee and on account of their interest, the membership of this committee was very often offered to the woman members. It can be said, on the basis of the above ananlysis, that mostly the woman members provided workable solutions on numerous problems by their efficiency and responsibility they exhibited while functioning in the committees also.

The important subjects, disposed of by the women members of the 11th and 12th assemblies, are as follows:-

- Development and empowerment of women.
- Education
- Basic facilities
- Local problems of their constituency.
- Protection of suppressed and backward classes.
- Preservation of culture and wild life and protection of archeological monuments.
- Local self-government and empowerment of Panchayati Raj.

Conclusion

The analysis, of women legislators' participation in various activites, indicates that woman members have generally been vocal on the floor of the house. They not only concentrate on women and soft issues like welfare of children and women, health and education, but they have also expressed their views on sensitive political matters like the motion of thanks, Governor's address, financial and law formulation issues etc. Such involvement provides the woman members' opportunities to express their criticicism or appreciation of the working of the government. By their intervention in the budgetery issues, the women members have displayed their ability to grasp economic realities and offer useful suggestions. Woman members do not behave differently than men with regard to a number of women's areas, as long as they constitute a small minority. Though, the woman members of both the assemlies have shown keen interest with the matters, as mentioned above, but woman legislators in the assembly also feel more accountable to their party. The impact of party is stronger than that of gender.

However, it is also true that the increased women's presence in legislative assemblies may not necessarily lead to improved representation of women interests and issues. In view of the changing the gender composition of elected assembilies, Anne Phillips (Phillips, 1995) argues that it is largely an enabling condition but it cannot present itself as a guarantee of improved representation of women interests. In other words, increased descriptive representation does not automatically lead to enhanced substantive representation. The extent, to which a relationship exists between the numerical presence of women and the representation of women's interests, is an emperical question. Woman legislators may also additionally disregard woman's interests and behave like their male counterparts. Though some female legislators were sensitive to the need of women and payed considerable attention to the woman issues, but this does not easily translate into an improved representation of their interests. On the other hand, some woman legislators were not anxious in giving special attention to issues having an impact on the lives of women and on the areas of traditional concern to women, such as, children welfare and education rather they were more concerned with their political loyalties to their parties rather than with woman issues. Some woman members were concerned to reach the goal of 'critical mass' stage that will allow them to advance their political position and gain influence in the policy-making process. This situation is the result of a limited representation of the women in the assemblies and to some extent this situation can be changed if women reservation bill is passed because than a sizeable number of women (33 %) can seek election in the parliament and to the state assemblies. Although reservation of seats in parliament and assembalies is not an end in itself but it can be a means to achieve gender equality in the law-making bodies. If more women are able to enter in these bodies, the participation of the women legislators in the debates and proceedings would get a boost, because the presnece of handful women in these bodies sometimes works to their disadvantage. In the absence of supporting groups they sometimes fail to voice their concerns; therefore, for more effective participation by the woman legislators, more women need to enter in these bodies and the political parties also need to make provisions for the reservation of seats for the women within their parties, so that their entry in these bodies becomes easier. On the other hand, the women also need to recognise collectively and critically the forces that limit them, and to work collectively and continuously to change the unequal power structures around them. In other words, they have to experience the process of empowerment. This is the process of gaining control over the self, the ideology and the resources – physical (like land and water), human, intellectual and financial – which determine power. Unless they would enter the critical mass stage (Batliwala, 1993), they would not be able to secure their political position and exercise influence in the policy-making process.

REFERENCES

Phillips, Anne. (1995), *The Politics of Presence.* Oxford : Oxford University. Press, p. 83.

Mahila Netritava Evam Mahila Sahabhagita, Avishkar Publishers, Jaipur, 2010, p. 253.

Mahila Netritava Evam Mahila Sahabhagita, Avishkar Publishers, Jaipur, 2010. pp. 256-57. www.rajassembly.nic.in

11th Legislative Assembly (Who's Who) Rajasthan Vidhan Sabha Secretariat, Jaipur.

12th Legislative Assembly (Who's Who) Rajasthan Vidhan Sabha Secretariat, Jaipur.

www.rajassembly.nic.in

Batliwala, Sarilata: *Empowerment of Women in South Asia : Concepts and Practices*, Sponsored by Asian-South Pacific Bureau of Adult Education and FAO's Freedom From Hunger Campaign, Action for Development, New Delhi, 1993, quoted from Desai Neerja and Thakkar Usha, *Women in Indian Society*, NBT 2001, p. 119.

16

Political Activism of Women in India: Importance and Problems

— ***Rakesh Singh Negi***

Man's political activism is the most essential element of his social, political and psychological development. In fact, people's socio-political activism and interest is the very fundamental basis of any democratic system of government. As democratic system mainly works, survives and flourishes by people's collaboration and active participation in the public affairs, therefore, people's participation and activism also ensures a strong, stable and accountable democratic system. The absence of political activism on the part of people will generate a lethargic and flailing democratic mechanism, which, at length, may create conducive situations for irresponsibility, corruption, bureaucratic hegemony and a host of other such vices, which are not good for the health and strength of any democarcy. People's participation in various debatable issues, under a political system, expressing their opinion, underlining the systematic infirmities and influencing the decisions of political set-up, could be termed as political activism. Actually, in the democratic mechanism, the importance of political activism is heightened by the very fact that the formation and operation of political institutions is also completed by the citizens. Such contribution of the citizens is possible only through awareness, about the issues and involvement and participation in the political process.

The development, dynamism and relevance of any nation-state are determined, to a great extent, by the awakening and activism of its citizens. The success of a political system could be measured by the political participation of its citizens. Political activism is not related to only having a formal knowledge about the state and its democratic organs, but also having an insightful and practical understanding of their functioning. Awareness, participation, activism, aptitude, knowledge of government system, political institutions, constitutions and democratic mechanism are the essential part of the political character of a modern, able, awakened and ideal citizen, because through political development, citizens are enlightened about the salient features of a democratic system, their activities and different bodies. Political participation, activism or awakening is the major characteristic of a community or society and it meaningfully expresses the political attitudes and inclinations of the members of that particular community. (Rawat, 2004, p. 78) The Indian constitution grants ample opportunities to all its citizens, irrespective of their gender, caste, creed or class, for equal participation in political systems in all the institutions, ranging from local self government to central bodies. As the constitution also grants equal opportunities to women to ensure their political participation and activism, therefore, political activism of the women is directly linked to their level of using the constitutional and statutory powers. In view of this, it can be said that every step which associates women with the making and advancement of political system could be called a symbol of their political development. (Kaushik, 2004, p. 123) and hence the very right of adult franchise and partaking of electoral process is also a part and parcel of their political activism. In Normon and Verba's view political participation consists of those legally justifiable activities of citizens, which are intended to elect political, officials and directly influence the decisions taken by them. Actually, political participation or activism is the spontaneous procedure of intervening in the selection of public policies, administrations or public affairs or election of government officials at a regional or national level. The level of activism may vary from person to person. Often it is noticed that women's involvement in political activities is relatively small and, therefore, their political activism is mostly average and marginal. This speaks volumes about small number of representatives and leadership of women in the political arena, despite their population and enactment of pro-women laws, policies and political initiatives. Although, there is no denying the fact that, in today's world, women are keeping pace with time and achieving new milestones in knowledge, skill and work capacities; they are skillfully participating in all works of life. Yet, their participation and dominance in political, organisational and governmental posts is relatively small. While there are ample examples that, if given opportunities, women, working on key posts, have left indelible impression of their leadership qualities and capacities and this presents a strong basis for their activism and participation in all such systems.

As far as women's political activism is concerned, a rapid growth has been seen in the last few decades, particulalry, since the 1990's and once reticent and confined within the walls of their houses, the women are now ensuring better participation in political demonstration, rallies, picketing, bandh etc. The women are even showing their activism in the religious demonstrations and activities. The example of religious activism of some Hindu women of Bijnour town in Western Uttar Pradesh, in October 1990, when they marched through the Muslim dominated areas of the town, shouting and wielding tridents in their hands, has been cited in some studies to showcase the religious activism of the simple and ordinary women of very small towns. (Basu, 1999, p.1) This indicates that if women are given opportunities and allowed to participate in different forums, they can be as active as the men. Such participation of the women may be exceptional, becasue, mostly their activism always remains limited, small and limited to a particular section of the women in the society. Infact, in practice women's activism is shaped by the traditional socialisation which adopts different parameters for judging the role, expectations and achievements of men and women. This process of socialisation while projects men as skillful, competitive and capable of taking self decisions, promotes the image of women as humble, sensitive, co-operative, dependent, tolerant, compromising, submissive and physically and mentally weak. On account of such socialisation, women are always hesitant to assert their leadership aspirations, which are not considered a natual quality of the women rather they are considered best in looking after the family, nuturing family and the elederly. Women's limited political activism is also the result of the male dominated society, which supports men's qualities of competitiveness, aggression and liberty, more than the women's qualities of compassion, understanding and tolerance etc. (Basu, 1999, p. 2)

Although, there is no denying that women have equal rights and privileges like men and by using these rights and privileges are gradually making their presence felt in almost all the areas like government, politics, education, science, social welfare, industry, commerce, trade unions etc. their working capacities, intellect, qualities, abilities and talent are changing the traditional social assumptions and taboos about them. But the women of the remote and rural areas are still untouched by such socio-political transformation, awareness and activism. Due to the double standards of socialisation and male-dominated society, a majority of women are still deprived of their rights. It is also unfortunate that despite representing 50 percent of the country's population and an integral part of 50 percent vote casting population, the women have not been included significantly in the decision-making process. Noticeably, only 47 women representatives were elected in the 13th Lok Sabha, which is the highest number of women members elected în Lok Sabha so far. Prior to this, in the 8th Lok Sabha 44 women were elected. Women's representation in the Parliament so far could not cross the 10 percent bench mark. As far as the state legislative assemblies are concerned, (shown in the following table-1) the average rate of women's representation has been 4.0; for example, in Bihar, it has been 3.4 percent, Haryana 4.4 percenr and Uttar Pradesh 4.7 percent.

Table 16.1: Women's Representation in State Legislative Assemblies

States	Year of election	No. of Seats	No. of women contes-tants	No. of elected women	Percen-tage of success-ful candi-dates	Percen-tage of women's repre-sentation
Bihar	1995	-	264	11	4.2	3.4
Orissa	1995	147	75	8	10.7	5.4
Assam	1996	126	45	8	13.33	4.8
Haryana	1996	90	93	4	4.3	4.4
Jammu & Kashmir	1996	87	15	2	13.0	2.3
Kerala	1996	141	55	13	23.6	9.2
Tamil Nadu	1996	234	156	9	5.8	3.8
Uttar Pradesh	1996	425	190	20	10.5	4.7
Uttar Pradesh	2002	403	-	26	-	-
Punjab	1997	117	52	7	13.5	5.9
Punjab	2002	117	-	8	-	-
Gujrat	1998	182	49	4	8.2	2.2
Himachal Pradesh	1998	68	25	6	24.0	8.8
Madhya Pradesh	1998	320	181	26	13.3	8.1
Meghalaya	1998	60	15	3	20.0	5.0
Delhi	1998	70	57	9	12.8	12.9
Rajasthan	1998	200	69	14	20.3	7.0
Tripura	1998	60	21	2	9.5	3.3
Goa	1999	40	10	2	20.0	5.0
Utarakhand	2002	70	-	4	-	-
Uttarakhand	2007	70	56	4	7.14	5.7
Chattisgarh	2003	90	-	5	-	-
Rajasthan	2003	200	-	12	-	-
Jharkhand	2005	81	-	13	-	-

Source : http://www. eci.gov .in/statistical reports/election statics.asp (compiled by the author).

The above table clearly points out that even in the present times, women's representation in the legislative assemblies has been marginal and low. As the table shows, in 1995, 264 women contested assembly election in Bihar only 11 women were elected in 1996, in Tamil Nadu 156 women contested election but only 09 were elected in Uttar Pradesh out of 190 women contestants only 20 were elected in 1996. Similarly, 181 women contested state legislative assembly election in 1998 in Madhya Pradesh but only 26 were elected and in Uttarakhand 56 women contested elections in 2007 but only 04 could be elected. This situation cannot be considered satisfactory from the point of women's political respresentation, particpation and activism. A look at women's particiaption and representation in the 14th Lok sabha elections also indicates the pathetic state of women's involvement in the political and decision-making process.

Table 15.2: Women's Participation, Represntation and Percentage of Polling in the 14th Lok Sabha Elections

S.N.	*State*	*No. of Seats*	*Partici-pation of women in Election*	*No. of Win*	*% of Polling*
1	2	3	4	5	6
1.	Andhra Pradesh	42	21	3	67.40
2.	Arunachal Pradesh	2	0	0	55.32
3.	Assam	14	6	0	65.36
4.	Bihar	40	14	3	51.62
5.	goa	2	1	1	56.94
6.	Gujarat	26	11	1	40.66
7.	Haryana	10	8	1	62.80
8.	Himachal Pradesh	4	2	1	59.03
9.	Jammu & Kashmir	6	4	1	29.02
10.	Karnataka	28	10	2	63.00
11.	Kerala	20	15	2	69.06
12.	Madhya Pradesh	29	30	2	38.80
13.	Maharashtra	48	29	5	50.50
14.	Manipur	2	1	0	64.88
15.	Meghalaya	2	0	0	58.86

1	2	3	4	5	6
16.	Mizoram	1	0	0	61.48
17.	Nagaland	1	0	0	90.23
18.	Orissa	21	9	2	63.64
19.	Punjab	13	10	2	60.21
20.	Rajasthan	25	17	2	44.02
21.	Sikkim	1	0	0	75.54
22.	Tamil Nadu	39	23	4	56.89
23.	Tripura	2	0	0	63.30
24.	Uttar Pradesh	80	61	7	41.20
25.	West Bengal	42	34	4	75.38
26.	Chattisgarh	11	12	1	45.50
27.	Jharkhand	14	13	1	48.13
28.	Uttarakhand	5	5	0	43.97
29.	Andaman & Nicobar Islands	1	1	0	63.81
30.	Chandigarh	1	1	0	50.11
31.	Dadra & Nagar Haveli	1	1	0	70.99
32.	Daman & Diu	1	0	0	75.06
33.	NCT of Delhi	7	15	1	44.57
34.	Lakshadweep	1	0	0	84.17
35.	Puducherry	1	1	0	74.91

Source: Women Participation and percentage of Polling. Election Commission of India General Elections, 2004 (14th Loksabha) http://www.eci.gov.in/statistical reports/L.S.2004/Vol. 1, LS2004.

As shown in the above table, that in most of the big states, women's participation has been from 2 to 7 seats. In Bihar for 40 Lok Sabha seats, 14 women contested and 03 were elected and the polling percentage was 51.62, in Karnataka for 28 seats 10 women contested and only 02 got elected and the percentage of polling was 63 percent, in Kerala also which is the most literate state of India for 20 seats 15 women contested and only 02 were elected, the polling percentage was 69.06 percent. In Madhya Pradesh 02 women were elected whereas for 29 seats there were 30 women candidates, the polling percentage was 38.80 percent. In Uttar Pradesh for 80 seats 61 women contested election and only 07 were elected. In Uttarakahnd 05 women contested for 05 Lok Sabha seats and none got elected, the polling perccentage was 43.97 percent. The above tables clearly show that despite being granted equal political freedom and opportunities by the constitution, the women's participation has remained low and insufficient. The small number of women's participation in assemblies and parliament, also points out towards the stark reality of the interplay of money and muscle power in the elections, due to which mostly the powerful, rich and influential class can only be successful in politics in today's political scene. The women, the poor and the marginalised sections of the society who lack muscle or money power mostly remain unable to secure their seats in the elections. As the reservation of 33 percent seats to the women in the Panchayat Raj Instituions have produced very good results and a large number of women taking advantage of such reservation have entered these institutions and by their participation in the decision-making process of these local bodies are making difference in the delivery system of the services-also therefore-more participation by the women is being advocated. At present there are about 3 million elected representatives at all levels of the panchayats and one-third of which are women. These members represent more than 2.4 lakh Gram panchayats, about 6,000 intermediate level tiers and more than 500 district panchayats. These panchayats cover about 96 per cent of India's more than 5.8 lakh villages and nearly 99.6 per cent of rural population. (http://enwikipedia.org/history_of panchayat_raj_in_india) In view of the success of the women's participation in the local bodies, it is being felt that the reservation of seats for the women in parliament and assembalies could be an answer to the problem of under representation of the women in these bodies, but unfortunately the bill to provide 33 percent reservation to the women in parliament and assemblies, despite being introduced in Rajaya Sabha, is yet to see the light of the day.

Since, women not only have compassion, but also a feel of the needs of the people and area, therefore, women's active participation in political process can create an atmosphere for speedy implementation of policies and other radical socio-political changes. Actually, women's political activism and equal participation is one of the greatest needs of our times, but by improving women's participation only in urban areas cannot bring good results; rather it needs to be improved in the rural and remote areas of the country also. As the women of the remote and rural areas are even deprived of various facilities necessary for development, therefore, for making a productive contribution and registering their activism, the women of the rural and remote areas need to be given equal opportunities for political participation and say in the mainstream political development. Actually effective measures and implementation of already existing laws/provisions are needed to boost women's activism, enhanced awareness and participation in the socio-political process.

The Importance of Women's Activism

Since ages, Indian community has been male-dominated and male child (son) preference society. A son is not only considered heir to paternal prosperities and carrying the family lineage further and the daughters are considered a 'burden'. This allows the gender disparity to set in from the beginning in the family and it transmits in the society also. The girl child is made to sacrifice her schooling, training opportunities needs, lesiure time and even food sometimes to look after siblings, giving a helping hand in the household and sometimes due to other socio-economic constraints and traditions. Women are expected to put her family and home first and then everything else and such expectation from the women not only hamper their chances of equal growth and opportunities but also constraint their participation and activism in socio-political affairs. However, interestingly, despite being the vicitms of a male-dominated society, women's reformation movements were also initiated and pioneered by the men. As women component of the society has always been the 'natural' victim of the social evils, therefore, the religious reformers and social thinkers also focused their attention on the plight of the women and with persistent efforts could bring changes in their socio-political status. During the entire period of freedom struggle and reformation movement both men and women worked hand in hand and in Renaissance period, the call of women awakening and reformation was actually heralded by the men. Even in our fast changing social conditions, whenever a mass movement stirs women, they are mostly supported by the reformist men as well as social workers and dynamic leaders. (Sharma, 2002, p. 68) On the basis of this, it can also be said that women's participation and activism can be increased more, if in place of hindrances, they are provided support by the men.

Women's activism in India actually started with the freedom struggle and the reformist movement of the 19th century. But unfortunately, after independence, only a small number of women preferred to enter the political arena and majority of them once again adopted their traditional chores. Since women's liberation movement and the development of women consciousness in India has primarily centred on the two factors: a mass uprising against social evils and women's participation in the freedom movement as well as other movements related to various socio-political and environmental movements from time to time in the different parts of India, therefore, these can be seen as the main symbols of women activism. The 'Chipko Movement' of 1970's in Uttarakhand, which was started by the rural women of the reomte villages of the Garhwal Himalayas, left an indelible impression world-wide. Later on, this small movement led by the women, because of the innovative and noble startegy of hugging trees to stop their cutting for commercial uses by the government contractors, not only became a synonym of environment conservation but also a source and ideal for future movements in other parts of India also. It attracted global focus on many fundamental issues of regional, national and international importance. (Nautiyal, 1996, p. 14) Taking cue from such movements, during the very turbulent time of 1970's, the Indian women also launched anti-liquor movements around the country, which were pioneered by the dynamic women like Mrinal Gore and Ahellya Rangekar. Rural women's participation and activism in the anti liquor and forest movements indicated that women can be instrumental in bringing changes in the laws, if the situation demands. Actually, in Uttarakhand, particularly the women have a history of participating in the movements launched from time to time. The women's participation in the movement for the creation of the Uttarakhand state in the 1990s was also totally spontaneous, and their sacrifices, for the cause and the role of the leading light of this movement, became a source of inspiration for others also. (Nautiyal, 2005) Ironically after the creation of the state in 2000, women were pushed to the backwaters, the presence of only 04 women in the house of 70 and no women member of parliament from Uttarakhand amply speaks about the state of women's represntation and participation in the political and decison-making bodies in Uttarakhand.

Women's activism is very important for changing the existing gender relations and bringing qualitative changes in the social and political set-up. Actually, it was Mahatma Gandhi, who highlighted the importance of women's activism, their rights, entry in the organisations and role in the socio-political arena. Gandhi believed that the women's traits like tolerance, sensitivity and self-control are best suited for bringing socio-political changes in the society. (Basu, and Bharti, 1990) Acknowledging their potential. Gandhi openly motivated women to participate in the freedom struggle and this experience of participating in the freedom movement generated a new kind of consciousness in the women to realise their potential. It also became a strong base of their activism, progress and development in the later periods. To ensure women's productive and qualitative activism, special focus was given on women welfare programmes after independence. Influenced by Gandhi, Nehru also wanted to ensure women's equal participation in the planned economy of India, because he also believed that without involving women in large numbers in socio-political activities, India cannot achieve its desired goals of developmentland gender equality. Keeping in view, the holistic and complete development democracy, secularism, social justice, equaltiy and liberty became the mantra of the new system. (Varma, 2005, p. 34) All kinds of gender biases were removed and equal political rights were granted to men and women under the article 15(1) of the constitution. Groups like Mahila Mangal Dals were formed and promoted in rural areas to improve women's awareness, activism and participation in socio-poitical affairs. Many welfare schemes were started in rural areas to provide health facilities and training of micro scale industries and the schemes related to poverty elimination of women were also launched. Significant result started coming during 1970's and 1980's. Internationally also, the United Nations Organisation initiated many path-breaking schemes for women's upliftment and a committee formed in 1974 to study women's condition around the globe prepared a report "Towards Equality' which, in later years, became an important document for working towards gender equality and encouraging women's activism, so that they can become part of the mainstream socio-political development. The reason behind these initiatives was the feeeling that without giving equal socio-political opportunities to half of the world's population and ensuring their activism, empowerment and involvement in the socio-political process, the total, wholistic and expected development of the women and the society at large is not possible. (John, 2008, p. 3-4) This new philosophy of 'Women Activism' and 'Women Empowerment' has produced significant changes in the socio-political arena with the result, provisions are being made to not only promote women's entry in politics, decision-making process but also to provide an atmosphere where they can play effective, constructive and positive role in the economic and social development of the society.

Supporting Elements of Women's Activism

As women's activism is a must for the wholistic development and effective implementation of the plans and schemes, therefore, there is a need to promote more and more activism of the women in the socio-political process. The following elements can be helpful in promoting women's activism.

Education

Education is an important tool of empowerment for everyone, because it is a source of light, intuition, insight, knowledge, awareness, right reasoning (viveka) and moral, physical, spiritual and mental development of a person. Thus, education is an essential exponent of activism and empowerment and helps one to develop all possible faculties as well as to understand the fundamental aims of life. It also provides a capabiltiy for ananlytical thinking and generates awareness about one's surroundings which in turn contributes for activism. The nations which have registered immense growth, progress and prosperity have achieved this growth, on the basis of their high quality, world-class eduational institutions and educated people. Education is a game changer for all; but particularly, for the women who have been the vicitims of all social evils and controls of the male dominated society. This has been a boon, as eduaction is radically changing the lives of the women globally. According to World Education Report 1995, women and girls are kept captivated within the forewalls of their houses in poor countries and not allowed eduation and literacy. The illiterate women breed illiterate girls and again these uneducated girls are married at a very tender age. This allows interminable continuation of a vicious cycle of poverty, illiteracy, child marriage and gender discrimination. Since in the Indian tradition, women have been the focal point of the life of a family and society. Therefore, women's education is a must for the development of the family and society as well as for their constructive activism in socio-political affairs. Women's spontaneous participation in different movements in India is an examle of their eagerness to be associated with issues and if provided equal opprtunities for education, development and participation. Indian women can radically change the life and system of the country. In a democratic society, the education system should be so shaped that even a common man should find something interesting in relations and in social works. It should also develop an ability to accept and assert social change of any magnitude. As women being sensitive to the issues of development, progress and sustainance, therefore, they have always been in the fore front of movements and agitations. But due to poor eduactional status of a majority of the rural and urban women, their activism is not valued. The lack of quality education not only makes women less confident, dependent on the males for any decisions but also apprehensive about their capabilites and qualities, to overcome this situation and allowing women to share their responsibilities, it is more than necessary to provide good quality education to them. However, it is also ironical that even after 64 years of independence, women's literacy in India has not crossed 80 percent mark. Though it has increased from 64.83 percent in 2001 to 74.04 percent in 2011, male literacy from 75.26 percent to 82.14 percent and female literacy from 53.67 percent to 65.46 percent with a reduced gender gap of 16.68 percent which was 18.30 percent in 1951 and 21.59 percent in 2001 but still much has to do to improve this situation. The situation of literacy can be explained through the following table:

Table 16.33: Total Literates and Literacy Rate by Sex in Indian States: 2011

S.N.	India	Persons	Males	Females	Persons	Males	Females
1	2	3	4	5	6	7	8
	India	778,454,120	444,203,762	334,250,358	74.04	82.14	65.46
1.	Jammu & Kashmir	7,245,053	4,370,604	2,874,449	68.74	78.26	58.01
2.	Himachal Pradesh	5,104,506	2,791,542	2,312,964	83.78	90.83	76.60
3.	Punjab	18,988,611	10,626,788	8,361,823	76.68	81.48	71.34
4.	Chandigarh#	809,653	468,166	341,487	86.43	90.54	81.38
5.	Uttarakhand	6,997,433	3,930,174	3,067,259	79.63	88.33	70.70
6.	Haryana	16,904,324	9,991,838	6,912,486	76.64	85.38	66.77
7.	NCT of Delhi#	12,763,352	7,210,050	5,553,302	86.34	91.03	80.93
8.	Rajasthan	38,970,500	24,184,782	14,785,718	67.06	80.51	52.66
9.	Uttar Pradesh	118,423,805	70,479,196	47,944,609	69.72	79.24	59.26
10.	Bihar	54,390,254	32,711,975	21,678,279	63.82	73.39	53.33
11.	Sikkim	449,294	253,364	195,930	82.20	87.29	76.43
12.	Arunachal Pradesh	789,943	454,532	335,411	66.95	73.69	59.57
13.	Nagaland	1,357,579	731,796	625,783	80.11	83.29	76.69
14.	Manipur	1,891,196	1,026,733	864,463	79.85	86.49	73.17
15.	Mizoram	847,592	438,949	408,643	91.58	93.72	89.40
16.	Tripura	2,831,742	1,515,973	1,315,769	87.75	92.18	83.15
17.	Meghalaya	18,17,761	9,34,091	8,83,670	75.48	77.17	73.78
18.	Assam	1,95,07,017	1,07,56,937	87,50,080	73.18	78.81	67.27
19.	West Bengal	6,26,14,556	3,45,08,159	2,81,06,397	77.08	82.67	71.16
20.	Jharkhand	1,87,53,660	1,11,68,649	75,85,011	67.63	78.45	56.21
21.	Orissa	2,71,12,376	1,53,26,036	1,17,86,340	73.45	82.40	64.36
22.	Chhattisgarh	1,55,98,314	89,62,121	66,36,193	71.04	81.45	60.59

1	2	3	4	5	6	7	8
23.	Madhya Pradesh	4,38,27,193	2,58,48,137	1,79,79,056	70.63	80.53	60.02
24.	Gujarat	4,19,48,677	2,39,95,500	1,79,53,177	79.31	87.23	70.73
25.	Daman & Diu#	1,88,974	1,24,911	64,063	87.07	91.48	79.59
26.	Dadra & Nagar Haveli#	2,28,028	1,44,916	83,112	77.65	86.46	65.93
27.	Maharashtra	8,25,12,225	4,62,94,041	3,62,18,184	82.91	89.82	75.48
28.	Andhra Pradesh	5,14,38,510	2,87,59,782	2,26,78,728	67.66	75.56	59.74
29.	Karnataka	4,10,29,323	2,28,08,468	1,82,20,855	75.60	82.85	68.13
30.	Goa	11,52,117	6,20,026	5,32,091	87.40	92.81	81.84
31.	Lakshadweep#	52,914	28,249	24,665	92.28	96.11	88.25
32.	Kerala	2,82,34,227	1,37,55,888	1,44,78,339	93.91	96.02	91.98
33.	Kerala	2,82,34,227	1,37,55,888	1,44,78,339	93.91	96.02	91.98
34.	Puducherry#	9,66,600	5,02,575	4,64,025	86.55	92.12	81.22
35.	Andaman & Nicobar Islands#	2,93,695	1,64,219	1,29,476	86.27	90.11	81.84

UT/Union Territory.

Source: http://www.census 2011.co.in

Though that is no denying that literacy among the women has increased but in some big and populous states like Uttar Pradesh, Bihar, Rajasthan, Madhya Pradesh, Andhra Pradesh and Jharkahnd, it is still below 60 percent which is not a good sign. In view of the role of education and literacy in generating awareness among the women and promoting activism among them, more work on this sector of human development is required.

Awareness

As explained above that awareness about one's surrounding is very important for women's activism and participation in the socio-political process. Only sound education system, social security, gender equality and economic self-dependence can make strong and awakened women. Their work potential, skill, qualities can be used and evolved best only if they are given equal respect, education and liberty and their awareness is also up to date. On the other hand, women's illiteracy makes them indifferent of social, economic and political participation and generally such women do not show any interest in the issues beyond their family affairs and they also remian least aware of national and international issues. Illiteracy and lack of awareness is the greatest stumbling block in women's way to politics. As awareness and activism go hand in hand, therefore, good quality education to it support is necessary. Women have proved their excellence in various walks of life viz. science, knowledge, religions, politics, ethics, social life etc. There are examples of women, who showed exemplary leadership qualities, like Sarojini Naidu, Vijay Laxmi Pandit, Indira Gandhi and more recently Mayavati and Sheela Dixit have also proved their courage, mental toughness and adventurous leadership acumen. These women could reach the pinnacle of power due to their hard work, leadership qualities and also education and awareness. In view of this, it is important to involve women in a large number in awareness generating training programmes, camps etc.

Reservation

'Reservation' literally means securing 'place' or providing opportunity for advancement of a particular group or class, which is/ are socially, economically and politically backward and marginal. The provision of reservation is mentioned under article 341 and 342 of the constitution of India. In fact, the makers of modern India were deeply aware of the socio-political and economic differences among its citizen and to bridge this gap as well as to promote social justice, they created special provisions by introducing the reservation system or affirmative action. In 1955, the Kelkar committee advised that 'social condition' in any community or caste should be the yardstick for measuring its poverty. The Mandal committee formed in 1978, recommended some constitutional reservation to address the problems of the extremely poor, the marginal sections of the society who have been the victims of social injustice in the country and for upgrading them socially, economically and politically. In 1990, the V.P. Singh Government enforced the recommendations of the Mandal commission which was followed by nation-wide agitation and unrest against the 27 percent OBC (Other Backward Class) reservation. Despite anti reservation movements across the country, it was considered a judicious move for bringing social parity and equality of opportunities. In 1992 for improving women's participation and activism in the political and decision-making process in the local bodies, a provision to reserve 33 percent seats was made and with the implementation of the 73rd Constitutional Amendment enacted in 1992 the roles of panchayats have become more important in rural and community development programmes. The rationale behind these amendments was that only through the effectiveness of the local bodies, the vision of good and decentralised governance in rural areas could be materialiseds, because the Panchayati Raj bodies are not only closely attached to the masses but they also have a strong foothold in every strata of the society. In view of the various divisions and inequalities in the communities and societal structure, the women, deprived and the marginal section of society have also been given reservation so that their active participation is ensured under the decentralied self-governance mechanism. With the provisions of this act which provides for the three tiers of the Panchayat Raj System, the government has transferred 14 out of 29 subjects along with all their procedures, programmes, accountability, rural level administrative units, personnel and the financial resources related to these subjects to village panchayats. Besides, watchdogs like Zila Panchayat Prakost (District Panchayat Cell) and Directorate of Panchayati Raj has also been established to strengthening and facilitating the works of Panchayati Raj bodies. This amendment has conferred a constitutional status to the panchayats and, more importantly for the first time, it has ensured 33 percent reservation for women in all the three tiers of the Panchayats as heads and members. In Uttarakhand and some other states, the reservation for women has been increased to 50 percent and with the result, a large number of women of all socio strata have entered the Panchayat Raj Institutions at all the three levels.

Actually, the concept of democratic decentralisation and the reservation for women have positively affected women's political activism, because now in a large scale, women are participating and contesting elections for the reserved and non-reserved posts of Gram Panchayat, Area Panchayat and District Panchayat. The reservation has allowed rural women to venture out of the security of their homes and move in a totally unknown and unfamiliar path. Actually, with the implementation of the 33 percent reservation for women in the local bodies, women's affiliation and association with political parties has also increased. Even in the election of the primary Panchayat Raj Institution, the Gram Panchayat, and the Village Pradhan, party consideration have become very important. No election is being contested without the support of a political party and this has not only introduced the power politics and the money game in these elections, but it has also made the post of the Village Pradhan political. Although with the implementation of this reservation an improvement in the condition of women, her role, participation and activism can be witnessed but this change is visible in the context of the educated women of the urban or rural areas. There are studies which have highlighted that in case of the illiterate women heads of the village panchayat a the Pradhan Pati (husband ruling by proxy) was found to be discharging the duites of the Pradhan. In such a situation, women in place of being empowered, just act as a rubber stamp or figure head of the organisation. But despite this, it can be said that reservation for the women in political bodies is an enabling factor and for increasing women's participation and activism in the entire decison-making bodies and organisations, it needs to be extended. Reservation for women in state assemblies and parliament therefore, need to be seen as a faciltaing factor for women's entry into politics and ensuring their enhanced activism.

Conclusion

Many promising signs can be noticed in the field of women activism and awareness in India today. Women are being more and more enlightened by the spread of education and mass awareness. With education and enlightment, they are transforming the age-old orthodoxy into a new world of equality, gender parity and awareness. Steps like reservation for women have brought noticeable changes in the lives of women and, consequently, women now enjoy a greater say in socio-political affairs. By bringing a sea change in the plight of the women, the reservation system can be called a justful means of equality, independence and activism. Reservation has created more socio-political opportunities and spaces for women. Acting as an inspired force, women have also realised the power of unity and economic and political liberation and by making use of the reservation they are also changing the contours of village development. However, for ensuring participation and activism of more women still much needs to be done at all levels. Commenting on the small number of women in the first Lok Sabha, Nehru had said, "I feel dejected that only a small number of women have won the election. We menfolk are totally responsible for this sad state of affairs; our laws, our society and our collective psyche is male-dominated. We have one archetypal mindset for women. But, ultimately, women will be the true builders of future for India." As time and again, the women have shown their potential, eagerness and efficiency, therefore, if the bill to provide 33 percent reservation to women in state assemblies and parliament can be passed and also be made a law, it would definitely break the barriers and by promoting their fruitful and much desired activism would also make the women the builders of modern India in the true sense of the term.

REFERENCES

Rawat, Brijmohan: *Nari Samanta Avum Sashaktikaran: 1990 ke Dasak Mein Uttaranchal Main ek Adhyayan*. Unpublished Ph.D. Thesis, HNB Garhwal University, 2004, p. 78.

Kaushik, Asha: *Nari Sashaktikaran: Vimarsh Avum Yatharth.* Jaipur: Pointer Publication, 2004, p. 123.

Basu, Amrita : "Women's Activism and the Vicissitudes of Hindu Nationalism". *Journal of Women's History,* Baltimore, Vol. 10, issue 4, p. 1, 1999 http:// enwikipedia.org/history_of panchayat_raj_in_india

Sharma, Om Prakash: *Samkaleen Mahila Lekhan,* Pooja Pakashan, Delhi, 2002, p. 68.

Nautiyal Annpurna: "Chipko Movement and the Women of Garhwal Himalaya". *Gandhian Perspectives,* Vol. IX, No. 2, 1996.

Nautiyal Annpurna: "Roots of Gender Disparity in Garhwal Himalaya: From Eco-Social Disparity to Eco-Political Activism". *Journal of South Asian Women Studies.* Vol. 10, No. 2, April 27, 2005.

Basu, Aparna and Raj, Bharti: *Women's Struggle: A History of All India Women's Conference 1927-1990.* Manohar Prakashan, New Delhi, 1990.

Varma, Sawalia: *Bihari Mahila: Jagriti Avum Sashaktikaran,* Avishkar Publishers, Jaipur, 2005, p. 34.

John Mary E.: *Women's Studies in India : A Reader.* Penguine Books, 2008.

Index

Z